Working and Walking in the Footsteps of Ghosts

Volume 1: The Wooded Landscape.

Edited by Ian D. Rotherham, Melvyn Jones and Christine Handley

Edited by Ian D. Rotherham, Melvyn Jones and Christine Handley

ISBN 978-1-904098-42-3

Published by:
Wildtrack Publishing, Venture House,
103 Arundel Street, Sheffield S1 2NT

Typeset and processed by Christine Handley

Supported by:
Sheffield Hallam University.
HEC Associates Ltd.
South Yorkshire Biodiversity Research Group.
Landscape Conservation Forum.

© Wildtrack Publishing and the individual authors 2003/2012.

All rights reserved. No part of this publication may be reproduced or transmitted in any form or by any means, electronic or mechanical, including photocopying, recording, or any information storage or retrieval system, without permission in writing from the publisher.

Working and Walking in the Footsteps of Ghosts: Volume 1 the Wooded Landscape

Contents

Part 1: The Wooded Landscape - Introduction and Overview   5
Ian D. Rotherham, Melvyn Jones & Christine Handley

Holocene Woodland History: a palaeoentomological perspective   11
Paul C. Buckland

South Yorkshire's Ancient Woodlands: Past, Present and Future   40
Melvyn Jones

Characterisation of the woodland flora and woodland communities in Britain using Ellenberg Values and Functional Analysis   66
Keith Kirby, D.G. Pyatt and John Rodwell

English Woodlands: Historical Landscapes and Archaeology   87
Della Hooke

'Therapy of the Green Leaf': the development of forest and woodland recreation in twentieth century Britain   103
Robert Lambert

The Ghosts at the Ends of the Earth: Tree-Land in Four Hemispheres   118
Oliver Rackham

Historical Diversity in the Woods of the Lower Wye Valley   133
George F. Peterken

The Age of Wood   147
Francis T Evans

Surveying the wood for the trees: the archaeology of Sheffield's Heritage Woodlands.   160
Nick Sellwood and Jim McNeill

Embracing spaces: wood pastures, open pastures and historical geography   **172**
Brian K. Roberts

Decaying Wood - Recycling in Arboreal Ecosystems   **182**
Andrew Cowan

'To stand in them is to feel the past': Pinewoods and Birchwoods in the Scottish Uplands.   **192**
Chris Smout

Woodland Transport: the evidence for Derbyshire and the West Riding of Yorkshire   **199**
David Hey

Oak, the footmark of ghosts   **205**
Frans Vera

Bringing the Ghost to Life: woodland ecology and landscape history   **210**
John Rodwell

Identifying and protecting archaeology in the woodland environment in Northern Scotland   **214**
Jonathan Wordsworth

The Use of Woodlands by Mammals - Past and Present   **218**
Derek W. Yalden

The work with old trees and saproxylic beetles in Östergötland, Sweden   **221**
Nicklas Jansson

Traditional Woodland Management: the Implications of Cultural Severance and Knowledge Loss   **223**
Ian D. Rotherham

Introduction
Ian D. Rotherham, Melvyn Jones and Christine Handley

The conference at which the chapters in this book were originally presented as papers – *Working and Walking in the Footsteps of Ghosts* – took place at Sheffield Hallam University between 29th May and 1st June 2003. The conference proceedings were published at the event as a bound volume of abstracts and longer papers. This was a landmark conference in a number of ways. First, it was a large conference attended by more than 300 delegates. Secondly, they came from all parts of Britain, from regions in England as far apart as Sussex and Cornwall in the south to Cumbria and Northumberland in the north, from Scotland, from Northern Ireland and the Republic of Ireland and from continental Europe – from Belgium, France, Hungary, Italy, the Netherlands and Sweden. Thirdly, it marked the tenth anniversary of the publication of the proceedings of the first national woodland conference in Sheffield organised by The Landscape Conservation Forum – *Ancient Woodlands: their archaeology and ecology – a coincidence of interest?* Finally, the delegates represented a very wide range of backgrounds – including academics, professional foresters, land managers, staff of regional Wildlife Trusts, representatives from the Forestry Commission, English Nature, English Heritage, Scottish Natural Heritage, the Woodland Trust and members of woodland conservation and wildlife groups.

The wide range of backgrounds of the conference delegates is reflected in the equally wide range of specialist research interests presented in the papers. In this volume, the first of two, they range from woodland history, historical geography, palaeontology and archaeology to woodland flora, woodland mammals, saproxylic beetles and woodland recreation.

In the first chapter, **Paul Buckland** discusses *Holocene Woodland History: a palaeoentomological perspective*. The paper grew out of reading Frans Vera's book *Grazing Ecology and Forest History* (2000) and subsequent discussions with the author and Keith Kirby of English Nature. He concedes that the fossil insect evidence provides a little support for the Vera hypothesis. He also points out that evidence suggests that the Atlantic forest was being modified by fire. In conclusion he goes on to state that this does not mean that we should ignore the dynamic forest system of growth, death and re-growth, influenced by 'natural' grazers and browsers.

In Chapter 2, **Melvyn Jones** writes about *South Yorkshire's Ancient Woodlands: Past, Present and Future*. He considers the place-name evidence for former woodland cover that was cleared between the seventh and twelfth centuries, charts the evolution of woodland management from wood pasture that was the dominant woodland land use at the time of Domesday and beyond. The chapter then consider the rise, decline and extinction of coppice management whose legacy is the 333 ancient woodland sites that survive across the region. In a final section, he shows that the growing awareness of the cultural importance and recreational potential of the surviving ancient woodlands is likely to guarantee their future survival.

Woodland flora is an important research topic and this is the theme of **Keith Kirby, D. Pyatt and John Rodwell's** paper in Chapter 3 on *Characterisation of the woodland flora and woodland communities in Britain using Ellenberg Values and Functional analysis*. They show how records from the National Vegetation Classification tables, Ellenberg Indicator Values and Functional Attributes have been used to characterise differences between plant species identified as 'woodland specialists', 'other woodland species' and 'non-woodland plants'. 'Woodland specialists' were by these tests shown to be more strongly associated with woodland habitats. Moreover, they were more likely to be recorded as decreasing in importance and may be more sensitive indicators of changes in woodland habitats than other species.

Della Hooke's study of *English woodlands: Historical Landscapes and Archaeology* in Chapter 4, drawing examples from various regions, considers a number of related topics. These include the identification of former heavily wooded regions in the modern landscape through their settlement patterns, place-names and communication networks and important woodland archaeological features, both those connected with woodland management and those not connected with woodland management. She also considers the 'living archaeology' of old worked trees such as pollards and holly trees once cropped for animal fodder. In the final section of her paper, she looks in detail at the role of woodland in the past, present and future in the Coalbrookdale region in Shropshire.

Robert Lambert in Chapter 5 examines woodland recreation in *'Therapy of the Green Leaf'*: the development of forest and woodland recreation in twentieth century Britain'. In the paper, he gives an overview of the rise of forest and woodland recreation looking at state, NGO and the private sectors. A particular focus is the Forest Park ideal across Britain. Among issues raised are the introduction of forest byelaws by the Forestry Commission, the holiday forest movement, people management and improving management for the needs of visitors.

In Chapter 6 **Oliver Rackham** has produced a thought provoking paper on **The Ghosts at the Ends of the Earth: Tree-Land in Four Hemispheres**. He defines tree-land in five ways: forest (closely spaced trees with a shade bearing ground flora), savanna (wood pasture), coppice, farmland trees and maquis. Based on his own worldwide fieldwork investigations he demonstrates how the methods of a British landscape archaeologist can be applied to other continents that contain other tree species, genera and families of trees and which have been managed by other civilisations.

Another regional study is that by **George Peterken** in Chapter 7. His subject is ***Historical Diversity in the Woods of the Lower Wye Valley***. The author describes the history of three woods, each with a different history. Lady Park Wood was, over a 700-year period, successively managed as a park, as a coppice-with-standards, as a beech-dominated high forest and since 1944 as a Forestry Commission research reserve. In contrast Cadora and Bigsweir woods, a collective name for a continuous belt of woodland along the Gloucestershire bank of the River Wye, was originally many separate small woods that was coniferised in the 1960s. Surviving native trees include high coppice stools, stubs and pollards of small-leaved lime. Finally, Hudnalls was a wooded common in the Forest of Dean. He concludes that the historical diversity of woodlands needs to be identified and historical features retained when management strategies are being devised.

Francis Evans in Chapter 8 examines ***The Age of Wood***. He discusses the ingenuity of engineers and craftsmen in achieving mastery over the constraints imposed by the natural characteristics of wood and timber. He describes in detail the myriad uses of wood and timber, from wood fuel, roof timbers and timber railway bridges to windmills, sailing ships and aircraft, reminding us that one of the most successful aircraft of the Second World War, the Mosquito, was built of wood.

There are two contributions specifically about the archaeology of woodlands. In Chapter 9 **Nick Sellwood** and **Jim McNeill** in their paper on ***Surveying the wood for the trees: the Archaeology of Sheffield's Heritage Woodlands*** describe the archaeological surveys, incorporating rapid walk-over surveys and detailed measured surveys, of twenty-three ancient woods in Sheffield as part of the Heritage Lottery Funded *Fuelling a Revolution: the woods that founded the steel country* project. They demonstrate how the surveys have resulted in sympathetic woodland management approaches and the management of recreational pressures.

In Chapter 10, historical geographer **Brian Roberts** in his paper ***Embracing Spaces: wood pastures, open pastures and historical geography*** analyses patterns and distributions of woodland and wooded commons through the analysis of three maps. The first is a map of England and Wales showing the distribution of woodland between the years 730 and 1086; the second is a map of County Durham based upon the reconstruction of common pastures about the year 1600; the third is a map of the small shire or multiple estate of Heighingtonshire also in County Durham. He stresses that the method (zooming in) may be as important as the content.

In Chapter 11, **Andrew Cowan** discusses *Decaying Wood – Recycling in Arboreal Ecosystems*. He makes the strong point that woodland managers need to recognise that a decaying wood habitat is a dynamic system of processes, which is constantly evolving as part of the arboreal ecosystem. He goes to state that the role of the woodland manager is careful guidance to support natural processes and not to impose a physical state or form that fit certain ideas of what is right. He concludes that woodland managers need to appreciate the ageing process of trees and tree longevity.

In Chapter 12 **Chris Smout** in his study of the *Pinewoods and Birchwoods in the Scottish Uplands*, writes with authority about the history of the 16,000 hectares of the much-loved Caledonian pinewoods. These unique woods are still found in less than one hundred woods in the Scottish Highlands. He also writes about the much less appreciated and therefore more threatened birchwoods, 40 per cent of which were lost between 1960 and 1990. He stresses the importance of the economic and social history as well as the ecological history of woods.

David Hey in Chapter 13 writes about *Woodland Transport: the evidence from Derbyshire and the West Riding of Yorkshire*. He writes not about guide stoops, packhorse bridges and causeys, but about the holloways created – through wear and tear – to transport charcoal to iron works, whitecoal to lead smelting ore hearths and pit props to collieries and ironstone mines. He uses a wide range of documentary records together with landscape evidence to explain the significance of these features. Most people take these for granted, but in the past, they were the lifeblood of local economies throughout Derbyshire and South Yorkshire, and indeed in the country as a whole.

Frans Vera in Chapter 14 explores the character of primeval woodland in *Oak, the footmark of ghosts*. In his paper, he underlines the main point made his then recent book *Grazing Ecology and Forest History* (2000) that the wildwood of the lowlands of Western and Central Europe was not a closed canopy forest but a mosaic of trees, shrubs and grassland, a park-like savanna landscape. He compares the wood pastures of medieval Europe grazed by horses, cattle and sheep to the mid-Holocene savanna grazed by aurochs and tarpan (wild horse) and the interglacial savannas grazed by rhinoceros, elephant, hippopotamus and giant deer. And, as in medieval wood pastures where it was an open growth solitary tree protected by groves of thorns, pollen analysis shows that oak was present in these ancient landscapes. Oak, states Vera, may be 'the footmark of a menagerie of ungulate ghosts'.

John Rodwell in Chapter 15 writes on the subject of ***Bringing the Ghost to Life: woodland ecology and landscape history***. In his paper, he describes how the National Vegetation Classification (NVC) can be used in a predictive fashion to develop past scenarios that can greatly inform landscape history and our understanding of the role that woodlands played in local and regional economies in former times. He cites examples of projects in South Yorkshire, West Yorkshire, Lancashire and Cheshire, and the European Vegetation Map which enables landscape patterns, including woodlands, to be understood on an international scale.

In Chapter 16 **Jonathan Wordsworth** in ***Identifying and protecting archaeology in the woodland environment of Northern Scotland***, looks at woodland archaeological surveys on a bigger scale. The author describes a range of recent archaeological work in areas such as the Rassal Ashwoods, the most northerly substantial ashwood in the UK, the great pinewoods edging the Cairngorm plateau and in the area of great natural beauty around Loch Sunart. He points out that archaeologists need to be able to recognise different types of former worked trees and features such as pitsteads and sawpits. In return, woodland managers need to be better equipped to recognise and protect archaeological features.

In Chapter 17 **Derek Yalden** discusses ***The use of Woodlands by Mammals – Past and Present***. He explores the woodland conditions that would have supported large populations of roe and red deer, elk, aurochs, wild boar and beaver in Britain. He concludes that dense high forest cover would not have supported these and besides river valley grasslands, woodland glades and considerable amounts of low-level scrub and young growth would have been present. He suggests that just over two-fifths of the land would have been deciduous woodland and just under one-fifth would have been grassland. He estimates that in Mesolithic Britain there would have been 1.2 million red deer (0.36 million now), 11.8 million red squirrels, 0.9 million wild boar, 80,000 aurochs and 60,000 elk.

In Chapter 18, **Nicklas Jannson** discusses ***The work with old trees and saproxylic beetles in Östergötland, Sweden***. The author describes the studies concerning old trees and their associated organisms carried out in this county in south-east Sweden since 1990. The organisms studied are lichens, fungi, beetles, pseudoscorpions and bats. In 1998, a project began of mapping all the old trees in the county. So far, 60,000 trees have been registered. The study of saproxylic beetles, that are dependent on decaying or dead wood, has targeted hollow old oaks, pollards, trees in old avenues and in parks. He discusses various beetle survey methods.

In the final chapter, Chapter 19, **Ian Rotherham** provides an overview of many of the issues and brings the research themes and recent paradigms more fully up-to-date with ***Traditional Woodland Management: the Implications of Cultural Severance and Knowledge Loss***. He reports on the developing and emerging concepts, and issues from research across Europe and based on long-term, in-depth, action research and field surveys in Sheffield. This is an appropriate way to end this first volume of two.

The papers gathered together in this volume, written by experts in their fields, demonstrate the breadth and quality of current research into woodlands from a very broad range of approaches. They make compelling reading and are full of ideas for further research.

Holocene Woodland History: a palaeoentomological perspective

Professor Paul C. Buckland
University of Sheffield

Introduction

The nature and form of lowland woodland in northwest Europe during the mid-Holocene, before extensive forest clearance (Landnám) has been the source of much discussion, largely based upon the palynological evidence. Most of this has concerned the processes of immigration and differential expansion and contraction of individual taxa (e.g. Tallantire, 1992; Bennett, 1995). The image of a landscape of closed forest lacking any substantial open spaces, of the 'massed tree trunks of the primaeval forest still waiting the axe', to quote Hoskins' (1977) view of early medieval wooded landscapes, has been challenged, most recently by Frans Vera (2000), who sees a much more varied landscape of old trees, forest lawns maintained by natural grazing pressure and more tangled forest boundary communities in the mid-Holocene in a dynamic cycle of death and regeneration (Figure 1). The interpretation of the pollen evidence has rarely considered any impact from large herbivores, and most overviews only acknowledge the large scale presence of grazers and browsers from early Neolithic clearance onwards (e.g. Godwin, 1975; Tipping, 1995). The work of Simmons, most recently summarised in his book on the history of upland moorland in England and Wales (Simmons, 2003) provides a notable exception, and he adds another important factor to the equation, the incidence of fire. Whilst from his earliest work (e.g. Simmons, 1969) has sprung a hare chased by many archaeologists working on the mesolithic (e.g. Mellars, 1976), there has been a recent trend toward accepting fire as part of the natural sequence, albeit with very long return periods in deciduous woodlands (Moore, J. 1996; 2000; Whitehouse, 2000), and the probability that mesolithic human activity had a significant impact (Simmons, 1996). Peter Moore (1973;1993) has reaffirmed his belief that upland moorland is at least partly anthropogenic in origin, and similar impacts should be sought in the more marginal lowland landscapes. The nature of species composition and frequency of large vertebrates in the mid-Holocene landscape has been approached by Yalden (1999; Marroo & Yalden, 2000), but the problem is bedevilled by the paucity of good bone assemblages and the wild component of early Neolithic assemblages is relatively small. Whilst there are sizeable early Holocene groups associated with archaeological sites, such as the now classic and much discussed bones from Star Carr in the Vale of Pickering, Yorkshire (Fraser & King, 1954; Legge & Rowley-Conwy, 1988; Rowley-Conwy, 1998), there are few mid-Holocene bone groups, and none are substantial. It is perhaps partly for these reasons that the impact of large grazers and browsers has largely been ignored and changes in the forest pollen spectra have been ascribed to other either climatic or anthropogenic causes.

The early Holocene medium to large herbivore assemblage from Star Carr includes aurochs, elk, red deer, and roe deer. Wild boar and beaver, also present, need to be considered as they are also likely to have had a significant impact on the landscape (Legge & Rowley-Conwy, 1988). Schadla-Hall (1988) adds horse from the nearby site of Seamer Carr, and this assemblage is repeated at the only other reasonably secure and sizeable mesolithic assemblage, at Thatcham in Berkshire (Wymer, 1962). To the list has to be added Irish deer, *Megaloceros giganteus*, which has radiocarbon dates down to *circa* 9250 BP in the Isle of Man and south-west Scotland (Gonzalez *et al.*, 2000). The latter, along with elk and horse, however, probably disappeared during the early Holocene, although it is difficult to see why. Whilst both horse and Irish deer might be regarded as animals essentially of the open steppe with only a slim hold on north-west Europe, much of Scotland in the mid-Holocene would not be significantly different from areas of Scandinavia where elk continues to thrive. The one possible Roman record of elk, from Newstead in the Borders, is probably redeposited from earlier peat (McCormick & Buckland, 1997) and its extinction is probably of early Holocene date. Unless human populations were greater than the archaeological record would suggest, it is tempting to equate this group of extinctions with the short, cold snap at *circa* 8200 BP, perhaps causing stress as a result of a significant reduction in carrying capacity and the most significant climatic downturn during the Holocene (Mayewski *et al.*, 1996; Alley *et al.*, 1997; Klitgaard-Kristensen *et al.*, 1998), an event which might also be relevant to changes in archaeological industries.

Greig (1996) provides regional summaries based upon the pollen evidence for the various regions of England. Wales is covered by Chambers (1996) in the same volume. Tipping (1995) presents a similar review of the Scottish evidence. The mid-Holocene landscapes of lowland England were dominated by lime (Greig, 1982), giving way to oak and elm to the west, oak and alder on wetter soils, and to oak hazel woodland in the uplands. The continuous pollen trace for pine on the poorer more acid soils and its presence in the plant macrofossil record from lowland bogs through into the Late Holocene (e.g. Legeard *et al.*, 2001) suggests that continuity of pine woodland on places like the Surrey and Hampshire heaths should not be ignored.

Fossil Insect Evidence

Although there had been some earlier work, notably by Henriksen (1931) and Lindroth (1948) in Scandinavia, it was only with the discovery of fossil beetles in organic silts at Upton Warren, Worcestershire (Coope *et al.*, 1961) and Chelford, Cheshire (Coope,

1959) that detailed research upon Quaternary insect assemblages began. Holocene forest faunas were first examined by Osborne at Shustoke in Warwickshire (Kelly & Osborne, 1965), and he presented his initial comments to the XIII Congress of Entomology in London in 1964 (Osborne, 1965). He pointed to the occurrence of deadwood species of coleoptera (beetles), including species now either extinct or extremely rare in Britain, in mid-Holocene fossil assemblages. Osborne later added several other species to the list (e.g. Osborne, 1972a). It was significantly extended by work by Buckland and Kenward (1973) on material from Thorne Moor in South Yorkshire, at *circa* 3000 BP still the most recent Old Forest (*Urwald*) assemblage from Britain (Buckland 1979), and with the more recent work by Roper (1996) and Whitehouse (1997; 2004), the peats of the Humberhead Levels have the longest list of nationally extinct species from any region. Girling (1982) also added significantly to the list with work in the Somerset Levels, and Robinson (2000) has specifically targeted the mesolithic / neolithic transition. It should be stressed, however, that so far only the beetles have been subjected to intensive study and that the distribution of sites examined both spatially and temporally remains patchy. Kenward's work in York in particular has provided long lists for the Anglo-Scandinavian period (Hall & Kenward, 1983; Kenward & Hall, 1995), but contemporary rural landscapes are less well served. The Roman countryside has several large assemblages from both urban and rural wells (e.g. Coope & Osborne, 1968; Girling, 1989a), as well some natural assemblages (e.g. Osborne, 1996). It is apparent from sites like Pilgrim Lock at Bidford-on-Avon, Warwickshire (Osborne, 1988) and the Wilsford shaft in Wiltshire (Osborne, 1969; 1989) that the later prehistoric landscape was already largely cleared and managed, but woodland is apparent at Thorne (Buckland, 1979), and older sites, away from direct evidence of human occupation, like many of Girling's (e.g. 1984; 1985) in the Somerset Levels, give some hint of the natural, relatively undisturbed landscape. A number of sites have faunas across the pollen zone VIIa/b boundary. Osborne's (1972a) series of sites along the edge of the Longmynd at Church Stretton are particularly useful, and West Heath Spa on the edge of London (Girling, 1989b) gives an indication of the nature of the first impacts upon the fauna of the forest by early agriculturalists. The latter site has been the basis of much discussion because of the presence of *Scolytus scolytus*, the elm bark beetle, in deposits predating the classic elm decline, one of the parameters used to define the VIIa/b boundary (Girling & Greig, 1985; Girling 1988; Moore, 1984). Table 1 lists the sites and their date ranges, which cover the period from the Early Holocene to the Neolithic.

Table 1: Early Holocene – Neolithic (Late Holocene) sites with insect faunas

Site	Range	Date from	Date to	Ref.
Glanllynau, Gwynedd	LG-EH			Coope & Brophy (1972)
Church Stretton, Salops.	LG-MH	>11048 ± 376		Osborne (1972a)
Holywell Coombe, Kent	LG-EH		> 9900 ± 100	Coope (1998)
West Bromwich, Warks.	LG-EH	>10025 ± 100	9080 ± 455	Osborne (1980)
Mingies Ditch, Oxon	LG-MH	>10860 ± 130	6540 ± 80	Robinson (1993)
Rodbaston, Staffs.	LG-EH	>10300 ± 170		Ashworth (1973)
Church Farm, Ches.	LG-EH	>9790 ± 60	7900 ± 50	Hughes *et al.* (2000)
Red Moss, Lancs.	LG-EH	<10850 ± 120	>9800 ± 700	Ashworth (1972)
Leicester	EH	9920 ± 100		Shackley & Hunt (1985)
Lea Marston, Warks.	EH	9550 ± 200	9450 ± 90	Osborne (1974)
Ripon, Yorks.	EH	9710 ± 60		Howard *et al.* (2000)
Bole Ings, Notts.	E-LH	< 8240 ± 60	> 2750 ± 60	Dinnin (1997)
Little Stretton, Salops.	EH	< 8101 ± 138	(VIa)	Osborne (1972a)
Church Stretton RS2, Salops	EH-MH	(VIa)	(VIIb)	Osborne (1972a)
Alcester, Warks.	EH	7440 ± 200	6930 ± 380	Shotton *et al.* (1977)
Norwich	EH- ?	?	?	Allison & Kenward (1994)
Etton, Cambs.	EH & MH	?	<> 4960 ± 90	Robinson (1999)
West Heath Spa	M-LH	(VIIa)	(VIII)	Girling (1989b)
Runnymede, Surrey	M-LH	< *circa* 5750	> *circa* 3950	Robinson (1991)
Abbot's Way, Somerset	M-LH	5500 ±	< 3980 ±	Girling (1976)
Baker Track, Somerset	M-LH	<> 4540 ± 80		Girling (1980)

Rowland's Track, Somerset	M-LH	> 4210 ± 90		Girling (1977)
Stileway, Somerset	LH	< 4470 ± 70		Girling (1985)
Silbury Hill, Wilts.	LH	4530 ± 110		Robinson (1997)
Shustoke, Warks.	LH	4830 ± 100		Kelly & Osborne (1965)
Sweet Track, Somerset	LH	5650 ± 70	4054 ± 45	Girling (1984)
Breiddin, Clwyd	LH			Buckland et al. (2001)

Key: LG = Lateglacial ~13,500-10,000 BP; EH = Early Holocene ~10,000-7000 BP; MH = 7000-5000 BP; LH = 5000- present day

Despite some past arguments to the contrary (cf. Dennis, 1977), it is unlikely that any significant elements in the biota survived the Last Glacial Maximum, and the present flora and fauna immigrated from *circa* 13,500 BP, with a significant return to high arctic conditions for about 1000 years down to 10,000 BP. Taken in the perspective of the Quaternary, the Holocene is only unique in the degree of human interference in the vegetational succession. For the purposes of discussion, a tripartite division of the present interglacial provides a usable framework: a) the Early Holocene during which the major forest trees immigrated from their refugia to the south (pollen zones IV – VI), b) the mid-Holocene with mixed deciduous woodland, the so-called Atlantic forest (pollen zone VIIa), and c) the Late Holocene, the post-Elm Decline landscapes of clearance and increasing human impact. The changes in the biota can be compared with those of previous interglacials, where there is no human interference in the succession. The rapidity of Late Glacial warming immediately into a Holocene at least as warm as present day was first indicated on insect faunas from sites at Church Stretton, Shropshire (Osborne, 1972a), Glanlynnau, Gwynedd (Coope & Brophy, 1972), and Red Moss, Lancashire (Ashworth, 1972), although it took the annual record of the ice cores, over twenty years later (Alley *et al.*, 1993) for the often precipitate nature of climate change to become more generally accepted. Given the vagaries of survival in refugia and differing patterns of post-glacial expansion, it might be expected that each interglacial would have a unique signal, but it now seems that nature occasionally has dealt what, in palynological terms, appears to be the same hand at least twice, although Coope (2001) has recently suggested that there may be unique elements in particular interglacial insect faunas. In pollen terms, however, sites previously regarded as all belonging to the last interglacial, the Ipswichian, can be shown to belong to two separate events, with type sites at Ipswich and Stanton Harcourt, better labelled using the numbered sequence derived from the oscillations apparent in the deep sea core sequence as Oxygen Isotope Stages as OIS 5e and 7, and the preceding

Hoxnian deposits belong to OIS 9 and 11. Similar elements of the Old Forest (*Urwald*) fauna appear in all. Whilst the Holocene (OIS 1) might be said at least in the Lowland Zone to be characterised by the small lime bark beetle *Ernoporus caucasicus*, discovered by Osborne (Kelly & Osborne, 1965) as a fossil before A. A. Allen (1969) added it to the modern British List, OIS 5e should, on the pollen evidence dominated by *Carpinus*, perhaps have the hornbeam scolytid *Scolytus carpini* as characteristic, although this is currently only known from two sites (Gaunt *et al.*, 1972; Keen *et al.*, 1999). It is perhaps hardly surprising that much of the deadwood fauna, having evolved in a Tertiary landscape of continuous habitat availability, should appear much the same whenever mature temperate mixed forest is reassembled (*cf.* Dinnin, 1992), and having co-evolved in this landscape it is equally hardly surprising that these species are the ones which are most under threat in the present fragmented landscape. The importance of dead wood habitats and their continuity has been the subject of much discussion on a European basis (*cf.* Harding & Rose, 1986; Kirby & Drake, 1993), but it should be remembered that old, unimproved grasslands are perhaps even more under threat. Their insect faunas, however, having evolved to be more mobile because of the transient nature of much of the open ground habitat through the Quaternary, are perhaps less likely to regional extinction. Table 1 summarises the present position with regard to extirpations from the British insect fauna during the Holocene. Decisions as to what to include have inevitably been somewhat arbitrary, but probable casual imports, such as the cerambycid *Hesperophanes fasciculatus* from Roman Alcester (Osborne, 1971), have been omitted, and others, like the dung beetle *Onthophagus fracticornis*, which might just be hanging on in a few localities (Hyman, 1992; 1994), have also been excluded.

Table 2: Extinctions from the British Holocene insect fauna, the fossil evidence, compared with earlier interglacial records. Species with 19th C records but now regarded as extinct are included. * indicates a species lacking woodland association. (for key to sites, see Appendix 1)

Taxon	Site	Interglacial
*Chlaenius sulcicollis	ST; MH;	TS; Itt (5e); Ave (7)
*Oodes gracilis	ST; AW; Go;	TS; Ips; Itt; Shr; De; TCP (5e)
*Gyrinus natator	Co; Cald; Bri;	
*G. colymbus	Lei	

Rhysodes sulcatus	Dav; Shu; BS; TM; Nsea	De; (5e)
Batrisus formicarius	Stil;	
Porthmidius austriacus	World;	
Dromaeolus barnabita	BoI; Run;	
Isorhipis melasoides	WHS; BS; Mist; TM	TCP (5e)
Buprestis rustica	TM	
**Dermestes laniarius*	Wil	TS (5e)
Zimioma grossum	Run; TM	
**Airaphilus elongates*	Wils; Rip; CS; ST; Sto; Dro;	Ips; Max (5e); HL (12)
Prostomis mandibularis	ST; TM	
Cryptolestes corticinus	HM;	
Pycnomerus terebrans	WHS; Min; Stil	TCP (5e)
Bothrideres contractus	Stil; TM;	Au (5e)
Mycetina cruciata	TM	
Rhopalodontus bauderi	TM	
**Leucohimatium* sp.	LeaM	
**Anthicus gracilis*	ST; AW; RT; Mea;	
Tenebroides fuscus	HM;	
**Onthophagus taurus*	Run; Pil; Flag;	TS; Ips; Els; De (5e);
**O. verticicornis*	Wil; Pil; Ming; Ast;	TS; Els; Wool; De (5e)

Aphodius quadriguttatus	Wil;	
A. scrofa	WHS;	
A. varians	Run; Min;	
Rhyssemus germanus		TS; Shr; Wool; (5e)
Pleurophorus caesus		TS; De; (5e)
Polyphylla fullo	Hib;	
Platycerus caraboides	Melt;	
Strangalia attenuate	ST;	
Cerambyx cerdo	Isle; Rams;	
Cathormiocerus validiscapus	Al;	SG (7);
Cyphocleonus trisulcatus	LeaM	
Rhyncolus elongates	HoC; World; TM;	
R. sculpturatus	TM	
R. strangulates	World;	
R. punctulatus	Stil; TM; HM;	

If clearings in the forest are regarded as transient habitats, then their insects, in contrast with the deadwood faunas, should therefore be more likely to appear in the fossil record, occurring in peat successions remote from woodland localities. Most, however, largely disappear between the open ground of the warmer parts of the Late Glacial and early Holocene and the extensive opening up of the *Urwald* by people. Some, like the thermophilous steppe genus *Leucohimatium*, present at Lea Marston in Warwickshire during the early Holocene (Osborne, 1974), probably also the warmest part of the present interglacial, do not return, but others become characteristic of the open landscapes, particularly of the chalk and limestones, Hammond's (1974) *cultursteppe*, from the Bronze Age onwards, although many had to wait until the Roman period to gain assisted passage. Several species, which one would regard as primarily inhabitants of old established grassland, do maintain a continuous trace through the Holocene, whilst becoming more common in post-clearance landscapes.

The large elaterid *Agrypnus murina* occurs in pasture and on woodland margins, where its larvae are predatory on those of *Melolontha, Phyllopertha* and other root feeders in grassland (Horion, 1953). It is present in the earliest Holocene at Lea Marston (Osborne, 1974) and West Bromwich (Osborne, 1980), both in Warwickshire, and later at Westward Ho in Devon (6810#140 BP) (Girling & Robinson, 1987), Bole Ings, Nottinghamshire (<6290#70) (Dinnin, 1997), and Church Stretton in Shropshire (pollen zone VIIa) (Osborne, 1972). The cockchafer, *Melolontha melolontha*, whose larvae develop on the roots of grassland in clearings in woodland is present at West Hampstead Heath in north London during pollen zone VIIa (Girling, 1989b) and at Bole Ings (Dinnin, 1997). It is important to note that Osborne (1972), long before the Vera hypothesis, interpreted the insect assemblage from the pollen zone VIIa landscape around the Church Stretton site as one in which "Large herbivores must have been present and it is suggested that this locality was occupied by grassland." He preferred to regard this as evidence of early human impact, but the associated dung fauna, largely *Aphodius* spp., extends back to early in the pollen zone, when it is unlikely there were settled human populations.

The insect fauna of herbivore dung, because of the transient nature of the habitat, is widely dispersed, and provides a trace after the animals in the absence of a direct fossil record. Many species, however, are able to exploit analogous accumulations of rotting plant debris, and occasional records of these have to be treated circumspectly. The scarabaeoid beetles which feed in dung are specific as to the depositional environment of the faeces, rather than the vertebrate species of origin. Thus, whilst aphodius zenkeri is normally found in deer droppings, it is the shaded habitat provided by forest or pasture woodland that is being exploited and the species is as likely to be in sheep, pony or cattle dung when these domestic animals are grazed in woodland localities (Landin, 1961). Whilst its present apparent expansion in range may relate to increasing roe deer populations (Skidmore, pers. comm.), the earliest Holocene records are from the Late Holocene at Langford in Nottinghamshire, *circa* 4000 BP (Howard *et al.*, 1999) and Stileway in the Somerset Levels, circa 4470 ± 70 BP (Girling, 1985). Most of the scarabaeoid dung fauna first appears in the Neolithic and the record is thereafter heavily biased towards research upon samples from archaeological sites. The large assemblage recovered by Osborne (1969; 1989) from the late Bronze Age well at Wilsford, is one of the few assemblages from the Chalk, and adds several members of the dung fauna to the list, including large numbers of individuals of acragas quadriguttatus, now extinct in Britain. Whilst a few sites have mid-Holocene records at the generic level for aphodius species, the site at Church Stretton in Shropshire having a continuous trace through pollen zones VIc and VIIa (Osborne, 1972), only one species, aphodius rufipes, has been recorded between the Late Glacial and the Neolithic, at Mingies Ditch in Oxfordshire in deposits of 6540±80 BP (Robinson, 1993). As Jessop (1986) records A. rufipes as a cuckoo parasite of geotrupes spiniger, it is probable that this species was also present. A. rufipes is fairly eurytopic but avoids open ground, although it flies readily. Koch (1989) notes it particularly from clearings in woodland and on pastures near woods.

Table 3: Earliest Holocene and Interglacial records for the scarabaeoid dung fauna. (For key to sites, see Appendix 1)

Taxon	Holocene	Interglacial
Typhaeus typhoeus	Wil – 3060 BP (LBA)	
Geotrupes mutator		
G. spiniger	ST – 5150 BP	
G. stercorarius	TatT – 2350 BP (IA)	
G. stercorosus	SLoch – Mid Holocene?	
G. vernalis	ST – 5150 BP	
G. pyrenaeus	ST – 5150 BP	
Onthophagus Taurus	Run - < 5400 BP (Neol.)	TS; Ips; Els; De (5e)
O. verticicornis	Wil – 3160 BP (LBA)	TS; Els; Wool; De (5e)
O. joannae	ST – 5150 BP	
O. nuchicornis	TatT – 2350 BP	TS (5e)
O. vacca	Wil – 3160 BP (LBA)	TS; Wool; TCP (5e)
O. fracticornis	Sil – 4750	
O. similes	CS – Zone VIIb	

O. coenobite	Wil – 3160 BP (LBA)	TCP (5e)
Onthophagus sp.	CS – Zone VIIa	Max; Wool; TCP (5e)
Aphodius fossor	Sil - 4750 BP	TS; Itt; De (5e); SG; SH; US;
A. haemorrhoidalis	Run - < 5400 BP (Neol.)	
A. brevis		
A. arenarius	Wil – 3160 BP	
*A. rufipes	Ming – 6540 BP	Itt; De (5e)
A. luridus	ST – 5150 BP	
A. depressus	West – 4840 BP	Shr; (5e) SH (7)
A. zenkeri	Lang – 4000 BP	
A. pusillus	Sil – 4750 BP	
A. coenosus		
+A. quadriguttatus	Wil – 3160 BP	
A. quadrimaculatus		
A. sticticus	BoI - < 6290 BP	
A. conspurcatus	Brigg – 3000 BP	
A. distinctus	Wil – 3160 BP	
A. paykulli	Bart – Late Roman	
A. obliteratus	TatT – 2350 BP (IA)	
A. contaminatus	Pil – 2900 BP	

A. sphacelatus	Sil – 4750 BP	
A. prodromus	Sil – 4750 BP	
A. consputus	ST – 5150 BP	TS; Shr; De (5e)
A. porcus	Run - < 5400 BP	De; TCP (5e)
A. scrofa	WHS – Zone VIIa/b	
A. merdarius	TatT – 2350 BP (IA)	
A. foetidus	Run - < 5400 BP	
A. lapponum	SLoch - ?Mid Holocene	
A. fimetarius	LS – Zone VIIa	Shr (5e)
A. foetens	Brigg – 3000 BP	
A. fasciatus	TinT – 3060 BP	SH (7)
A. ater	TatT – 2350 BP (IA)	
A. constans	Wil - 3160 BP (LBA)	
A. borealis		
A. nemoralis		
A. sordidus	TinT -3060 BP	
A. ictericus	Wil – 3160 BP (LBA)	
A. rufus	ST – 5150 BP	
A. plagiatus	Go - (IA)	
A. niger		

A. varians	Run – (BA)	
A. lividus	Emp – (Rom)	
A. granarius	ST – 5150 BP	
++*Aphodius* sp.	CS	

Table 4: Earliest Holocene records of other species associated with dung (probable Roman or later introductions excluded). (For key, see Appendix I)

Taxa	Earliest Holocene	Interglacial
Cercyon atomarius	Run - < 5400 BP	
C. haemorrhoidalis	Run - < 5400 BP	
C. melanocephalus	Wil – 3160 BP (LBA)	Itt; Shr (5e); Ave; Cam; SG; Mars; SH; US (7)
C. lateralis	Drag – (Rom)	
C. atricapillus	Run – (LBA)	
C. terminatus	Run – (LBA)	
C. pygmaeus	Run - <5400 BP	
Megasternum boletophagum	CS zone VIIa	Itt; Shr; Wool; De; TCP (5e); Ave; Cam; Mars; US; TT (7)
Cryptopleurum minutum	CS zone VIIa	Itt; Shr; De (5e); Ave; Cam; SG; Mars; US;
Sphaeridium bipustulatum	Run - <5400 BP	TS; Shr; Wool; De (5e); SG (7)
S. scarabaeoides	Radley – 3250 BP	

Onthophilus striatus	CS – zone VIIa/b	
Atholus 12-striatus	Run - < 5400 BP	
Paralister purpurescens	HoC – 9280 BP, then Wil -3160 BP (LBA)	
Hister bisexstriatus	Run < 5400 BP	
Oxytelus piceus	BS – (BA)	Wool (5e);
O. laqueatus	CS – zone VIIa	
Anotylus sculpturatus	ST – 5150 BP	TS (5e); US (7)
A. complanatus	BoI - < 6290	SG (7)
A. tetracarinatus	Brigg – 2600 BP	
Platystethus arenarius	Ming – 6540 BP	De; TCP (5e); Cam; SG; Mars; US (7);
Leptacinus batychrus	Run – (BA)	
Gyrohypnus punctulatus	Shu – 4830 BP	TS (5e); SG (7)
G. fracticornis	Shu – 4830 BP	
G. angustatus	Run - < 5400	Au (5e)
Xantholinus glabratus	Sil – 4750 BP	
Philonthus laminatus	Brigg – 2600 BP	
P. politus	Eil – (Neo.) (then Rom.)	
Ontholestes tesselatus	Fish – (IA)	
O. murinus	Cald – zone VII	

Platydracus fulvipes	TM - < 4500 BP	
P. stercorarius	Abb – (Neo.)	
P. pubescens	Wil – 3160 BP (LBA)	
Quedius fuliginosus	TM - < 4500 BP	
Tachinus signatus	Shu – 4830 BP	
T. marginellus	Shu – 4830 BP	
Autalia rivularis	TM – 3000 BP	
Tinotus morion	Brigg – 2600 BP	

Amongst the remainder of the essentially obligate dung fauna, it is again the Church Stretton borehole which provides hints of the presence of large herbivores in the mid-Holocene. The histerid *Onthophilus striatus*, which Skidmore (1991) records largely from horse dung in Britain, although known from a wider range of habitats on the continent (Koch, 1989; see also Donisthorpe, 1939), appears in a sample straggling the pollen zone VIIa/b boundary. In the absence of any evidence for proximity of human occupation, it seems likely to be related to natural habitats. The more eurytopic hydrophilid *megasternum boletophagum*, which Skidmore (1991) notes in large numbers in herbivore dung, also occurs early in zone VIIa at Church Stretton, with *cryptopleurum minutum*, also often in dung, from the overlying sample. No significant elements of the large carrion fauna have been recorded from pre-Landnam deposits (Table 5).

Table 5: Earliest Holocene records of large carrion fauna.(For key, see Appendix I)

Taxa	Earliest Holocene
Nicrophorus humator	Whit – (Rom)
Necrodes littoralis	Brigg – 2600 BP
Thanatophilus rugosus	Wil – 3160 BP (LBA)

T. sinuatus	Wil – 3160 BP (LBA)
Dermestes lardarius	Run - (BA)
Omosita discoidea	Run – (BA)
O. colon	Run – (BA)
Nitidula bipunctata	Wil – 3160 BP (LBA)

The Interglacial Record

In terms of analogues for a warmer Holocene, the previous interglacial, the Ipswichian (Eemian), Oxygen Isotope Stage 5e, with summer temperatures of the order of three degrees celsius warmer than present on the fossil beetle evidence (Coope & Beesley, 1987), provides interesting parallels. There is no evidence for the presence of hominids in the British Isles, yet abundant evidence of open ground taxa at the period of maximum warmth and forest expansion. Species which are particularly favoured by human activity, such as the ground beetles *Calathus fuscipes* and *Pterostichus melanarius*, are present, and there is a remarkable suite of dung beetles, including the presently Sicilian 'endemic' *Onthophagus massai* from several sites. The fauna in part reflects the presence of large herbivores; elephant, rhinoceros and hippopotamus, which fail to return in the present interglacial, but the warmer nature of the maximum is also apparent. Rackham's (1998) view of temperate savannah is clearly more appropriate for this interglacial. In the present interglacial, the open ground taxa are less evident in the early – mid-Holocene record, although in part this may reflect the paucity and nature of sites examined. Continuous sequences through much of the Holocene are only available from Church Stretton (Osborne, 1972) and Bole Ings (Dinnin, 1997) and these have problems in working from limited samples from boreholes. The trace, however, is sufficient to provide some support for Vera's hypothesis on the variegated nature of Holocene forests. Large vertebrate grazers must have played an important part in the maintenance of this varied landscape, but the incidence of natural fire, particularly in regions on poor soils still dominated by pine, rather than mesolithic pyromania, should also be reconsidered. Tidy deciduous forest with little dead wood may not be particularly flammable, but return the dead wood with many standing moribund trees and the recipe for occasional lightning struck fires becomes available, providing habitat for a range of insects that have evolved to exploit this transient habitat. Whitehouse and Eversham (2002) have recently discussed the fossil record of the pyrophilic carabid *Pterostichus angustatus* from Hatfield Moors, South Yorkshire, and pointed out the problems of habitat continuity for such species through the mid-Holocene, a point equally valid for even more fire dependent species (*cf.* Wikars, 1992), such as the buprestid *Melanophila acuminata* (Danks & Foottit, 1989; Palm, 1951), apparently largely restricted to the Surrey heaths (Levey, 1977; Alexander, 2002) yet omitted from the Red Data Book lists (Hyman, 1992; 1994).

Conclusion

Much has yet to be learnt regarding the nature of 'natural' woodland. A more integrated approach to the fossil record is the best approach, provided it is based upon a sound knowledge of the present ecology of species. Palaeoecology can also inform decisions on conservation issues, although managers of present reserves rarely have access to the knowledge of the long term past trajectories of their landscapes. It is problem which needs addressing. Whilst sites like Thorne and Hatfield Moors have been extensively researched for their Late Holocene coleoptera record, similar studies of apparently less damaged habitats, like the New Forest for example, are lacking. The insect record does provide a little support for the Vera hypothesis, but the picture is not one of warm temperate savannah, as appeared in the last interglacial. The reasons for this are complex, but the relative warmth of the Ipswichian, perhaps accompanied by seasonal drought concentrating herbivores on the floodplains, where inevitably palaeoecological samples come from, and the extinction from the European fauna of elephant, rhinoceros and hippopotamus, would have had a significant impact on the nature of wetland forest, where deer, aurochs and boar in the mid-Holocene were unable to have similar impact. Anthropogenic impact, if this is the reason for Late Pleistocene overkill of large mammals, had therefore already started by the early Holocene. The Atlantic forest, in itself further modified by fire, was more dense than that of previous interglacial, simply because Man had already started to modify the grazing regime. This does not mean however that the dynamic nature of the forest system of death and re-growth, influenced by 'natural' grazers and browsers, can be ignored.

Acknowledgments

This paper grew out of a reading of Frans Vera's book and subsequent discussions with him and Keith Kirkby of English Nature, to both of whom primary acknowledgment is made. The research was funded by English Nature through ECUS at the University of Sheffield as part of their project to examine 'naturalistic grazing regimes', and was designed to provide the longer term framework for management projects. The review is here largely limited to the fossil insect data, and will later be extended to other sources of evidence. The comments of Damian Hughes (ECUS) and Eva Panagiotakopulu on a previous draft of the text are also acknowledged.

References

Alexander, K.N.A. (2002) *The invertebrates of living and decaying timber in Britain & Ireland. A provisional annotated checklist.* Peterborough, English Nature.

Allen, A.A. (1969) *Ernoporus caucasicus* Lind. and *Leperesinus orni* Fuchs (Col., Scolytidae) in Britain. *Entomologist's Monthly Magazine*, **105**, 245-249.

Alley, R.B., Mayewski, P.A., Sowers, T., Stuiver, M., Taylor, K.C. and Clark, P.U. (1997) Holocene climatic instability: a prominent, widespread event 8,200 yr ago. *Geology*, **25**, 483-486.

Allison, E.P. and Kenward, H.K. (1994) IV. Insects. In Ayers, B.S. Excavations at Fishergate, Norwich 1985. *East Anglian Archaeology*, **68**, 45-48.

Ashworth, A.C. (1972) A Late-glacial Insect Fauna from Red Moss, Lancashire, England. *Entomologica Scandinavica*, **3**, 211-224.

Ashworth, A.C. (1973) The Climatic Significance of a Late Quaternary Insect Fauna from Rodbaston Hall, Staffordshire, England. *Entomologica Scandinavica*, **4**, 191-205.

Bennett, K.D. (1995) Post-glacial dynamics of pine (*Pinus sylvestris* L.) and pinewoods in Scotland. Aldous, J. R. (ed.) *Our pinewood heritage*. Farnham, Forestry Commission, RSPB, 23-39.

Buckland, P.C. (1979) *Thorne Moors: a palaeoecological study of a Bronze Age site.* Birmingham, Department of Geography, University of Birmingham. (173pp).

Buckland, P.C. and Kenward, H.K. (1973) Thorne Moors: a palaeoecological study of a Bronze Age site. *Nature*, **241**, 405-406.

Buckland, P.C., Parker Pearson, M., Wigley, A. and Girling, M.A. (2001) Is there anybody out there? A reconsideration of the environmental evidence from the Breiddin Hillfort, Powys, Wales. *Antiquaries Journal*, **81**, 51-76.

Chambers, F.M. (1996) Great Britain - Wales. Berglund, B.E., Birks, H.J.B., Ralska-Jasiewiczowa, M. and Wright, H.E. (eds.) *Palaeoecological events during the last 15 000 years. Regional synthesis of palaeoecological studies of lakes and mires in Europe.* J. Wiley & Sons, Chichester.

Coope, G.R. (1959) A Late Pleistocene insect fauna from Chelford, Cheshire. *Proceedings of the Royal Society of London*, **B151**, 70-86.

Coope, G.R. (1998) Insects. Preece, R.C. and Bridgland, D.R. (eds.) *Late Quaternary environmental change in North-west Europe: Excavations at Holywell Coombe, South-east England*. Chapman & Hall, London.

Coope, G.R. (2001) Biostratigraphical distinction of interglacial coleopteran assemblages from southern Britain attributed to Oxygen Isotope Stages 5e and 7. *Quaternary Science Reviews*, **20**, 1717-1722.

Coope, G.R. and Beesley, A.R. (1987) How warm was the Ipswichian interglacial: evidence from insect assemblages. *International Union for Quaternary Research XII international Congress: Program with Abstracts*, Ottawa.

Coope, G.R. and Brophy, J.A. (1972) Late Glacial environmental changes indicated by a coleopteran succession from North Wales. *Boreas*, **1**, 97-142.

Coope, G.R. and Osborne, P.J. (1968) Report on the Coleopterous Fauna of the Roman Well at Barnsley Park, Gloucestershire. *Transactions of the Bristol and Gloucestershire Archaeological Society*, **86**, 84-87.

Coope, G.R., Shotton, F.W. and Strachan, I. (1961) A Late Pleistocene fauna and flora from Upton Warren, Worcestershire. *Philosophical Transactions of the Royal Society of London*, **B244**, 379-421.

Danks, H.V. and Foottit, R.G. (1989) Insects of the boreal zone of Canada. *Canadian Entomologist*, **121**, 625-690.

Dennis, R.L.H. (1977) *The British Butterflies. Their origin and establishment*. E.W. Classey, Faringdon.

Dinnin, M.H. (1992) *Islands within Islands: the development of the British entomofauna during the Holocene and the implications for conservation*. University of Sheffield, Sheffield.

Dinnin, M. (1997) Holocene beetle assemblages from the Lower Trent floodplain at Bole Ings, Nottinghamshire, UK. *Quaternary Proceedings*, **5**, 83-104.

Donisthorpe, H.S.J. (1939) *A preliminary list of the Coleoptera of Windsor Forest*. Lloyd & Co, London.

Fraser, F.C. and King, J.E. (1954). Faunal remains. Clark, J.G.D. *Excavations at Star Carr*. Cambridge University Press, Cambridge.

Gaunt, G.D., Coope, G.R., Osborne, P.J. and Franks, J.W. (1972) *An interglacial deposit near Austerfield, South Yorkshire*. HMSO, London.

Girling, M.A. (1976) Fossil Coleoptera from the Somerset Levels: the Abbot's Way. *Somerset Levels Papers*, **2**, 28-33.

Girling, M.A. (1977) Fossil insect assemblages from Rowland's track. *Somerset Levels Papers*, **3**, 51-60.

Girling, M.A. (1980) The fossil insect assemblage from the Baker Site. *Somerset Levels Papers*, **6**, 36-42.

Girling, M.A. (1982) Fossil insect faunas from forest sites. Limbrey, S. and Bell, M. (eds.) *Archaeological Aspects of Woodland Ecology*. British Archaeological Reports, Oxford **S146**, 129-146.

Girling, M.A. (1984) Investigations of a second insect assemblage from the Sweet Track. *Somerset Levels Papers*, **10**, 79-91.

Girling, M.A. (1985) An old forest beetle fauna from a Neolithic and Bronze Age peat deposit at Stileway. *Somerset Levels Papers*, **11**, 80-83.

Girling, M.A. (1988) The bark beetle *Scolytus scolytus* (Fabricius) and the possible role of elm disease in the early Neolithic. Jones, M. (ed.) *Archaeology and the Flora of the British Isles*. Oxford University Committee for Archaeology Monograph, **14**, 34-38.

Girling, M.A. (1989a) The insect fauna of the Roman well at the Cattle Market. Down, A., *Chichester Excavations*. Philimore, Chichester. **6**, 234-241.

Girling, M.A. (1989b) Mesolithic and later landscapes interpreted from the insect assemblages of West Heath Spa Hampstead. Collins, D. and Lorimer, D., *Excavations at the Mesolithic Site on West Heath, Hampstead 1976-1981*. British Archaeological Reports, Oxford **217**, 72-89.

Girling, M.A. and Greig, J.R.A. (1985) A first fossil record for *Scolytus scolytus* (F.) (Elm Bark Beetle): its occurrence in Elm Decline deposits from London and the implications for Neolithic Elm Disease. *Journal of Archaeological Science*, **12**, 347-352.

Girling, M.A. and Robinson, M. (1987) The Insect Fauna. In Balaam, N.D., Bell, M.G., David, A.E.U., Levitan, B., McPhail, I.R., Robinson, M. and Scaife, R.G., Prehistoric and Romano-British Sites at Westward Ho!, Devon. Archaeological and Palaeoenvironmental Surveys, 1983 and 1984. Balaam, N.D., Levitan, B. and Staker, V. (eds.) *Studies in palaeoeconomy and environment in South West England*. British Archaeological Reports, Oxford, **181**, 239-246.

Godwin, H. (1975) *History of the British flora: a factual basis for phytogeography*. Cambridge University Press, Cambridge.

Gonzalez, S., Kitchener, A.C. and Lister, A.M. (2000) Survival of Irish Elk into the Holocene. *Nature*, **405**, 753-754.

Greig, J.R.A. (1982) Past and present lime woods of Europe. Bell, M. and Limbrey, S. (eds.) *Archaeological Aspects of Woodland Ecology*. British Archaeological Reports, Oxford, **S146,** 23-56.

Greig, J.R.A. (1996) Great Britain - England. Berglund, B.E., Birks, H.J.B., Ralska-Jasiewiczowa, M. and Wright, H.E. (eds.) *Palaeoecological events during the last 15 000 years. Regional synthesis of palaeoecological studies of lakes and mires in Europe*. J. Wiley & Sons, Chichester.

Hall, A.R., Kenward, H.K., Williams, D. and Greig, J.R.A. (1983) Environment and living conditions at two Anglo-Scandinavian sites. *Archaeology of York*, **14(4)**.

Hammond, P. M. (1974) Changes in the British Coleopterous Fauna. Hawksworth, D. L. *The Changing Flora and Fauna of Britain*. London, Systematics Association Special Volume **6**. Academic Press, London.

Harding, P.T. and Rose, F. (1986). *Pasture-woodlands in lowland Britain*. Institute of Terrestrial Ecology, Huntingdon.

Henriksen, K.L. (1931) Undersøgelser over Danmark-Skånes kvartære Insektfauna. *Videnskabelige Meddelelser fra Dansk naturhistorisk Forening*, **96**, 77-355.

Horion, A. (1953) *Faunistik der Mitteleuropäischen Käfer, 3. Malacodermata, Sternoxia (Elateridae - Throscidae)*. G. Frey, Munich.

Hoskins, W.G. (1977) *The Making of the English Landscape*. Hodder & Stoughton, London.

Howard, A.J., Keen, D.H., Mighall, T.M., Field, M.H., Coope, G.R., Griffiths, H.I. and Macklin, M.G. (2000) Early Holocene environments of the river Ure near Ripon, North Yorkshire, UK. *Proceedings of the Yorkshire Geological Society*, **53**, 31-42.

Howard, A.J., Smith, D.N., Garton, D., Hillam, J. and Pearce, M. (1999) Middle to Late Holocene environments in the Middle to Lower Trent valley. Brown, A.G. and Quine, T. A. *Fluvial processes and environmental change*. J. Wiley & Sons, Chichester.

Hughes, P.D.M., Kenward, H.K., Hall, A.R. and Large, F.D. (2000) A high-resolution record of mire development and climatic change spanning the Late-glacial-Holocene boundary at Church Moss, Davenham (Cheshire, England). *Journal of Quaternary Science*, **15**, 697-724.

Hyman, P.S. (1992) *Review of the scarce and threated Coleoptera of Great Britain. Part 1*. Joint Nature Conservancy Council, Peterborough.

Hyman, P.S. (1994) *Review of the scarce and threated Coleoptera of Great Britain. Part 2*. Joint Nature Conservancy Council, Peterborough.

Keen, D.H., Bateman, M.D., Coope, G.R., Field, M.H., Langford, H.E., Merry, J.S. and Mighall, T.M. (1999) Sedimentology, palaeoecology and geochronology of Last Interglacial deposits from Deeping St James, Lincolnshire, England. *Journal of Quaternary Science*, **14**, 411-436.

Jessop, L. (1986) *Dung beetles and chafers. Coleoptera: Scarabaeoidea* (new ed.). Royal Entomological Society of London Handbooks for the Identification of British Insects, 5,11, London.

Kelly, M.R. and Osborne, P.J. (1965) Two faunas and floras from the alluvium at Shustoke, Warwickshire. *Proceedings of the Linnean Society of London*, **176**, 37-65.

Kenward, H.K. and Hall, A.R. (1995) *Biological evidence from 16-22 Coppergate*. Council for British Archaeology, York.

Kirby, K.J. and Drake, C. M., (eds.) (1993) Dead wood matters: the ecology and conservation of saproxylic invertebrates in Britain. *English Nature Science*, **7**. English Nature, Peterborough.

Klitgaard-Kristensen, D., Sejrup, H.-P., Haflidason, H., Johnsen, S. and Spurk, M. (1998) A regional 8,200 cal yr cooling event in northwest Europe, induced by final stages of the Laurentide ice-sheet deglaciation? *Journal of Quaternary Science*, **13**, 165-169.

Koch, K. (1989) *Ökologie. Die Käfer Mitteleuropas*. Goecke & Evers, Krefeld.

Landin, B.-O. (1961) Ecological Studies on Dung-Beetles. *Opuscula Entomologica* Suppl., **19**.

Legeard, J.G.A., Thomas, P.A. and Chambers, F.M. (2001) Using fire scars and growth release in subfossil Scots pine to reconstruct prehistoric fires. *Palaeogeography, Palaeoclimatology, Paleoecology*, **164**, 87-99.

Legge, A.J. and Rowley-Conwy, P.A. (1988) *Star Carr revisited: a re-analysis of the large mammals*. Birkbeck College, London.

Levey, B. (1977) *Coleoptera Buprestidae*. Handbooks for the Identification of British Insects, V,1(b). Royal Entomological Society of London, London.

Lindroth, C.H. (1948) Interglacial insect remains from Sweden. *Årsbok Sveriges geologiska undersökning*, **C42**, 1-29.

McCormick, F. and Buckland, P.C. (1997) *The Vertebrate Fauna*. Edwards, K.J. and Ralston, I.B.M. (eds.) Scotland. Environment and Archaeology 8,000 BC to AD 1000, 83-103. J. Wiley & Sons, Chichester.

Maroo, S. and Yalden, D.W. (2000) The mesolithic mammal fauna of Great Britain. *Mammal Review*, **30**, 243-248.

Mayewski, P.A., Buckland, P.C., Edwards, K.J., Meeker, L.D. and O'Brien, S. (1996) *Climate change events as seen in the Greenland ice core (GISP2)*. Pollard, T. and Morrison, A. (eds.) The early prehistory of Scotland. 74-86, Edinburgh University Press, Edinburgh.

Mellars, P.A. (1976) Fire ecology, animal populations and man: a study of some ecological relationships in prehistory. *Proceedings of the Prehistoric Society*, **42**, 15-45.

Moore, J. (1996) Damp squib: how to fire a major deciduous forest in an inclement climate. Pollard, T. and Morrison, A. (eds.) The early prehistory of Scotland. 62-73, Edinburgh University Press, Edinburgh.

Moore, J. (2000) Forest fire and human interaction in the early Holocene woodlands of Britain. *Palaeogeography, Palaeoclimatology, Palaeoecology*, **164**, 125-137.

Moore, P.D. (1973) The influence of prehistoric cultures upon the initiation and spread of blanket bog in upland Wales. *Nature*, **241**, 350-353.

Moore, P.D. (1984) Hampstead Heath clue to historical decline of elms (Find of Dutch elm disease beetle in pre-elm decline level). *Nature*, **312**, 103.

Moore, P.D. (1993) *The origin of blanket mire revisited.* Chambers, F.M. (ed.) Climate Change and Human Impact on the Landscape. 217-225, Chapman & Hall, London.

Osborne, P.J. (1965) *The effect of forest clearance on the distribution of the British Insect fauna.* Proceedings XII International Congress of Entomology, London, 1964. London, 556-557.

Osborne, P.J. (1969) An insect fauna of Late Bronze Age date from Wilsford, Wiltshire. *Journal of Animal Ecology*, **38**, 555-566.

Osborne, P.J. (1971) An insect fauna from the Roman site at Alcester, Warwickshire. *Britannia*, **2**, 156-165.

Osborne, P.J. (1972a) Insect faunas of Late Devensian and Flandrian age from Church Stretton, Shropshire. *Philosophical Transactions of the Royal Society of London*, **B263**, 327-367.

Osborne, P.J. (1974) An Insect Assemblage of Early Flandrian Age from Lea Marston, Warwickshire and Its Bearing on the Contemporary Climate and Ecology. *Quaternary Research*, **4**, 471-486.

Osborne, P.J. (1980) The Late Devensian Flandrian transition depicted by serial insect faunas from West Bromwich, England. *Boreas*, **9**, 139-147.

Osborne, P.J. (1988) A late Bronze Age insect fauna from the River Avon, Warwickshire, England: its implications for the terrestrial and fluvial environment and for climate. *Journal of Archaeological Science*, **15**, 715-727.

Osborne, P.J. (1989) Insects. In: Ashbee, P., Bell, M. and Proudfoot, E., *Wilsford shaft excavations 1960-62*. English Heritage, London, 96-99.

Osborne, P.J. (1996). An insect fauna of Roman date from Stourport, Worcestershire, U.K., and its environmental interpretation. *Circaea*, **12**, 181-189.

Rackham, O. (1998) Savannah in Europe. Kirby, K.J. and Watkins, C. (eds.) *The ecological history of European forests*. CABI, Wallingford, 1-24.

Robinson, M.A. (1991) The Neolithic and Late Bronze Age insect assemblages. Needham, S. *Excavation and Salvage at Runneymede Bridge 1978: The Late Bronze Age waterfront site*. British Museum Press, London, 277-326.

Robinson, M. (1993) The scientific evidence. Allen, T.G. and Robinson, M.A., *The prehistoric landscape and Iron Age enclosed settlement at Mingies Ditch, Hardwich-with-Yelford Oxon*. Oxford Archaeological Unit, Thames Valley Landscapes. The Windrush Valley 2, Oxford, 101-141.

Robinson, M. (1997) The insects. Whittle, A. *Sacred mound holy rings. Silbury Hill and the West Kennet palisade enclosures: a Later Neolithic complex in north Wiltshire*. Oxbow Monographs, Oxford, **74**, 36-46.

Robinson, M. (1998) Insect assemblages. Pryor, F. *Etton. Excavations at a Neolithic causewayed enclosure near Maxey Cambridgeshire, 1982-7*. English Heritage Archaeological Report, London, **18**, 337-348.

Robinson, M. (2000) Coleopteran evidence for the Elm Decline, Neolithic activity in woodland, clearance and the use of the landscape. Fairburn, A. S. *Plants in Neolithic Britain and beyond. Neolithic studies group seminar papers*, **5**. Oxbow Books, London, 27-36.

Roper, T. (1996) Fossil insect evidence for the development of raised mire at Thorne Moors, near Doncaster. *Biodiversity and Conservation*, **5**, 503-521.

Rowley-Conwy, P. (1998) Faunal remains and antler artifacts. Mellars, P. and Dark, P. (eds.) *Star Carr in context*. McDonald Institute for Archaeological Research, Cambridge, 99-110.

Schadla-Hall, R.T. (1988) The early post glacial in eastern Yorkshire. Manby, T.G. (ed.) *Archaeology in eastern Yorkshire: essays presented to T. C. M. Brewster*. Sheffield, Dept. of Archaeology & Prehistory, University of Sheffield, 25-34.

Shackley, M. and Hunt, S.-A. (1985) Palaeoenvironment of a mesolithic peat bed from Austin Friars, Leicester. *Transactions of the Leicestershire Archaeological & Historical Society*, **59**, 1-12.

Shotton, F.W., Osborne, P.J. & Greig, J.R.A. (1977) The fossil content of a Flandrian deposit at Alcester. *Proceedings of the Coventry and District Natural History and Scientific Society*, **5**, 19-32.

Simmons, I.G. (1969) Evidence for vegetation changes associated with Mesolithic man in Britain. Ucko, P.J. and Dimbleby, G.W. (eds.) *The Domestication and Exploitation of Plants and Animals*. London, Duckworth, 111-119.

Simmons, I.G. (1996) *The environmental impact of later mesolithic cultures: the creation of moorland landscapes in England and Wales*. Edinburgh University Press, Edinburgh.

Simmons, I.G. (2003). *The moorlands of England and Wales. An environmental history 8000BC - AD 2000*. Edinburgh University Press, Edinburgh.

Skidmore, P. (1991) *Insects of the Cow Dung Community*. Field Studies Council, Shrewsbury.

Tallantire, P.A. (1992) The alder (*Alnus glutinosa* (L.) Gaernt.) problem in the British Isles: a third approach to its palaeohistory. *New Phytologist*, **122**, 717-731.

Tipping, R. (1995) The form and fate of Scotland's woodlands. *Proceedings of the Society of Antiquaries of Scotland*, **124**, 1-54.

Vera, F.W.M. (2000) *Grazing ecology and forest history*. CABI, Wallingford.

Whitehouse, N.J. (1997) Silent witnesses: an 'Urwald' fossil insect assemblage from Thorne Moors. *Thorne & Hatfield Moors Papers*, **4**, 19-54.

Whitehouse, N. (2000) Forest fires and insects: palaeoentomological research from a sub-fossil burnt forest. *Palaeogeography, Palaeoclimatology, Palaeoecology*, **164**, 247-262.

Whitehouse, N. (2004) Mire ontogeny, environmental and climatic change inferred from fossil beetle successions from Hatfield Moors, eastern England. *The Holocene*, **14**, 79-93.

Whitehouse, N.J. and Eversham, B.C. (2002) A fossil specimen of *Pterostichus angustatus* (Duftschmidt) (Carabidae): implications for the importance of pine and fire habitats. *The Coleopterist*, **11**, 107-118.

Wikars, L.-O. (1997) *Effects of forest-fire and the ecology of fire-adapted insects*. Uppsala University, Uppsala.

Wymer, J. (1962) Excavations at the Maglemosian sites at Thatcham, Berkshire, England. *Proceedings of the Prehistoric Society*, **28**, 329-361.

Yalden, D. (1999) *The history of British mammals*. T & A D Poyser, London.

Appendix I : Key to site name abbreviations

Abb = Abbot's Way, Somerset (Girling, 1976)
Al = Alcester, Warks. (Shotton et al., 1977)
Ast = Aston Mills, Worcs. (Whitehead, 1989)
Au = Austerfield, Notts. (Gaunt et al., 1972)
Ave = Averley, Essex (Coope, 2001)
Bart = Barton Court Farm, Oxon. (Robinson et al., 1984)
BoI = Bole Ings, Notts. (Dinnin, 1997)
Brigg = Brigg, Lincs. (Buckland, 1981)
BS = Baker Site, Somerset (Girling, 1980)
Bre = Breiddin, Clwyd (Buckland et al., 2001)
Cald = Caldicott, Gwent (Osborne, 1997)
Cam = Histon Road, Cambridge (Coope, 2001)
CS = Church Stretton, Salops. (Osborne, 1972)
Co = Cowick, W Yorks. (Hayfield & Greig, 1989)
Dav = Church Moss, Davenham, Ches. (Hughes et al., 2000)
De = Deeping St. James, Lincs. (Keen et al., 1999)
Drag = Dragonby, Lincs. (Buckland, 1996)
Dro = Droitwich, Worcs. (Osborne, 1974b)
Eil = Eilean Domhnuill a Spionnaidh, N Uist (Warsop, 2000)
Els = Elsing, Norfolk (Coope, 2001)
Emp = Empingham, Rutland (Buckland, 1986)
Fish = Fisherwick, Staffs. (Osborne, 1979)
Flag = Flag Fen, Cambs. (Robinson, 1992)
Go = Goldcliff, Gwent (Smith et al., 1997)
Hib = Hibaldstow, Lincs. (Girling, unpubl.)
HL = High Lodge, Suffolk (Coope, 1992)
HM = Hatfield Moors, S Yorks. (Whitehouse, 2004)
HoC = Holywell Coombe, Kent (Coope, 1998)
Ips = Bobbitshole, Ipswich, Suffolk (Coope, 2001)
Isle = Isleham, Cambs. (Duffy 1968; Buckland & Kenward, 1973)
Itt = Itteringham, Norfolk (Coope, 2001)
Lang = Langford, Notts. (Howard et al., 1999)
LeaM = Lea Marston, Warks. (Osborne, 1974a)
Lei = Leicester (Girling, 1984b)
LS = Little Stretton, Salops. (Osborne, 1972)
Mar = Marsworth, Bucks. (Murton et al., 2001)
Max = Maxey, Cambs. (Davey et al., 1991)
Mea = Meare, Somerset (Girling, 1979)

Melt = Melton, E Yorks. (Wagner, in Constantine, 1994)
MH = Meare Heath, Somerset (Girling, 1982)
Min = Minsterley, Salops. (Osborne, 1972)
Ming = Mingies Ditch, Oxon. (Robinson, 1993)
Mist = Misterton Carr, Notts (Osborne, in Girling, 1982)
NSea = North Sea floor (Blair, 1935)
Pil = Pilgrim Lock, Bidford-on-Avon, Warks. (Osborne, 1988)
Radley = Radley, Oxon. (Robinson, 1996)
Rams = Ramsey Heights, Cambs. (Harding & Plant, 1978)
Rip = Ripon, N Yorks (Howard *et al.*, 2000)
RT = Rowland's Track, Somerset (Girling, 1977)
Run = Runnymede, Surrey (Robinson, 1991)
SG = Stoke Goldington, Bucks. (Green *et al.*, 1996)
SH = Stanton Harcourt, Oxon. (Briggs *et al.*, 1995)
Shr = Shropham, Norfolk (Coope, 2001)
Shu = Shustoke, Warks. (Kelly & Osborne, 1965)
Sil = Silbury Hill, Wilts. (Robinson, 1997)
SLoch = South Lochboisdale, S Uist, Outer Hebrides (Dinnin, 1996)
ST = Sweet Track, Somerset (Girling, 1984a)
Stil = Stileway, Somerset (Girling, 1985)
Sto = Stourport, Worcs. (Osborne, 1996)
TatT = Tattershall Thorpe, Lincs. (Chowne *et al.*, 1986)
TCP = Tattershall Castle Pit, Lincs. (Girling, 1980)
TinT = Tinney's Track, Somerset (Girling, 1982)
TM = Thorne Moors, S Yorks. (Buckland, 1979; Roper, 1996; Whitehouse, 1997)
TS = Trafalgar Square, London (Coope, 2001)
TT = Tattershall Thorpe, Lincs (Coope, 2001)
US = Upper Stensham, Worcs. (de Rouffignac *et al.*, 1995)
West = Westward Ho, Devon (Girling & Robinson, 1985)
Whit = Whitton, Glamorgans. (Osborne, 1981)
WHS = West Heath Spa, London (Girling, 1989)
Wil = Wilsford, Wilts. (Osborne, 1969)
Wils = Wilsden, Worcs. (Shotton & Coope, 1983)
Wool = Woolpack Farm, Fenstanton, Cambs. (Geo *et al.*, 2000)
World = Worldsend, Church Stretton, Salops. (Osborne, 1972)

South Yorkshire's Ancient Woodlands: Past, Present and Future

Melvyn Jones
Sheffield Hallam University

Over a weekend in the late winter of 1993 a group of supervised volunteers coppiced an area of 0.25 hectares in Ecclesall Woods in south-west Sheffield. This was one of a series of four experiments in the city's woods. Although some thinning and glade creation had recently taken place in other South Yorkshire woods, most notably in Bowden Housteads Wood in Sheffield and Scholes Coppice in Rotherham, these experiments were the first attempts for almost a century to re-introduce coppice-with-standards management, with a view to testing the economic viability of the limited re-introduction of coppicing regimes and associated crafts, their ecological impact and to evaluate visitor reaction to intensive management in well-visited woods (Jones & Talbot, 1995).

An important forerunner of the heightened interest in woodland conservation and the selective re-introduction of active management in South Yorkshire's woods had been the growing realisation of the substantial number of ancient woods that had survived in the region, a wider appreciation of their significant role in the region's economic development and a clearer understanding of how they had been exploited in the past.

The rest of this paper discusses the history of South Yorkshire's ancient woods and examines their present and possible future state.

A diverse and many-layered landscape

The very varied physical environment of South Yorkshire, its geology, topography and soils, has had an immense influence on the way in which human beings over thousands of years have created the complex human landscape of the region (Figure 1). In the extreme west beyond Penistone and Bradfield are bleak uninhabited moorlands developed on the gritstones and shales of the Millstone Grit series. The skyline is periodically dominated by westward facing edges at their highest approaching 550 metres above sea level and cut though by the headwaters of the Derwent and the Don and its tributaries. The altitude decreases eastwards and eventually when the exposed Coal Measures are reached, the country takes on a more rolling appearance and drops from about 245 to less than forty metres in a dozen miles (nineteen kilometres) between Grenoside and Thurnscoe. Another distinct but lower edge made of Magnesian Limestone is then met with, rising to nearly 110 metres at Hickleton, beyond which is a low plateau of fertile agricultural country. This gives way at Doncaster and beyond to a flat, lowland, part of the Humberhead

Levels, floored by Triassic rocks (Sherwood Sandstone and Mercia Mudstone) covered with glacial and post-glacial gravels, clays and silts, in places only a few metres above sea level.

Figure 1. South Yorkshire: location and solid geology.

Figure 2. South Yorkshire: present-day distribution of ancient woodland sites (including replanted sites. Source: Eccles (1986).

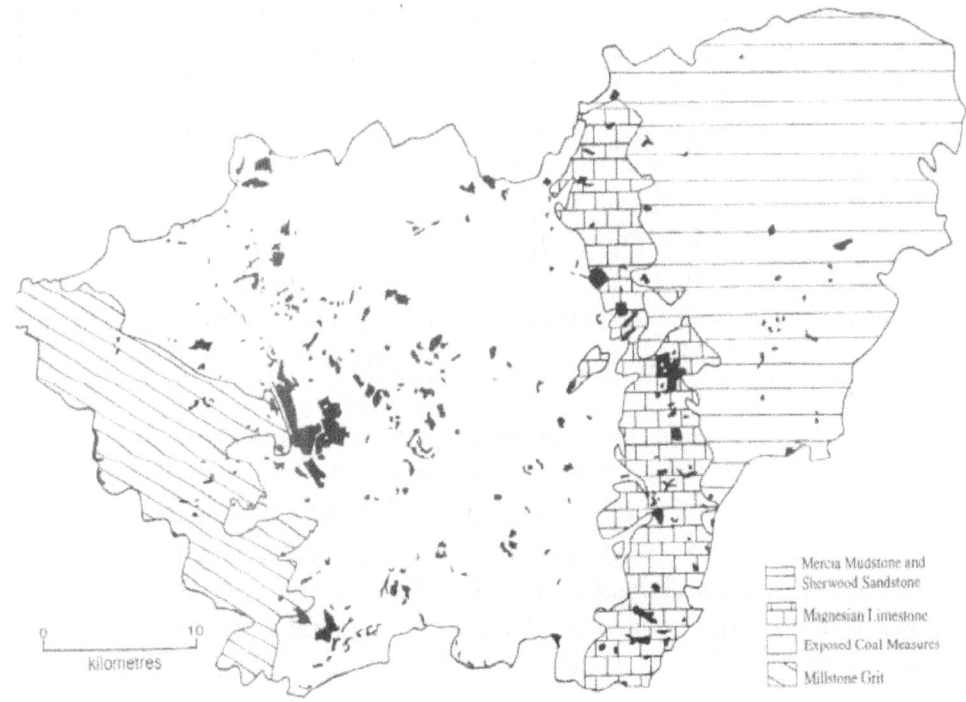

According to the Nature Conservancy Council's woodland inventory (Eccles, 1986) there are 333 ancient woodland sites in South Yorkshire covering 4,451 ha or just 2.8 percent of the land surface (Figure 2). Only one woodland exceeds 200 ha in size, with nine between 50-200 ha. Forty-seven percent are less than five hectares. Ancient woodland is unevenly distributed across South Yorkshire, with less than seven percent of surviving sites on the Millstone Grit, only 7.5 percent in the Humberhead Levels, and twelve percent in the Magnesian Limestone belt. This means that nearly three-quarters of the surviving sites are on the extensive exposed Coal Measures. The topographic variety of this zone means that the observer is everywhere aware of woodlands in the landscape even though they cover only a small fraction of the land area. They clothe the scarps and back slopes of the highest edges, and on lower ground they cling to narrow scarps, and hang on steep valley sides right into the heart of the major urban areas.

The rest of the paper looks chronologically and thematically at South Yorkshire's woodland history.

The wildwood and its clearance

The woodland history of the British Isles in general and of South Yorkshire in particular began about 13,000 years ago at the end of the last Ice Age when glaciers and ice sheets melted, frozen ground thawed and climatic conditions ameliorated to the point where trees could move in again from those parts of Europe that had lain beyond the grip of ice and freezing conditions. Analysis of pollen grains has enabled the colonisation process to be reconstructed (Birks, Deacon & Peglar, 1975; Huntley & Birks, 1983; Huntley, 1998). First came the pioneer arctic trees, birch, willow and aspen, the first two still being the first trees to colonise bare ground where the region's 'smokestack' industries have been demolished. Later came pine and hazel, then alder and oak; later still came elm and lime and finally ash, holly and maple. Beech and hornbeam did not get as far as South Yorkshire. The later trees found it more difficult to spread because the bare ground had already been occupied by the early colonisers. There was a long period of adjustment as particular species consolidated their dominance in particular localities, failed to gain a foothold in others or were pushed out by other, more invasive species.

Two interesting glimpses of the fully developed 'wildwood' in South Yorkshire, as Rackham (1976) termed the country's primaeval forests, comes from pollen analysis and the remains of fallen trees subsequently buried beneath peat deposits. Conway (1947) and Hicks (1971) made studies of pollen in the peat deposits on the moorlands to the west of Sheffield and suggested that by 4,000 BC the area was covered by a mixed oak forest with the canopy broken by areas of damp heath and alder-birch carr. More recent studies in the Humberhead Levels using the evidence of both pollen analysis and buried trees have suggested that before the drowning of the wildwood there, between 3,500 and 2,500 BC, there was on Thorne Moors a mixture of carr woodland in the wettest areas, deciduous woodland dominated by oak on clay-silts and native pine forest on the sands; and on the sands and gravels of Hatfield Moors native pine woodland (with oak locally present) and heathland (Dinnin, Ellis & Weir, 1996). The existence of pines buried in the peat on Hatfield Moors had been known about since at least the late seventeenth century and the antiquarian Joseph Hunter wrote about 'firs' being found in the peat up to 'thirty yards in length' (Hunter, 1828, p.154).

The early inhabitants of the wildwood, Mesolithic hunter-fisher-gatherers, would have made little impact on their environment and have left virtually nothing behind but their tools and their weapons. At Deepcar, for example, what appears to have been a temporary camp beside the River Don, where flint tools had been prepared, yielded more than 23,000 artefacts (including debris from working flints). There were signs of a shelter, possibly a windbreak, around three hearths (Radley & Mellors, 1964). The pastoralist and arable farmers of the succeeding Neolithic, Bronze, Iron, and Romano-British periods would have had a considerable impact on the wildwood. Now not only finds of stone and metal tools, hut circles, burial mounds and other earthworks (e.g. the many earthworks surveyed by L.H. Butcher (Beswick & Merrills, 1983)) but cropmarks from aerial photographs taken during periods of drought all indicate a long occupation of the region that must have been accompanied by much woodland clearance by axe and by grazing by domesticated animals. Derek Riley recorded cropmarks for more than two decades in South Yorkshire and they have established the existence of networks of fields not only in the very fertile Magnesian Limestone belt, but also on the clay-covered Sherwood Sandstone to the east and on the Coal Measures to the west (Riley, 1980).

It was the Anglo-Saxon (from the seventh century), Scandinavian (from the tenth century) and the later medieval occupants of the region, who left behind, in the names they gave to farms, hamlets and villages, widespread evidence of a countryside once covered by and gradually cleared of woodland. Some of these names tell us about the composition of the woods, names such as Lindrick (Old English for 'lime-tree strip', the name of a district which straddles the South Yorkshire-Nottinghamshire border and where there was a wood called *bosco de lyndric* first recorded in 1199; and Ewden and Agden, both deep valleys in the west of the region and first recorded as Udene (yew valley) in 1234 and Aykeden (oak valley) in 1329 (Smith, 1961).

But it is the woodland clearance names that are most instructive. Many of these must indicate large clearings that had existed for many generations before the Anglo-Saxons and Scandinavians entered the region and they were merely renaming them in their own languages. The Old English -leah (woodland clearing), which gives us names such as

Heeley, Tankersley and Cantley is the most widely distributed, with forty occurrences on the 1:50,000 OS sheets (110 and 111) covering the region. Another widely distributed Old English element is -feld (10 occurrences) which means a treeless area in an otherwise well wooded landscape, as in Sheffield, Darfield and Hatfield. The Old Norse element for clearing is -thwaite (twelve occurrences) as in Ouslethwaite, Butterthwaite and Hangthwaite. As Figure 3 shows, woodland clearance names are unequally distributed across the region with the vast majority in the Coal Measure country, particularly in the western half of that zone. Significantly the Magnesian Limestone belt, long thought to be the most attractive area in South Yorkshire for early settlement, has only three names indicative of a wooded countryside (Woolthwaite, Firbeck and Woodsetts) suggesting much woodland clearance there before the appearance of the Anglo-Saxon and Danish Viking name-givers.

Figure 3. South Yorkshire: Old English and Old Norse woodland and woodland clearance names depicted on 1:50,000 OS sheets 110 and 111.

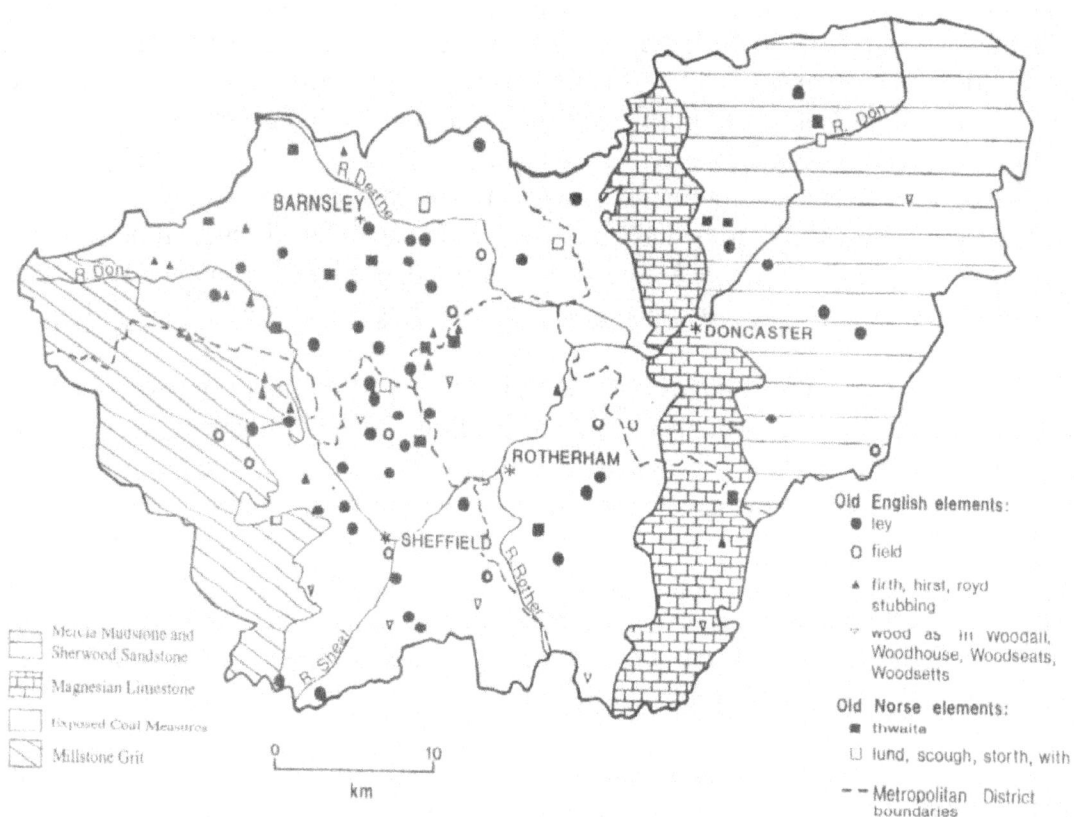

Domesday woodland

If we take the Domesday returns at their face value, then woodland cover had been drastically reduced by the eleventh century and the countryside was not covered by the boundless woodland of people's imagination. Rackham (1980) has calculated that the Domesday survey of 1086 covered twenty-seven million acres of land of which 4.1 million were wooded, that is fifteen percent of the surveyed area. His figure for the West Riding of Yorkshire is sixteen percent. My own calculation for South Yorkshire is just under thirteen percent. By way of comparison, woods today, including plantations, cover just over six percent of the region. What this means is that in the eleventh century, South Yorkshire was relatively sparsely wooded even by today's standards.

The Domesday surveyors in South Yorkshire in 1086 gave woodland measurements for each manor in almost every case in leagues (twelve furlongs or 1.5 miles) and furlongs (220 yards or one-eighth of a mile) and in most cases recorded how woods were utilised. When the data are mapped (Figure 4) noticeable variations in the distribution and types of woodland are clearly discernible. In the western half of the region, in the

Figure 4. South Yorkshire: Domesday woodland.

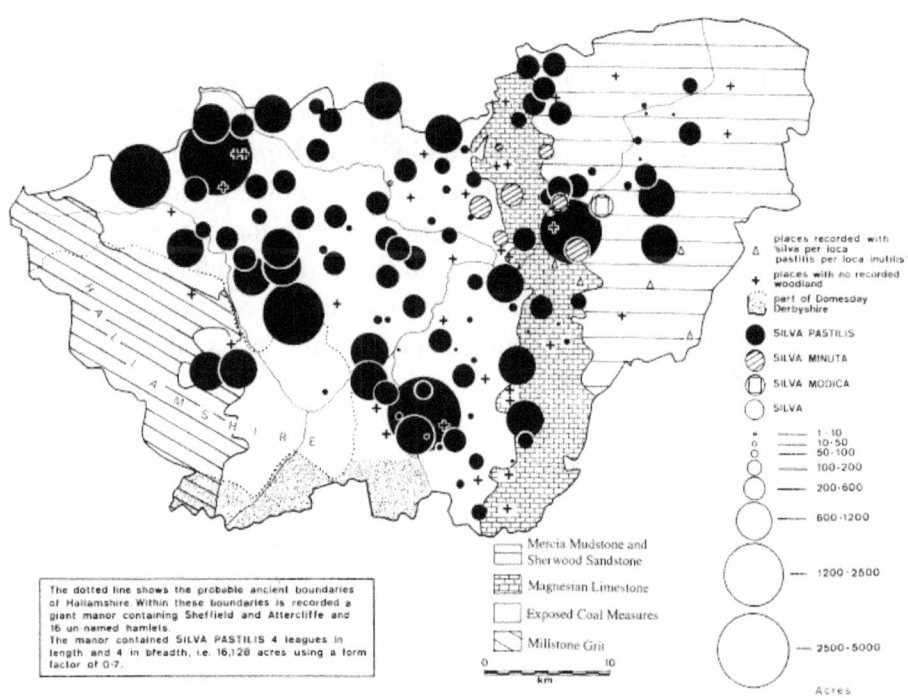

Millstone Grit country and on the Coal Measures, woodland was relatively extensive with a substantial number of communities having more than 1,000 acres of woodland. In contrast, in the Magnesian Limestone belt and in the Humberhead Levels further east, the picture was different. In those areas woodland was more scattered, and amounts in individual communities were generally smaller than to the west. Additionally, the Magnesian Limestone belt, although only covering about one-eighth of the land area of the region, contained nearly a third (ten out of thirty-three) of the places in which woodland was not recorded at all. This underlines the point made earlier about the lack of woodland clearance place-names suggesting very early clearance of woodland on the Magnesian Limestone.

The types of woodland recorded in South Yorkshire at Domesday also suggest a shortage of woodland in some places in the east of the region, particularly in the Magnesian Limestone belt, and a relative abundance further west. When woods were relatively abundant and populations relatively small, they would have been able to be exploited for timber and underwood **and** as pastures for cattle, sheep and pigs, i.e. as wood pastures. As populations grew and more woodland was cleared and the increased number of grazing animals prevented the regeneration of the remaining woodland, woods had to be fenced to prevent animals entering them and a type of management which gave a continuous and self-renewing supply of timber and underwood had to be introduced, i.e. coppicing.

Domesday woodland in South Yorkshire was described in four main ways: as *silva*, *silva modica*, *silva minuta* and *silva pastilis*. *Silva* is simply woodland. The meaning of *silva modica* is not clear; *silva minuta* is coppice; and *silva pastilis* is wood pasture. Of the 112 manors in which woodland was recorded, eight had coppice woods and 102 had wood pastures. All eight occurrences of coppice woods were in the eastern half of the region, two in the eastern part of the Coal Measures and six on the Magnesian Limestone. On the other hand, although wood pastures were found throughout South Yorkshire they were very extensive and the only type of woodland found in the Millstone Grit country and throughout most of the Coal Measures.

The survival and decline of wood pasture

For at least five centuries after the Domesday survey the wood pasture tradition continued to be strong and for the first half of that period was the dominant form of woodland management. In the medieval period and beyond wood pastures were found on wooded commons, in chases and in deer parks.

A number of documents emphasise the continued dominance of wooded commons. For example in 1161 the monks of the Cistercian abbey of Kirkstead in Lincolnshire were granted land in Kimberworth to mine ironstone and operate two bloomeries and two forges. Their fuel was to be dead wood (*mortuus nemus*) from the wooded common, not from coppice woods. They were also granted permission to graze their draught animals on the common. In the same year the monks of Ecclesfield Priory were given the right to pasture their flocks every year from January to Easter in a large wood in the valley of the River Don, the surviving parts of which were coppice woods four centuries later (Eastwood, 1862). Finally, in 1332 in the *inquisitione post mortem* of Thomas de Furnival, lord of the manor of Sheffield (Curtis, 1918), eleven localities were listed under the heading of pastures in moors, woods and commons, including Greno Wood, Beeley Wood and Bowden Houstead Wood, all of which by Elizabethan times were coppice woods in which animals were not welcome.

Wood pasture on wooded commons persisted beyond the medieval period particularly in the west of the region. In about 1650, for example, Loxley Common, covering more than 1,500 acres, was said to be: 'one Great Wood called Loxley the herbage common and consisteth of great Oake timber'. About ten years earlier the much smaller common called Walkley Bank was said to have: 'a great store of rough Oake trees & some bircke [birch] woods'. In the same year another wooded common, Stannington Wood (215 acres), was said to consist of: 'pt of rough Timber & pt of Springe wood' (Bright Papers, BR24). In John Harrison's survey of the manor of Sheffield in 1637 some magnificent trees were described growing in a wooded common in Rivelin Firth (the private forest of the lords of the manor of Sheffield):

"Item Hawe Park lyeth open to Rivelin Firth ... This piece is full of excellent timber of a very great length & very Streight & many of them of a great bigness before you come to a Knott in so much that it hath been said by Travellers that they have not seene such Timber in Christendome." (Ronksley, 1908, p.152).

Wood pasture on wooded commons was almost entirely extinguished during the second half of the eighteenth century and the first third of the nineteenth century under the Parliamentary Enclosure acts. Figure 5 shows Stannington Wood in 1637 and as it was portrayed, subdivided into many square and rectangular enclosures, following parliamentary enclosure.

Wood pasture was also found on three chases (private forests) in South Yorkshire in the medieval period and beyond. Forest, of course in this context does not imply woodland but that Forest Law applied in the area relating to the hunting of deer, the grazing of animals, the felling of timber and the clearing of land. Forests were not fenced and could include within their boundaries woodland, heath, fen, farmland and settlements.

Figure 5. The wooded common, Stannington Wood, in 1637 and as it was depicted on the Six-Inch OS sheet in 1850-512, following its enclosure in 1805.

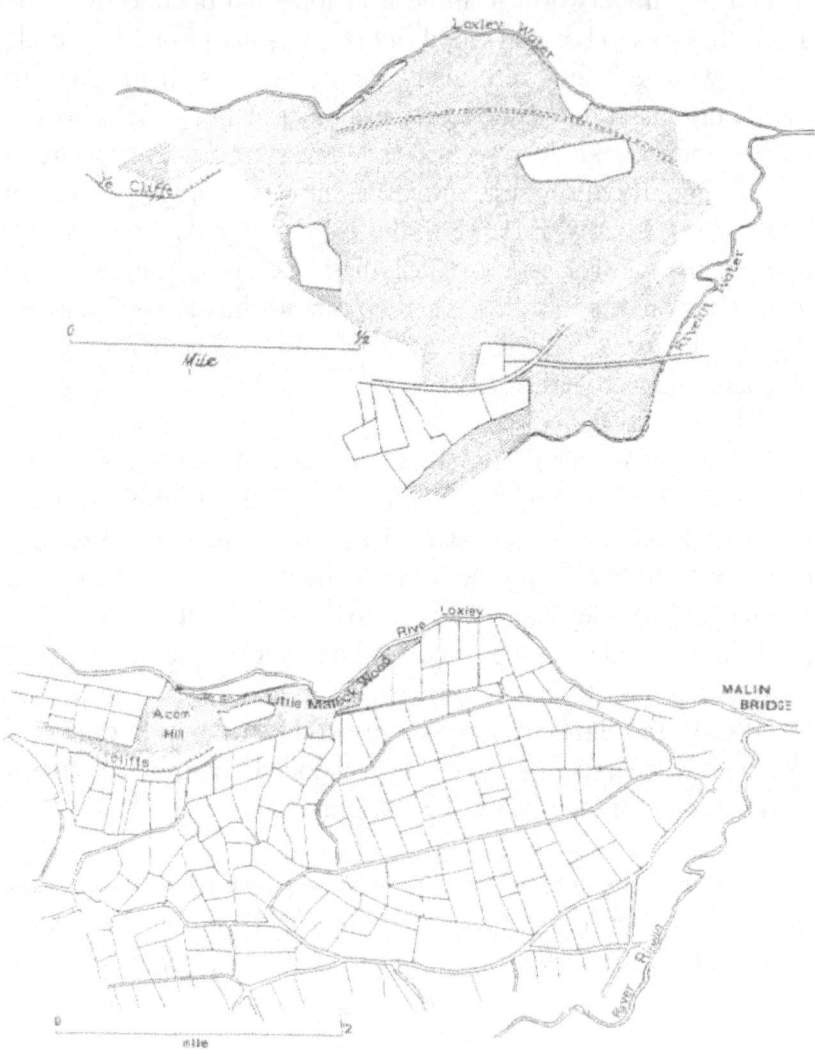

From shortly after the Norman Conquest until 1347 the low-lying and often inundated 70,000 acres (28,330 ha) of Hatfield Chase were the private forest of the de Warennes of Conisbrough Castle. The chase then reverted to the Crown until the early seventeenth century (it was freed from Forest Law in 1629) when it was drained by the Dutch engineer, Vermuyden. The last royal hunt took place here in 1609 when it is said the royal party in a flotilla of 100 boats pursued 500 deer that had taken to the water:

'... their horned heads raised seemed to represent a little wood' (Hunter, 1828, p.156). Although there were some oak woods in Hatfield Chase, it was not well wooded, the main areas of woodland occurring in the form of alder and willow carrs.

On the western extremities of South Yorkshire was Rivelin Chase, the generic name of a group of adjacent private forests of the medieval lords of Sheffield. This chase included Rivelin Chase proper, the Forest of Fulwood, Loxley Chase (including Loxley Common already referred to above) and a number of other areas under Forest Law called 'firths'. Rivelin Chase contained large areas of moorland on land over 300 metres and also extensive valley woodlands. In a *compotus* (account) of the foresters for Bradfeld (Bradfield) and Ryvelinge (Rivelin) for September 1441-September 1442, reference is made of pasturing plough cattle and pigs (*pannagio porcorum*), selling branchwood (*ramaylis*) for charcoal making and holly (*hussis*) for winter-feed for animals (Thomas, 1924). In John Harrison's survey of the manor of Sheffield in 1637, a large grassy clearing called: 'ye Old Laund reserved for ye Deare' was mentioned, it: 'being Invironed with Rivelin [Firth]' (Ronksley, 1908, p.152). A laund was the name for a treeless compartment within a park or chase. John Evelyn, writing in his book *Silva* in the late seventeenth century, said that Rivelin, apart from Hawe Park, was now: 'destitute' of its mighy oaks, but he described one that had been recently felled, called 'the Lord's Oak' whose trunk was twelve yards (thirty-six feet or eleven metres) in circumference (Evelyn, 1706 edition, pp. 228, 232). The tree was most likely a sessile oak, the largest stem diameter on record for which is thirty-six feet and ten inches in girth at breast height (White, 1995). Those parts of Rivelin Chase which still survived into the eighteenth century were enclosed under Parliamentary Enclosure acts.

On a much smaller scale than Hatfield Chase and Rivelin Chase, was Wharncliffe Chase, the private forest of the Wortley family (Earls of Wharncliffe), which had been developed on the high plateau above the River Don bounded by the dramatic Wharncliffe Crags (Figure 6). It was extended southwards in Elizabethan times. In order to create the New Park, as part of the extension was called, tenants were evicted and two hamlets depopulated (Hey, 2002). The wooded part of the chase, once famed for its ancient cork-screw oaks and large old hollies, was described by Joseph Hunter in the early nineteenth century as: 'the remains of that primaeval forest which once covered the whole of the southern parts of Yorkshire' (Hunter, 1831, p. 307). There were still 200 head of deer on the chase in the 1820s according to Hunter. This number had been reduced to just forty red deer in 1945 and the severe winter of 1946-47 is said to have killed off all but eight (Clinging & Whiteley, 1980). Red deer, probably descendants of the Whancliffe Chase herd, still roam widely throughout the Wharncliffe area.

Figure 6. Wooded commons, chases, deer parks and spring woods as depicted on Peter Perez Burdett's map of Derbyshire (first edition 1767, revised and reprinted in 1791) which extended for a dozen miles into South Yorkshire.

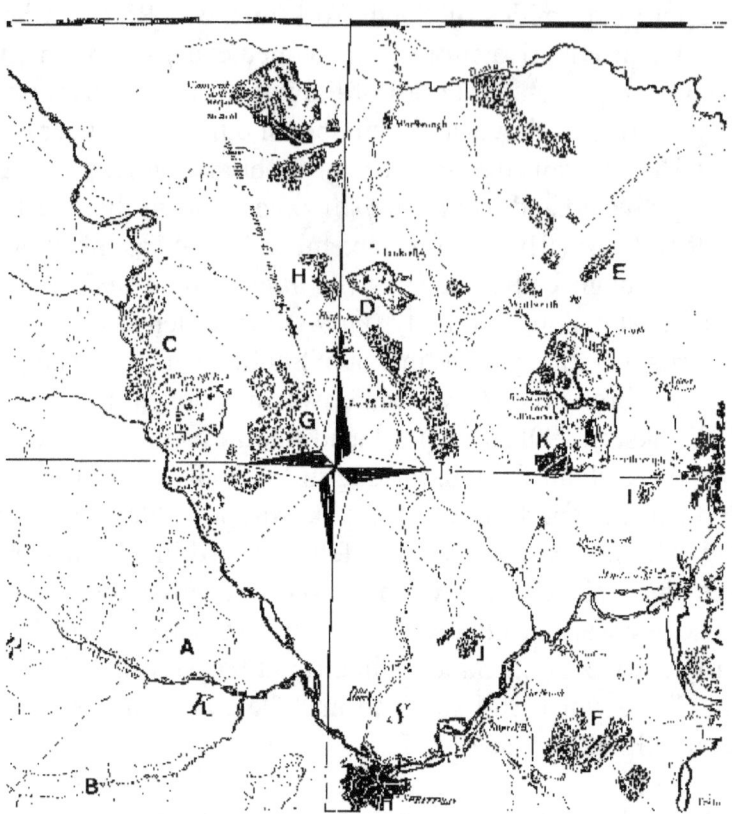

A= Loxley Common; B = Rivelin Firth; C = Wharncliffe Chase; D = the much reduced Tankersley deer park; E and F = two deer parks converted to coppice woods, Rainborough Park (E) and Tinsley Park (F); G, H, I, J = selected coppice-with-standards woods, Greno Wood and the adjacent Hall Wood, Wheata Wood and Prior Royd (G), West Wood (H), Bassingthorpe Spring (I) and Wincobank Wood (J); K = a coppice wood incorporated into a landscaped park and 'cut into walks for beauty', Scholes Coppice.

Deer parks, large and small, sometimes well wooded and sometimes only moderately so, studded South Yorkshire in the medieval period. Medieval deer parks were symbols of status and wealth. Unlike commons and chases, deer parks were areas of private land bounded by a wall or a cleft-oak fence (the park pale), in which the owner kept deer, hares, rabbits and (rarely) wild boar and fish in fishponds to provide his family and guests with a reliable source of meat and fish, and grew timber and underwood. As all the deer belonged to the Crown, from the beginning of the thirteenth century it was necessary for a landowner to obtain a licence – a right of free warren – from the king to hunt deer on his demesne and to create a park. The parks at Sheffield and Conisbrough predated the issuing of royal licences and so must have been of twelfth century or even earlier (possibly Saxon) origin. In South Yorkshire the bulk of the grants of free warren were made in the period from 1250 to 1325 when forty-four of the known seventy grants were made Jones, 1996a). No grants were made in the thirty years following the Black Death (1349) but there were then twenty-one grants between 1379 and 1400. The last known medieval grant of free warren was in 1491-92 when Brian Sandford was granted permission to create a park at Thorpe Salvin. This grant is notable for the fact that it was accompanied by a gift of twelve does from the king's park at Conisbrough: 'towards the storing of his parc at Thorp' (quoted by Hunter, 1831, p 309.). The last known grant of free warren was in 1637 when King Charles I permitted the 2nd Viscount Castletlon to create a deer park at Sandbeck (Rodgers, 1998).

Most of the grants of free warren were to lay lords such as the locally important Fitzwilliams, Bosvilles and de Vavasors, and also to the heads of the great Norman dynasties whose ancestors had accompanied the Conqueror to England in 1066: the de Warennes of Conisbrough Castle, the de Furnivals of Sheffield Castle and the de Buslis of Tickhill Castle. Religious houses were also granted free warren and the Prior of Worksop Priory created a park at Rykenildthorpe (Thorpe Salvin) Wood and Monk Bretton Priory created a park on its demesne at Rainborough in Brampton where there is still a forty-eight ha oval-shaped wood called Rainborough Park.

Although there are records of deer parks without trees, they usually contained woodlands intermingled with grassy or heathy areas (launds or plains) with scattered, often pollarded, trees. The park livestock could graze in the open areas and find cover in the woodlands (except newly-cut coppices which were protected for a number of years). Sheffield Park (Figure 7), the largest park in South Yorkshire, which covered nearly 2,500 acres (over 1,000 hectares) and was eight miles (nearly thirteen kilometres) in circumference, contained in the seventeenth century one coppice wood, Morton Bank, together with thousands of large, ancient oaks. John Evelyn described one oak whose trunk was thirteen feet (four metres) in diameter and another that was ten yards (9.2 metres) in circumference. Another large oak was so big that when it was felled and lying on its side two men on opposite sides on horseback could not see each other's hats. Even more impressive was his report that in an open area called Conduit Plaine there was another oak tree whose boughs were so far spreading that he estimated (giving all his calculations) that 251 horses could stand in its shade. (Evelyn, 1706, p. 230).

Besides coppices and holts (timber woods), there was another type of wood found in South Yorkshire's deer parks and on wooded commons and in chases. These were separate woods or compartments within woods in which the dominant tree was holly

Figure 7. The 2,462 acre Sheffield deer park in 1637. It had a typical shape, a rounded rectangle, and although 971 acres were let to tenants by that time (shown by stippling) it still contained 1,000 fallow deer (after Scurfield, 1986).

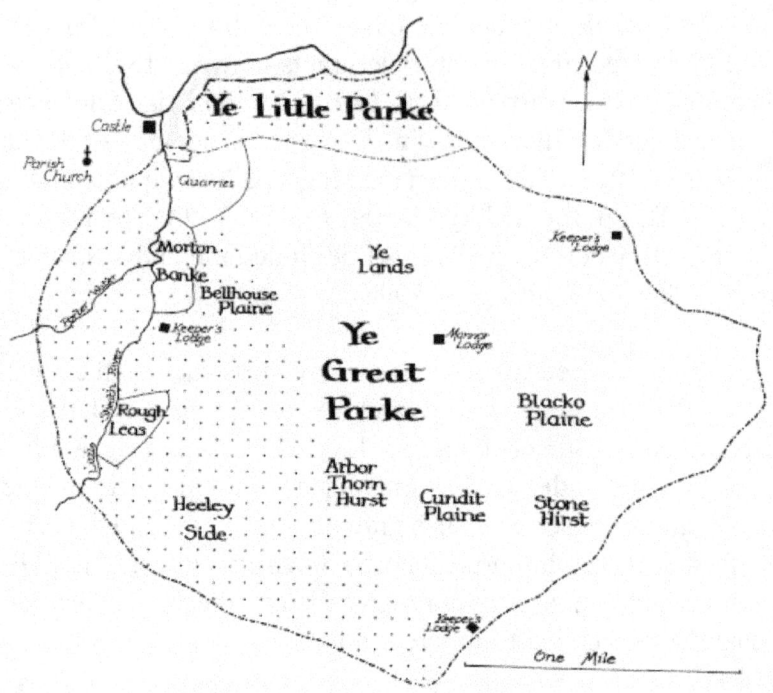

and which were called holly hags (Spray & Smith, 1977; Spray, 1981). The holly was cut on rotation like other coppiced or pollarded trees. In a lease of Tankersley Park in 1653, for example, it was stipulated that the deer had to be fed by: 'serving them with holley to be cutt therein in winter' (Hall, 1937, p. 181). John Harrison, in his survey of the manor of Sheffield in 1637 recorded twenty-seven separate 'Hollin Hagges' that were rented by farm tenants from the Earl of Arundel. They were also found in Rivelin Chase where they were apparently plundered by farmers in harsh winters. As late as 1710 the Duke of Norfolk's woodward noted in his accounts a payment of four shillings to Henry Bromhead: 'for him and horse going 2 days in ye great snow to see if any one croped Holling' (Arundel Castle Manuscripts, ACM S283).

Between the late fifteenth and eighteenth centuries many surviving South Yorkshire medieval deer parks either changed their function (to become the landscaped adornment to a country house) and hence their appearance, or, most commonly, ceased to be parks altogether. Well-wooded parks often simply became large coppice woods while retaining their original names, as in the case of Hesley Park and Cowley Park between Chapeltown and Thorpe Hesley, which together mark a medieval park of the de Mountenay family, and which had become coppice woods of 163 and 135 acres respectively by 1637. Similarly, the 400-acre Tinsley Park, between Sheffield and Rotherham, had by 1657 become ten coppice woods and three holts. Other parks simply reverted to farmland. In the case of Kimberworth Park, which still contained deer in 1635, the first steps leading to its eventual total disparkment had taken place by 1649 when a farm of about 140 acres was carved out of it. By 1671 the whole park had been leased, the remaining 600 acres being let to Lionel Copley, the ironmaster, whose main interests lay in mining the ironstone which outcropped in the park and the coppice woods that could be felled and made into charcoal. Between 1671 and 1732, when the then owner, the Earl of Effingham, had a survey made, the whole park, with the exception of the surviving woodland, had been divided into farms and the park had disappeared (Jones, 1996b).

The rise, decline and extinction of coppice woods

In the centuries following the Domesday survey, although, as we have seen, the wood pasture tradition in South Yorkshire continued to be strong, in the form of wooded commons, chases and deer parks, coppice management gradually became dominant in order to conserve wood supplies which were in danger of becoming seriously depleted as the population grew and more woodland was permanently cleared for agriculture.

Throughout the region the form of coppice management called coppice-with-standards, which combined the production of underwood with that of single-stemmed timber trees, emerged as the most important form of woodland management, in economic terms, during the middle ages and continued to be so until at least the middle of the nineteenth century.

The earliest-known surviving documentary record of coppice-with-standards management in South Yorkshire is a lease written in Latin at the relatively late date of 1421. The lease concerns un-named woods on a farm at Norton (then part of Derbyshire) and contains a number of clauses concerning the right to cut underwood and timber, charcoal burning and keeping animals out of the woods for three or four years after cutting (Hall, 1914). The woods on the farm are referred to as le Spryng bosci, 'spring' being the usual name for a coppice-with-standards in South Yorkshire from the fifteenth to the nineteenth century.

Two other late medieval records of coppice-with-standards have also survived, both in the same geographical area as the 1421 record. The first dated 1462, and written in English, refers to a number of woods in Norton parish including 'herdyng wood', the old name for the present Rollestone Wood (Hall,1914). The lease noted that the lessees had been granted permission by the lord of the manor 'to fell downe cole (i.e., to make into charcoal) and carry the said Woddes', preserving for the owner 'sufficiaunt Wayvers after the custom of the contre'. Wavers, or weavers, as they were more frequently written, were the young timber trees left to grow among the felled underwood. Wavers were also mentioned in the second document, which was written in 1496, also in English, and refers to two woods in the Sheaf Valley in Sheffield one of which was Hutcliff Wood, which still survives. The two woods were the property of Beauchief Abbey and the lease records that the 'abbot of Beacheff' had granted permission to the lessees 'to cooll (i.e. to make into charcoal) ii certen wodds', the woods to be left 'weyverd workmonlyke'. Significantly, the document also refers to a bloom hearth (a primitive furnace) and a dam (the local name for a pond at a water-powered industrial site) (Beauchief Muniments, BM 994). As we shall see, undoubtedly the increasing dominance of coppice management, at least in the western half of the region, was closely related to the expansion of metal smelting and related trades such as nail-making and edge tool manufacture.

Coppice management was also a feature of the eastern part of the county. At the dissolution of Roche Abbey in the Magnesian Limestone belt in 1546, a grant to Henry Tyrrell included sixty acres of coppice woods in four separate woods two of which (Norwood and Hell Wood) have survived to the present day. Two other woods belonging to the abbey, including a spring wood of fifteen acres, is also listed. There were also 800 oaks and ashes of sixty and eighty years' growth in the abbey's coppice woods and in other places in the abbey demesnes: 'parte tymbre and part usually cropped and shred' (Aveling, 1870, p. 131). This reference to shredding – the cutting off of side branches to produce a crop of poles and leaf fodder for animals – is the only instance of this practice that I have found in documents relating to woodland management in South Yorkshire.

By the early seventeenth century spring wood management appears to have been general. In an undated document written for the Seventh Earl of Shrewsbury, the major landowner in south-west Yorkshire, who succeeded to the title in 1590 and died in 1616, forty-nine spring woods were listed. Significantly, they were listed as belonging to the Earl's forges and contained reference to charcoal making such as:' Granowe Spring – 20 years ould redie to cole – 100 ac' and: 'Thorncliff Spring one half about 9 years old tother halfe coalable – 30 ac' (Shrewsbury Papers at Lambeth Palace Library, 698, Fol. 3). In 1637 John Harrison, in his survey of the manor of Sheffield, listed thirty-six spring woods in which the underwood varied in age from four years to forty. Maps of large compartmented coppice woods also survive from this period (Figure 8).

By this time the iron industry in south-west Yorkshire had achieved a high degree of sophistication and was increasingly characterised by a large measure of vertical integration and horizontal combination (Hopkinson, 1963). By the 1650s, the most powerful ironmaster in the region was Lionel Copley (Goodchild, 1996) who entered into a succession of agreements with local landowners to fell and coal their spring woods.

Figure 8. Redrawn version of the firsst-known map of Ecclesall Woods of mid-seventeenth century date. The site was divided into 20 separate coppice woods at that date, each one at a different stage of regrowth (the second number below the woodland name indicates the age of the underwood). Source: WWM MP 46.

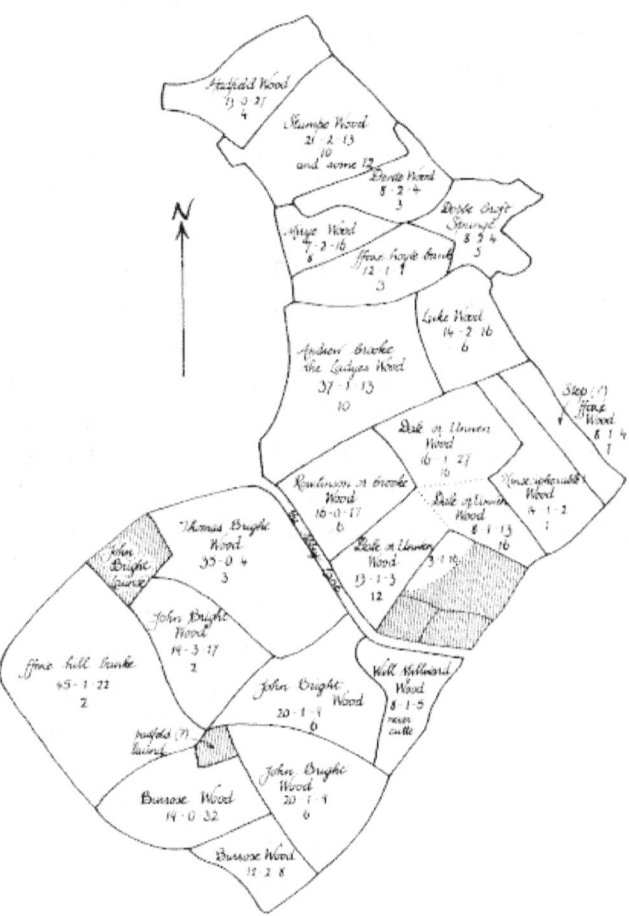

The surviving leases illustrate contemporary coppice practice. For example, in 1657 the second Earl of Strafford of Wentworth Woodhouse entered into a ten-year agreement with Copley to fell the underwood and selected timber trees in thirteen of the Earl's woods. Under the contract Copley was to cut 1,000 cords of wood (in South Yorkshire, a pile of wood four feet wide, eight feet long and four feet high) each year for charcoal making. He was allowed to cut: 'young timber trees, Lordings, Black Barks, powles, coppices and Springwoode' together with 'the Bark thereof'. The lessee was also instructed to make sure that 'all the said Springwoode [is] well and sufficiently weavered' and that coppice was: 'workmanlike cutt downe … and the stowens [stools] thereof neare to the roote so as best preserve for future growth and next springing thereof'. He was also asked to burn the 'Ramell' in places that would be:'least prejudiciall to the weavers and Springwood which shall be left to grow'.

Between the last quarter of the sixteenth century and the middle of the eighteenth century in the woods along the south-western boundaries of South Yorkshire (and in neighbouring North Derbyshire) was another woodland industry making a fuel for smelting ore and sustaining the management of the region's woods as spring woods. The ore was lead and the fuel was whitecoal (Kiernan, 1989). Local landowners are known to have been very active in the lead trade and they obtained their ore from the Peak District and smelted it at water-powered smelters called ore hearths using a mixture of whitecoal and charcoal as fuel. Whitecoal was small slivers of wood, dried in a kiln until all the moisture was driven out. According to William Linnard, charcoal and whitecoal were mixed together in lead smelting because 'charcoal made too violent a fire, and wood alone was too gentle' (Linnard, 1982, p. 76). In 1657 Ecclesall Woods were leased to a 'lead merchant' who was permitted to make 'charcole or whitecole' and to 'make & cast pitt & kilnes for the coaleing of the same' (Wentworth Woodhouse Muniments, WWM D 365). There are today in Ecclesall Woods some 300 surviving charcoal hearths and about 140 whitecoal kilns (Ardron & Rotherham, 1999), the latter in the form of deep round holes, usually on sloping ground, with a spout at the down-slope end (Figure 9).

To the east, coppice-with-standards management was also important. On the Duke of Leeds' estate centred on Kiveton Park in the Magnesian Limestone belt, there were seventeen woods in the early 1700s in Harthill, Thorpe Salvin and North and South Anston, five of them described in 1739 as 'timber woods', and another eight as spring woods including the surviving Anston Stones Wood, Hawks Wood, Lob Wells Wood and Old Spring Wood. Among the products made from the timber and wood cut in these woods during the period in question were hop poles, scaffold poles, cordwood, pit wood ('puncheons'), heft wood, hazel hoops, hedge bindings, and perhaps most interesting of all, 562 'straite oaken trees' which were taken by: 'land and water to his majestys yard at Chatham' in 1701 and which yielded £473 in income (Duke of Leeds' Archive, DD5/35).

Various aspects of eighteenth-century spring wood management in South Yorkshire are well illustrated in two schemes devised by Thomas Wentworth, first Marquis of Rockingham who inherited the Wentworth estates in 1723. In 1727 he devised what he called 'A Scheme for making a yearly considerable Profit of Spring Woods in Yorkshire' and in 1749 what he described as 'A Scheme for a Regular Fall of Wood for 21 years …'. In the 1749 scheme, a twenty-one-year rotation was used so that the woods coppiced in 1749 would be cut again 1771. This meant that the Marquis' 876 acres (355 ha) of

Figure 9. A whitecoal pit in Ecclesall Woods.

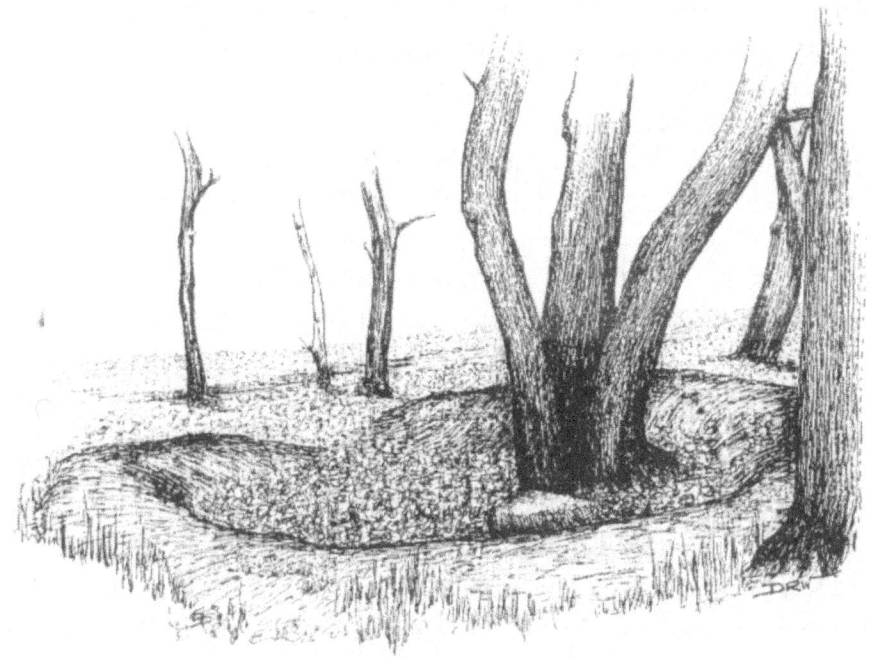

coppice-with-standards woodland in South Yorkshire would produce a regular crop of 40 acres of underwood a year. The Marquis stipulated that there were to be five black barks (mature timber trees, forty to sixty years old) and seventy wavers (sapling timber trees) left in every acre of felled coppice (WWM A1273).

The Marquis of Rockingham was fortunate that on his estate, besides hundreds of acres of coppice woods he also had deposits of ironstone, and he linked the charcoaling of the former with the mining of the latter. In 1749 he wrote that 'whereas it is the Iron Men that keep up the Price of the Wood, especiall care must be taken that the Iron Stone be never let for a longer time than the Woods are agreed for' (WWM A1273). But this was the beginning of the end. By 1780 the lead ore hearths had been replaced by coal-fired cupola furnaces and by the end of the eighteenth century iron furnaces were converted to or were rebuilt to use coke and new ironworks were, from the first, coke fired. The market for whitecoal, therefore, disappeared and that for charcoal was reduced, although it was still in demand locally for the production of blister steel in cementation furnaces. Nationally, coppicing did not decline in the immediate aftermath of the loss of the market for charcoal for iron smelting, and one author has suggested that the first half of the nineteenth century may be regarded as 'the golden age of traditional English woodmanship (Collins, 1992). This was not the case in South Yorkshire; its golden age was in the seventeenth and eighteenth centuries when production of charcoal and whitecoal were at their height (Jones, 1997; Jones, 1998).

During the nineteenth century the surviving coppice-using industries could not sustain coppice-with-standards management in the region. As a result more and more coppice woods were gradually converted into high forests (Figure 10). In essence they were becoming plantations and forestry was replacing woodmanship (Jones, 1998). The changes in Ecclesall Woods after about 1850, mirror changes that were taking place, or would take place in the next half century, in other coppice woods throughout the region (Jones & Walker, 1997). In Ecclesall Woods sales from 1775 until 1847 were entered under some variation of the title of a 'fall of wood' or 'falls of wood' or 'fall of coppis' But planting was also under way, there being a prolonged period of planting between 1830 and 1845 and planting took place either in Ecclesall Woods specifically or in woods in general on the estate of which Ecclesall Woods were part from the early 1860s until the end of the nineteenth century. A timber sale was recorded for the first time in 1848, again in 1851, and then continuously almost every year until the end of the century. No more sales of falls of wood are recorded after 1847. Those purchasing wood and timber from Ecclesall Woods also changed dramatically between the 1750s and 1900: between the 1750 after 1850 the main customers were ironmasters wanting coppice and branchwood for charcoal making or colliery owners purchasing pit wood; but from the 1850s industrial customers were replaced by timber merchants, William Toplis, a Chesterfield timber merchant, being the sole buyer at the Ecclesall woods annual timber sales on twenty-seven out of the thirty annual sales that took place between 1869 and 1900-01.

Similar changes were also taking place in the many woods on the Duke of Norfolk's Sheffield and Rotherham woods. In 1898 the Duke's forester (a term that had supplanted the earlier 'woodward'), began to plant heavily in the declining coppice woods. In Hesley Wood he planned to plant 100 acres (forty hectares) with ash, elm, sycamore, birch, lime, sweet chestnut and beech eight feet apart and 'filled up' at four feet intervals with larch. Another forty hectares were to be planted in the same way in Smithy Wood, fifty hectares in Greno Wood, twenty-five hectares in Beeley Wood, sixteen hectares in Bowden Housteads Wood, ten hectares in Hall Wood and eight hectares in Woolley Wood.

By the end of the nineteenth century coppicing and its related trades and industries had all but disappeared (Figure 11).

Figure 10. A typical South Yorkshire Coal Measure wood in 1650 (coppice-with-standards with only native species of trees and shrubs); in 1890 (converted to high forest with the planting of non-native species including conifers); and in 1980 (neglected, even-aged high forest with little understorey surviving).

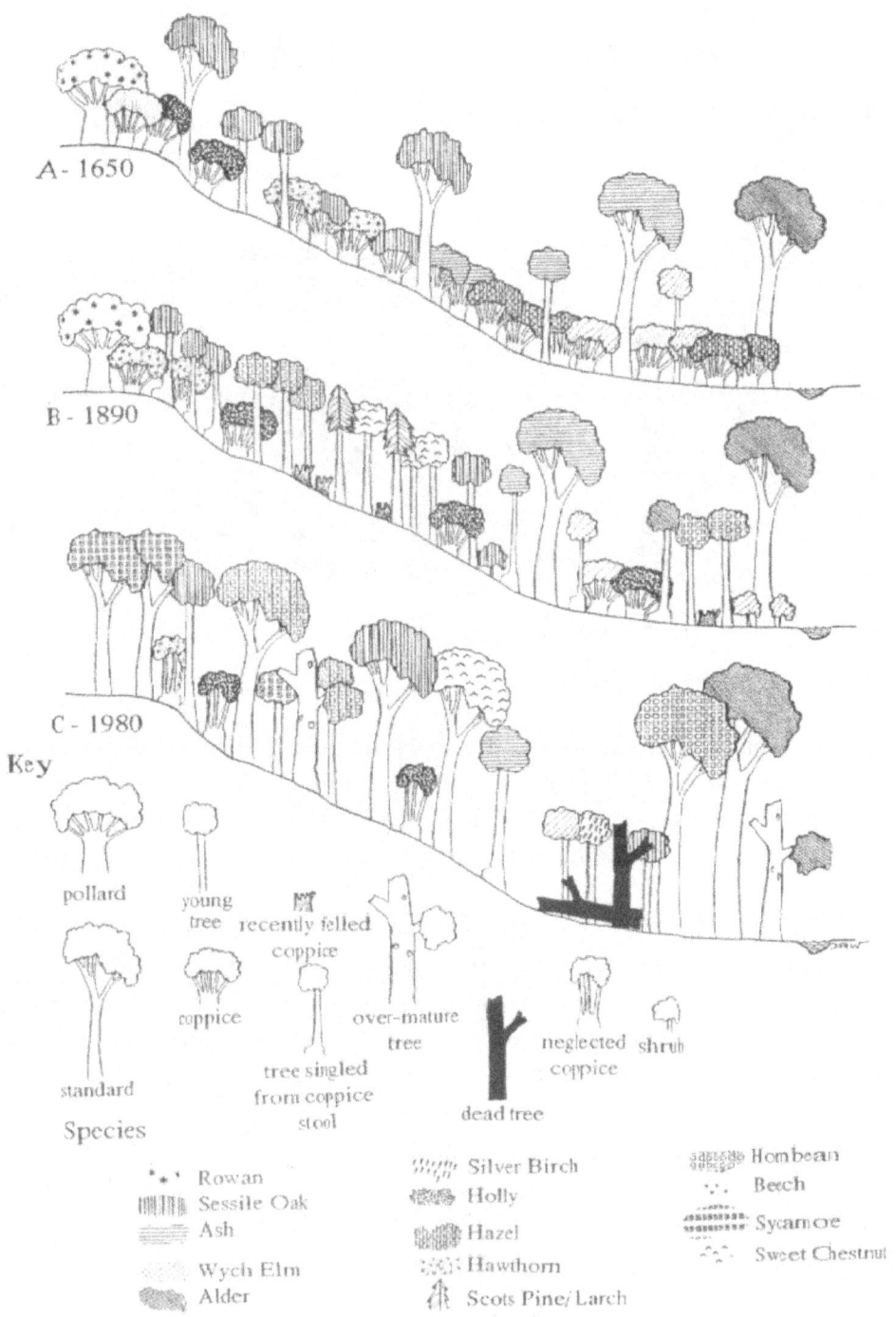

Figure 11. Drawing based on a photograph found in a Sheffield attic of a very late felling for charcoal making in a South Yorkshire wood. Source: Mrs A. Laurent.

The present and the future

Forestry management, including coniferous plantings, has continued to be important right up to the present time in some parts of the region, particularly on the still private estate woodlands and those woodlands managed by Forestry Enterprise (Wharncliffe Wood) and Fountain Forestry (Greno Wood).

Many other woodlands have come into local authority ownership through gift or by purchase, but since their acquisition they had until recently only been managed, if managed at all, on a 'care and maintenance' basis, and by the 1980s were even-aged with dense canopies and poorly developed shrub layers. In a good number of woods the ground layer had disappeared altogether in large sections where the canopy was particularly dense especially where beech had been planted (Figure 12). Local residents were increasingly afraid of walking through the woods because they were dark and gloomy and engendered a fear of personal attack. The more accessible woods were also sometimes heavily vandalised and full of litter. After many centuries of intensive

Figure 12. Dense Beech Canopy.

management and careful protection, the twentieth-century attitude seemed, at best, to leave the woods to their own devices, and at worst to abuse them unmercifully or to threaten to clear them for the sake of progress.

Things began to change for the better about twenty years ago. In Sheffield, the City Council's Recreation Department had created a Moorland and Amenity Woodland Advisory Group (MAWAG) in the 1970s made up of council officers and representatives from outside organisations including the voluntary sector. The City Council approved a Woodland Policy, put together by MAWAG, in 1987. Its primary aim was the protection and perpetuation of the more than forty ancient woods surviving within the city boundaries. The policy was largely enshrined in the City Council's *Sheffield Nature Conservation Strategy* document published in 1991. Meanwhile, work began during the winter of 1988 on the implementation of a management plan for Bowden Housteads Wood, an inner city ancient wood that had remained unmanaged since its purchase from the Duke of Norfolk in 1814. Other management plans and practical projects followed including the coppicing experiments described in the opening section of this paper.

Similar developments took place in Rotherham where there are more than twenty ancient woods in public ownership. Management plans were drawn up for a number of woods and the implementation of the management plan for Scholes Coppice was awarded a Centre of Excellence Award by the Forestry Commission in 1995.

In Barnsley, one of the most exciting projects under the auspices of the Countryside Action in the Rural Environment (CARE) Project was the purchase from the Forestry Commission in 1989 by Tankersley Parish Council of Broad Ing Wood, a plantation of sycamore and Japanese larch on an ancient woodland site. Members of the local community, with professional advice, transformed the site from a close-set plantation into an amenity wood with a semi-natural character and carpets of bluebells.

A major influence on local attitudes to woodland management in the last decade has been the South Yorkshire Forest Project (now Partnership). This project, established in 1991, was one of twelve 'community forest' projects established across the country. South Yorkshire Forest covers most of the Coal Measure country in Sheffield, Rotherham and Barnsley and among its objectives are commitments to protect areas of historical, archaeological and ecological interest (i.e., the existing ancient woodlands). Following a year of public consultation, the South Yorkshire Forest's first plan was published in 1994, which established a policy framework and a strategic approach to woodland management through the Project area.

In 1997, the South Yorkshire Forest Team put together a £1.5m bid to the Heritage Lottery Fund for a five-year action plan to restore thirty-five ancient woodlands in Sheffield, Rotherham and Barnsley – called ***Fuelling a Revolution – The Woods that founded the Steel Country***. In February 1999 it was announced that the bid had been successful and a five-year Heritage Woodlands Project was launched in September 1999. Since that time there has been much activity on a broad front connected with the project – archaeological surveys, the preparation of management plans, active woodland management programmes, interpretation for local communities, commissioning of public art works and the development of educational materials and programmes, including the publication in Sheffield of a 'big book' – Sheffield Woodland Detectives (Jones & Jones, 2002) – for the literacy hour pitched at year three pupils. There is also a *Fuelling a Revolution* website – www.heritagewoodsonline.co.uk – which provides general and site-by-site information about the heritage woodlands and their restoration.

The future of South Yorkshire's many publicly-owned ancient woods looks much better than it did two decades ago. Awareness of their cultural importance has been raised to a much higher level and interest in their economic as well as recreational potential has been re-awakened. But it cannot be emphasised enough that woodland management is not a one-off event; it needs to be continuous and long term. The work that is currently taking place is very encouraging but it is just the beginning. The challenge, as everyone involved knows only too well, is to sustain it in the medium- and long-terms.

Acknowledgements

I would like to thank the owners and guardians of the following archive collections for permission to consult and quote from the documents in their care:

In Sheffield Archives: Arundel Castle Manuscripts; Beauchief Muniments; Bright Papers; Wentworth Woodhouse Muniments.
In Yorkshire Archaeological Society's Archives, Leeds: Duke of Leeds Archives.
In Lambeth Palace Library, London: Shrewsbury Papers.

I also wish to thank Bob Warburton for drawing the final versions of the maps and other illustrations.

References

Ardron, P.A. and Rotherham, I.D. (1999) Types of charcoal hearth and the impact of charcoal and whitecoal production on woodland vegetation. *The Peak District Journal of Natural History and Archaeology*, **1**, 35-47.

Aveling, J. (1870) *The History of Roche Abbey*. Robert White.

Beswick, P and Merrills. D. (1983) L.H. Butcher's survey of early settlements and fields in the southern Pennines. *Transactions of the Hunter Archaeological Society*, **12**, 16-50.

Birks, H.J.B., Deacon, J. and Peglar, S. (1975) Pollen maps for the British Isles 5,000 years ago. Proceedings of the Royal Society, London, **B189**, 87-105.

Clinging, V. and Whiteley, D. (1980) Mammals of the Sheffield Area. S*orby Record Special Series*, **3**.

Collins, E.J.T. (1992) *Woodland and woodland industries in Great Britain during and after the charcoal iron era*. In: Metaille, J. P. (ed) *Protoindustries et Histoire des Forets* (Les Cahiers de l'ISARD 3) University of Toulouse, pp. 109-120.

Conway, V.M. (1947) Ringlinglow Bog, near Sheffield, Part 1, Historical. *Journal of Ecology*, **34**, 149-181.

Curtis, E. (1918) Sheffield in the fourteenth century. Two Furnival inquisitions. *Transactions of the Hunter Archaeological Society*, **1**, 31-53.

Dinnin, M., Ellis, S and Weir, D. (1996) *The palaeoenvironmental survey of the West, Thorne and Hatfield Moors*. In: R. Van de Noort and S. Ellis (eds) *Wetland Heritage of the Humberhead Levels*. Humber Wetlands Project, University of Hull, pp. 81-156.

Eastwood, J. (1862) *History of the Parish of Ecclesfield.* Bell & Daldy.

Eccles, C. (1986) *South Yorkshire Inventory of Ancient Woodland.* Nature Conservancy Council, Peterborough.

Evelyn, J. (1706 edition) *Silva or a Discourse of Forest-Trees.* 4th edition, Scott, Chiswell, Sawbridge and Tooke.

Goodchild, J. (1996) Lionell Copley, a seventeenth century capitalist. In *Aspects of Rotherham: Discovering Local History, Volume 2.* Wharncliffe Publishing, pp. 28-36.

Hall, T.W. (1914) *Descriptive Catalogue forming the Jackson Collection.* J. W. Northend Ltd.

Hall, T.W. (1937) *Incunabula of Sheffield History.* J. W. Northend Ltd.

Hey, D. (2002) *Historic Hallamshire: history in Sheffield's countryside,* Ch 9, 'The Dragon of Wantley'. Landmark Publishing, Ashbourne.

Hicks, S.P. (1971) Pollen-analytical evidence for the effect of pre-historic agriculture on the vegetation of North Derbyshire. *New Phytology*, **70**, 647-667.

Hopkinson, G.G. (1963) The charcoal iron industry in the Sheffield region, 1550-1775. *Transactions of the Hunter Archaeological Society*, **8**, 122-151.

Hunter, J. (1828-1831) *South Yorkshire.* 2 Vols. J.B. Nichols & Son.

Huntley, B. (1998) The Post-glacial History of British Woodlands. In M.A. Atherton & R.A. Butlin (eds), *Woodland in the Landscape: Past and Future Perspectives.* PLACE Research Centre, University College of Ripon & York St John, pp. 9-25.

Huntley, B. and Birks, H.J.B. (1983) *An atlas of past and present pollen maps for Europe: 0-13,000 BP.* Cambridge University Press, Cambridge.

Jones, J. and Jones, M. (2002) *Sheffield Woodland Detectives.* LD Design & Print for Sheffield Heritage Woodlands Team.

Jones, M. (1996a) Deer in South Yorkshire: An Historical Perspective. *Journal of Practical Ecology and Conservation*, Special Publication, **No.1**, 11-26.

Jones, M. (1996b) The medieval deer park at Kimberworth. In: M. Jones (ed) *Aspects of Rotherham: Discovering Local History, Volume 2*. Wharncliffe Publishing, pp. 115-135.

Jones, M. (1997) Woodland management on the Duke of Norfolk's Sheffield estate in the early eighteenth century. In M. Jones (ed) *Aspects of Sheffield: Discovering Local History, Volume 1*. Wharncliffe Publishing, pp. 48-69.

Jones, M. (1998) The rise, decline and extinction of spring wood management in south-west Yorkshire. In: C. Watkins (ed) *European Woods and Forests: Studies in Cultural History*. CAB International, pp. 55-71.

Jones, M. and Talbot, E. (1995) Coppicing in urban woodlands: a progress report on a multi-purpose feasibility study in the city of Sheffield. *Journal of Practical Ecology and Conservation*, **1**, 48-54.

Jones, M. and Walker, P. (1997) From coppice-with-standards to high forest: the management of Ecclesall Woods, 1715-1901. In I.D. Rotherham and M. Jones (eds) *The Natural History of Ecclesall Woods, Pt. 1, Peak District Journal of Natural History and Archaeology,* Special Publication, **No. 1**, 11-20.

Kiernan, D. (1989) *The Derbyshire Lead Industry in the Sixteenth Century*. Derbyshire Record Society.

Linnard, W. (1982) *Welsh Woods and Forest: History and Utilization*. National Museum of Wales.

Rackham, O. (1976) *Trees and Woodlands in the British Land*scape. J.M. Dent & Sons Ltd.

Rackham, O. (1980) *Ancient Woodland: its history, vegetation and uses in England*. Edward Arnold.

Radley, J. and Mellars, P.A. (1964) A Mesolithic structure at Deepcar, Yorkshire, England, and the affinities of its associated flint industry. *Proceedings of the Prehistoric Society*, **30**, 1-24.

Riley, D. (1980) *Early Landscapes from the Air*. University of Sheffield.

Rodgers, A. (1998) Deer parks in the Maltby area. In M. Jones (ed) *Aspects of Rotherham: Discovering Local History, Volume 3*, Wharncliffe Publishing, pp. 8-30.

Characterisation of the woodland flora and woodland communities in Britain using Ellenberg Values and Functional Analysis

K.J. Kirby[1], D.G. Pyatt[2] and J. Rodwell[3]
English Nature[1], Forestry Commission Research Agency[2] and Unit of Vegetation Science, Lancaster University.

Summary

Records from the National Vegetation Classification tables, Ellenberg Indicator Values and Functional Attributes developed by the Unit of Comparative Plant Ecology (Sheffield) were used to characterise differences between plant species independently identified as 'woodland specialists' (based on ancient woodland indicator lists), 'other woodland species' and 'non-woodland' plants. Species that had been proposed as possible 'woodland specialist' species were shown by these independent tests to be more strongly linked to woodland habitats, and to be more shade and stress-tolerant than the other groups.

Introduction

In evaluations for nature conservation purposes, the number of ancient woodland indicators or of woodland species (which includes but goes wider than ancient woodland indicators) has been used to compare sites and stands (Goodfellow and Peterken, 1981; Kirby, 1993; NCC, 1989; Peterken, 1974,1977a; Rose, 1999). Such species lists supplemented historical information in deciding which woods should be included in the ancient woodland inventories (Spencer and Kirby 1992). Defining groups of woodland and ancient woodland species can also simplify (and speed up) survey work by concentrating surveyor's attention on those species most likely to be significant in the interpretation and use of the results (Peterken, 1977b).

However, the definitions of what should be included as ancient woodland indicators, as a woodland species, or classed as a 'non-woodland' plant are inevitably to a degree arbitrary - how much more frequent in ancient woodland does a species have to be to count as an indicator; how often does a species need to occur in woodland for it to be included on the woodland list? Are there other, independent, ways in which the validity of such groupings could be assessed?

In this paper we compare the occurrence of different groups of species (Table 1) in the tables for different vegetation types collected for the National Vegetation Classification (Rodwell, 1991a *et seq.*). Ellenberg Indicator Values (Ellenberg, 1988; Ellenberg *et al.*, 1992; Hawkes *et al.*, 1997; Hill *et al.*,1999; Pyatt, 1997; Pyatt and Suarez, 1997) and Functional Attributes as developed by the Unit of Comparative Plant Ecology at the University of Sheffield (UK) (Grime, 1979; Grime *et al.*, 1988; Hodgson *et al.*, 1995) were then used to characterise the groups (Table 2).

Table 1. Definition Of Woodland Groups

(a)' Woodland specialists': those that had been suggested as ancient woodland indicators based on the following lists

P Phillipson personal communication	Peak District	86
Peterken 1981	Lincolnshire	55
Rackham 1980 (plus Rose 1999)	Eastern England	51 (83)
R J Hornby & F Rose, published in Marren 1992 and Rose 1999.	South-east England	86
As above	Southern England	86
As above	South-west England	88
J. Buchanan & R. Fuller, in Lister & Whitbread 1988	Carmarthenshire	31
Gulliver 1995	North Yorkshire	25
A. Horsfall, personal communication	Dorset	38
Somerset Environmental Record Centre, personal communication	Somerset	20
J. Day, personal communication	Worcestershire	95
Tidswell 1990	Angus	23

(b) 'Other woodland species': other species considered to be commonly associated with woodland and included on the Nature Conservancy Council's woodland survey card (Kirby, 1988; Peterken, 1977b).
(c) 'Non-woodland species': species found in a range of NVC habitat tables, excluding the above two groups.
The basis for these groupings and how they were derived is given in the text.

Table 2. Summary of the Ellenberg and Functional Attribute Approaches

(i) Ellenberg Indicator Values (Ellenberg, 1988; Hill *et al.*, 1999)
Values have been assigned on a 1-9 (12) scale for a species's affinity for/tolerance of a range of factors.

T Temperature: low values equate to tolerance of low temperature regimes.
K Continentality: low values are indicative of more Atlantic distributions for a species
R Soil reaction: low values indicate occurrence in acid soil conditions
F Soil moisture:
1. Plants of extreme dryness, 2. Between 1 and 3; 3. Dry site indicators, 4. Between 3 and 5; 5. Moist site indicators, 6. Between 5 and 7; 7. Damp site indicators, 8. Between 7 and 9; 9. Wet site indicators; 10-12. Flooded/aquatic conditions.
L Light:
1. Plants in deep shade, 2. Between 1 and 3; 3. Shade plants, 4. Between 3 and 5; 5. Plants of half shade, 6. Between 5 and 7; 7. Generally in well-lit places; 8. Light-loving plants; 9. Plants of full light.
N Soil nitrogen:
1. Sites poor in available N, 2. Between 1 and 3; 3. More often N-deficient soils, 4. Between 3 and 5; 5. Average N availability, 6. Between 5 and 7; 7. More often N-rich sites, 8. Between 7 and 9; 9. Extremely rich N soils.

(ii) Functional Attributes.
Attributes considered in the functional attribute analysis programs used in this study (Hodgson *et al.* 1995; for further detail of the attributes see Grime *et al.* 1988)

(a) Strategy type: C Competitive, S Stress-tolerant, R Ruderal, CR Competitive-Ruderal, SC Stress-tolerant competitive, SR stress-tolerant ruderal, CSR intermediate CSR strategist
(b) Commonest habitat type in which species occurred in surveys in central England.
(c) Number of polycarpic perennials (more likely to occur in undisturbed conditions).
(d) Regenerative strategy (production of persistent soil seed bank, production of widely dispersed seeds, seed weight).
(e) Geographical distribution in Europe -number of species showing some latitudinal or longitudinal bias to their distribution.
(f) Present status (whether increasing or decreasing in Britain, where data available)
(g) Height of mature plants

Methods

'Woodland Specialists', 'Other Woodland Species' and 'Non-Woodland' Species

In Lincolnshire woods Peterken (1974) and Peterken and Game (1984) showed that there was a strong association between the distribution of some vascular plants and the history of the site, more particularly whether it was ancient woodland as defined by Peterken (1977a). Ancient woodland indicator plants have also been identified elsewhere in Europe and North America (eg. Hermy, 1994, Hermy *et al.,* 1993, Verheyen *et al.,* 2003).

Twelve lists of ancient woodland vascular plants suggested for different parts of Britain were combined, totaling 158 ground flora species, excluding trees and shrubs. In some cases there was independent historical information to show that the species listed were in fact associated more with ancient than recent woodland sites; in other instances the lists were based on the opinions of experienced surveyors. All authors stressed that it is the occurrence of a number of indicator species in a wood that should be used in interpreting site history, not the presence of individual species.

In this paper, however, how strongly a species indicates ancient woodland is not the prime concern; rather the hypothesis to be tested is that as a group they are more strongly attached to woodland habitats and show a distinct set of characteristics compared to other species. Therefore they are referred to in the analysis subsequently as 'woodland specialists'.

Many other vascular plants commonly occur in woodland and may be the dominant species in the ground flora, without being confined to such vegetation. These include species found mainly in woodland edges and clearings. Ratcliffe (1977) categorised 236 species as 'exclusively or mainly in woodland' or 'species of a wider amplitude, but with a strong representation in woodland'. This list was modified and expanded to 344 species in the light of comments by experienced surveyors in the Nature Conservancy Council (Peterken, 1977b; Kirby, 1988). Of these 158 are the 'woodland specialists' already noted, leaving 186 'other woodland' species, i.e. those that frequently occur in British woodland but may also regularly occur in other habitats. These 'other woodland species' were expected to show a lesser affinity for woodland habitats than the 'woodland specialists', but more than that shown by those plants classed as 'non-woodland' species.

A broad sample of 'non-woodland' species for comparison was then derived from the National Vegetation Classification habitat tables.

National Vegetation Classification (NVC) Lists

The NVC is broken down into broad habitat types (swamps, mires, mesotrophic grassland, calcareous grassland, upland and acidic grassland, heath, sand dunes, maritime cliff habitats, and woodland) (Rodwell 1991a, *et seq.*) which are then broken down into communities. Aquatic habitats and salt marshes were excluded from this analysis.

The aim was to identify all vascular plants (excluding trees and shrubs) listed in a computerised version of the plant lists for the above nine habitats. In practice problems with the species codings meant that a few (probably fewer than twenty) were missed, but 850 species were identified, including some of the woodland species listed already. When the latter were excluded 640 species were left that formed the 'non-woodland' category used in this analysis. The distribution of the 'non-woodland' species across the different habitat types was compared with that of the woodland species.

Ellenberg and Functional Attribute Analysis

'Woodland specialist', 'other woodland' and 'non-woodland' species were compared in terms of their Ellenberg scores (Table 2) (Ellenberg, 1988; Hill *et al.*, 1999). Ellenberg values are on an ordinal scale and the steps between values are not equal. Therefore, as well as comparing mean values for the species groups, the distribution of values within the groups was tested using chi-squared analysis for each factor. Only species for which non-zero values were available for the various factors were used.

Functional Attribute data (Table 2) based on Grime *et al.* (1988) were also used to compare the three groups of species.

Results

Distribution of "Woodland Specialist" and "Other Woodland" species among different NVC habitats

Most "woodland specialist" and "other woodland" species (as defined above) were recorded from the NVC woodland tables, and most of the species in the NVC woodland tables fell into these categories (Table 3). There were 134 woodland species not recorded in the NVC woodland section, but some of these are uncommon, so their absence from the NVC data may simply reflect the nature of the NVC sampling programme.

Table 3. Overlap between the lists for 'Woodland Specialists' and "Other Woodland" Species and those contained in the NVC Woodland Community Tables.

	In NVC woodland tables	Not in NVC woodland tables	Total
All species	331	653	984
'woodland specialists'	102	56	158
"Other woodland" species	108	78	186
'non-woodland' species	121	519	640

There was no significant difference (chi-squared test) in the relative number of 'woodland specialists' found in the NVC woodland lists compared to the number of 'other woodland species', but both were more abundant than 'non-woodland species'. The 'woodland specialists' were less abundant outside the woodland section of the NVC (Table 4) comprising only about nine percent of the lists from non-woodland habitats. Some did however occur across a range of conditions from grassland to mires (Table 5, 6). The 'other woodland' species contributed about twenty-three percent of the species in the lists for most non-woodland vegetation and included species such as *Pteridium aquilinum*, *Arrhenatherum elatius*, *Calluna vulgaris* and *Urtica dioica*.

Table 4. Occurrence of 'woodland specialist' and 'other woodland' species in the NVC tables for non-woodland types.

Vegetation type	S	M	MG	CG	U	H	SD	MC	W
Number of species in tables	197	327	254	298	248	175	258	162	331
Number of 'woodland specialists'	12	26	33	27	36	22	10	17	102
Number 'other woodland'	58	78	69	58	56	38	57	27	108
% 'woodland specialists'	6	8	13	9	14	13	4	7	31
% 'other woodland'	29	23	27	19	22	21	22	17	33

Key to vegetation type
S = swamps; M = mires; MG = mesotrophic grassland; CG = calcareous grassland; U = upland and acidic grassland; H = heaths; SD = sand dunes; MC = maritime cliffs; W = woodland.

Table 5. Woodland specialists most frequently recorded from other NVC habitats and those not recorded in non-woodland tables at all.

Common in non-woodland	Number of habitats	Not in non-woodland tables	
Viola riviniana	7	Aconitum napellus	Lathraea squamaria
Primula vulgaris	6	Adoxa moschatellina	Lathyrus sylvestris
Anemone nemorosa	5	Elymus caninus	Luzula forsteri
Stachys officinalis	5	Allium ursinum	Lysimachia nemorum
Holcus mollis	5	Aquilegia vulgaris	Lythrum portula
Luzula sylvatica	5	Bromopsis benekenii	Maianthemum bifolium
Serratula tinctoria	5	Campanula latifolia	Melampyrum sylvaticum
Alchemilla filicaulis	4	Campanula patula	Melica nutans
Blechnum spicant	4	Campanula trachelium	Melica uniflora
Brachypodium sylvaticum	4	Cardamine impatiens	Melittis melissophyllum
Geranium robertianum	4	Carex digitata	Milium effusum
Geranium sanguineum	4	Carex elongata	Moehringia trinervia
Geum rivale	4	Carex laevigata	Monotropa hypopitys
Hypericum pulchrum	4	Carex pallescens	Myosotis sylvatica
Lathyrus linifolius	4	Carex pendula	Narcissus pseudonarcissus
Oxalis acetosella	4	Carex remota	Neottia nidus-avis
Silene dioica	4	Carex strigosa	Orchis purpurea
Solidago virgaurea	4	Carex sylvatica	Orobanche hederae
Trollius europaeus	4	Cephalanthera damasonium	Paris quadrifolia
Vaccinium myrtillus	4	Cephalanthera longifolia	Phyllitis scolopendrium
Valeriana officinalis	4	Circaea x intermedia	Platanthera chlorantha
Viola palustris	4	Convallaria majalis	Poa nemoralis
		Ceratocapnos claviculata	Polygonatum multiflorum
		Daphne laureola	Polygonatum odoratum
		Daphne mezereum	Polystichum setiferum
		Dipsacus pilosus	Primula elatior
		Dryopteris aemula	Pulmonaria longifolia

Common in non-woodland	Number of habitats	Not in non-woodland tables	
		Dryopteris carthusiana	*Pyrola minor*
		Epipactis leptochila	*Ribes nigrum*
		Epipactis phyllanthes	*Ribes rubrum*
		Epipactis purpurata	*Rosa arvensis*
		Equisetum sylvaticum	*Ruscus aculeatus*
		Euphorbia amygdaloides	*Sanicula europaea*
		Festuca altissima	*Scirpus sylvaticus*
		Festuca gigantea	*Sibthorpia europaea*
		Gagea lutea	*Stellaria nemorum*
		Galanthus nivalis	*Tamus communis*
		Galium odoratum	*Veronica montana*
		Gnaphalium sylvaticum	*Vicia sylvatica*
		Helleborus foetidus	*Viola odorata*
		Helleborus viridis	*Viola reichenbachiana*
		Hordelymus europaeus	*Wahlenbergia hederacea*
		Hymenophyllum tunbrigense	
		Hypericum androsaemum	
		Iris foetidissima	
		Lamiastrum galeobdolon	

'Non-woodland' species made up about a third of those in the NVC woodland tables (Table 6), but tended to be found in only one or two woodland communities; only fourteen occurred in more than three and only one was recorded from more than seven of the twenty-five woodland and scrub communities. The commonest 'non-woodland' species, often associated with wet conditions, were: *Carex nigra* (5 woodland communities) *Carex pilulifera* (4), *Cerastium fontanum* (4), *Epilobium palustre* (5), *Equisetum fluviatile* (5), *Erica cinerea* (4), *Galium uliginosum* (4), *Hydrocotyle vulgaris* (5), *Oenanthe crocata* (4), *Phalaris arundinacea* (7), *Phragmites australis* (6) *Poa pratensis* (4), *Ranunculus acris* (10) and *Senecio jacobaea* (4).

Table 6. Communities in which selected 'woodland specialists' were recorded outside woodland.

Anemone nemorosa	M26; MG3; CG11,12,14; U4,5,16,17; H12,16,18;
Hyacinthoides non-scripta	U17,20; MC12
Hypericum pulchrum	M13,15,25,37; CG8,,9,10,13,14; U17; H3,6,8,10,16,20,21
Lathyrus montanus	MG3; CG10,11,13,14; U4,17; H12,16
Mercurialis perennis	MG2; U17,24
Orchis mascula	MG3; CG13; U17
Polystichum aculeatum	CG13; U20
Primula vulgaris	MG2; CG10,13; U16,17,19; H10; SD8; MC3,9,12
Ranunculus auricomus	M26

Key for vegetation type
S = swamp, M = mire, MG = mesotrophic grassland, CG = calcicolous grassland, U = upland and acidic grassland, H = heath, SD = sand dune, MC = maritime cliff. The number following the letter is the community number within each broad vegetation type.

Ellenberg Values for different groups of species

Differences between groups for Ellenberg moisture values were significant, with 'non-woodland' species having the highest mean values (Table 7) because of the inclusion of species from the mire and swamp habitats. However there were also relatively more 'non-woodland' species (twenty-seven percent of total) in the lower (dryer) half of the Ellenberg scale for moisture; i e. woodland species (both specialist and other categories) tend to occupy the mid-range of conditions.

Nitrogen values were also significantly different between the groups, the 'non-woodland' mean being lower than for woodland species; within the woodland groups there was no difference in the mean values, but the 'other woodland species' were slightly more frequent at both high and low ends of the nitrogen spectrum than 'woodland specialists'.

Table 7. Mean Ellenberg Values for 'Woodland Specialists', "Other Woodland" species and 'Non-Woodland' species.

	'Woodland specialists'	'Other woodland' species	'Non-woodland' species	P for mean
Total number of species considered	158	186	640	
Species with Ellenberg scores	158	182	619	
(a) Mean moisture values	5.7	5.9	6.5	<0.001
No. of species with value <5	16 (10%)	28 (15%)	170 (27%)	
Chi-squared value for distribution differences = 152; 14 df; p=<0.001				
(b) Mean nitrogen values	4.7	4.9	3.8	<0.001
No of species with value <5	61 (33%)	75 (41%)	389 (63%)	
Chi-squared value for distribution differences = 93; 12 df; p=<0.001				
(c) Mean light values	5.2	6.2	7.6	<0.001
No. of species with value <6	96 (51%)	52 (29%)	3 (<1%)	
Chi-squared value for distribution differences = 581; 12 df; p=<0.001				

Note: Only species with non-zero Ellenberg values have been included in the analysis for each factor. In column 5 p = significance of difference of means for each groups, based on one-way anova for each factor separately.

The three groups were most clearly separated in terms of light values with 'woodland specialists' having the lowest values of all, i.e. most shade-tolerant. Sixty-one percent had an Ellenberg value of five or less suggesting that they are typically found in conditions of half-shade or darker.

No significant differences were found between mean values or in the distribution of values using chi-squared for 'woodland specialists', 'other woodland' species, and 'non-woodland' species for soil reaction (R) and continentality (K). The temperature scores showed no difference in mean values, but the values for woodland species were more concentrated in the middle of the range (fairly warm conditions on a European scale) than the scores for 'non-woodland' species.

Functional Attributes of different woodland groups

'Woodland specialists' included the greatest proportion of stress-tolerant species and the lowest ruderal element; 'non-woodland' species showed the highest ruderal element; while 'other woodland' species had the highest competitive element (Table 8). Other differences that may be linked to the strategy differences are that woodland species tended to be taller than 'non-woodland' species, with the 'other woodland' group having relatively the most species in the tallest classes. 'Woodland specialists' had the most polycarpic perennials, potentially long-lived herb species, that may require stable conditions.

Table 8. Comparison of Functional Attributes for Different Groups of Species.

	'Woodland specialists'	'Other woodland' species	'Non-woodland' species	chi-sq. significant
(a) Strategy type				
Number of species considered	105	145	347	
Number of S or S/int.	45	32	115	$p<0.001***$ df = 6
Number of C or C/int.	11	22	21	
Number of R or R/int.	3	14	66	
Number of Intermediate (int.)	46	77	145	
Number of polycarpic perennials	100	118	235	$p<0.001***$
Number with present status decreasing	85	52	187	)) $p<0.001***$)
Number with present status increasing	5	46	65	

Number of species with:				
Western distribution	18	11	36	No significant difference between groups.
Eastern distribution	6	3	5	
Southern distribution	68	83	214	
Northern or slightly northern distribution	13	8	27	

'Woodland specialists' had the highest proportion of species with woodland as their main habitat (based on surveys around Sheffield), consistent with their occurrence in the NVC tables. 'Woodland specialists' had the highest proportion of species believed to be decreasing in abundance across the country, although the basis for how the data underlying this categorisation was made is unclear.

The differences between the groups in terms of seed and dispersal characteristics were weak, but the data were more limited for these (only 105 species across all three groups). In other studies short-distance dispersal mechanisms have been identified as being characteristic of ancient woodland indicators (Hermy *et al.*, 1993).

Differences with respect to geographical distribution between the groups were small.

Discussion

Four approaches to characterising the woodland flora have been brought together, although each in itself has limitations. The National Vegetation Classification data are a sample survey and did not include even coverage for all woodland types across the country, so cannot by themselves provide a definitive listing of what species occur in British woodland. The Ellenberg Values were subjectively derived originally. With the Functional Attribute approach the habitat data comes from a relatively small area of central England. The basis for classing a plant as an ancient woodland indicator (and hence for it entering our category of 'woodland specialists') was often unspecified by those who provided the lists. However because these four ways of describing the flora are derived independently of each other, the common threads that emerge when they are put together are likely to represent real ecological patterns.

There are less than 100 species virtually restricted to woodland in Britain because of a high shade requirement or some mycorrhizal or parasitic/saprophytic link to trees or their litter (Ratcliffe, 1977). Hence it is not surprising that many 'other woodland' species are recorded from 'non-woodland' NVC habitat categories. However they do have different characteristics to the 'non-woodland' category and so there seems no reason not to continue to regard these species as woodland species for woodland survey and evaluation purposes. There is also a case for adding to the 'other woodland' species category some of those species that regularly occur in wet woodland such as *Oenanthe crocata*.

Suggested ancient woodland indicators, grouped together here as 'woodland specialists', were more strongly linked to the woodland environment than 'other woodland species'. 'Woodland specialists' occurred less often in other habitat types, both in the NVC and in the Sheffield surveys; they tend to have a higher proportion of long-lived stress-tolerant species; and they had lower Ellenberg light scores. The Functional Attributes analysis also classed them as more likely to be declining in abundance than other species, which is a justification in conservation terms for paying particular attention to them.

Peterken (1974) noted that indicators may occur in 'non-woodland' situations. *Anemone nemorosa* is considered a good ancient woodland indicator in parts of lowland England, but less weight can be put on its occurrences in areas where calcareous grassland types (CG11,12 and 14) also occur. The use of the NVC tables allows this issue to be approached in a more systematic way. Indicator lists for an area should concentrate on species that were not recorded in other habitats in the NVC tables or those for which the 'alternative habitats' are not common in their region, and also on species which have similar Functional Attributes and Ellenberg Values to known ancient woodland indicators.

The application of these different ways of characterising the woodland flora provides a useful way of describing woodland plants assemblages as others have shown for different suites of species (eg Verheyen *et al.*, 2003). It is being developed, using the same approaches, on the woodland community and sub-community tables within the National Vegetation Classification and in the interpretation of long-term botanical change within woods.

Acknowledgments

We wish to thank John Hodgson at the Unit of Comparative Plant Ecology at Sheffield for data and help with the functional attributes; and various colleagues who provided comments and criticism on drafts, in particular Tim Rich and Martin Hermy. KJK would like to thank David Foster and a Bullard Fellowship for the time to work up some of the material at Harvard Forest.

References

Ellenberg, H. (1988) *The vegetation ecology of central Europe.* Cambridge University Press, Cambridge.

Ellenberg, H., Weber, H.E., Dull, R., Wirth, V., Werner, W. and Pauliben, D. (1992) *Zeigerwerte von Pflanzen in Mitteleuropa.* [Indicator values for plants in central Europe.] *Scripta Geobotanica*, **18**, 1-248.

Goodfellow, S. and Peterken, G.F (1981) A method for survey and assessment of woodlands for nature conservation using maps and species lists: the example of Norfolk woodlands. *Biological Conservation*, **21**, 177-195.

Grime, J.P. (1979) *Plant strategies and vegetation processes.* John Wiley & Sons, Chichester.

Grime, J.P., Hodgson, J.G. and Hunt, R. (1988) *Comparative plant ecology.* Unwin Hyman, London.

Gulliver R. (1995) Woodland history and plant indicator species in north-east Yorkshire, England. In Butlin, R. and Roberts, N. (eds.) *Ecological relations in historic time*, Blackwell, Oxford.

Hawkes, J.C., Pyatt, D.G. and White, I.M.S. (1997) Using Ellenberg indicator values to assess soil quality in British forests from ground vegetation: a pilot study. *Journal of Applied Ecology*, **34**, 375-387.

Hermy, M. (1994) Effects of former land use on plant species diversity and pattern in European deciduous woodlands. In Boyle, T.J.B. and Boyle, C.E.B. (eds.) *Biodiversity, temperate ecosystems and global change*, 123-144. Springer-Verlag, Berlin.

Hermy, M., Van Den Bremt, P. and Tack, G. (1993) Effects of site history on woodland vegetation. In Broekmeyer, M.E.A., Vos, M. and Koop, H. (eds.) *European forest reserves*, 219-232. Pudoc, Wageningen.

Hill, M.O., Mountford, J.O., Roy, D.B. and Bunce, R.G.H. (1999) *Ellenberg's indicator values for British plants: ECOFACT Volume 2 Technical Annex*. Institute of Terrestrial Ecology, NERC and DETR, London.

Hodgson, J.G., Colasanti R.and Sutton, F. (1995) *Monitoring grasslands*. English Nature (Research Report 156), Peterborough.

Kirby, K.J. (1988) *A woodland survey handbook*. Nature Conservancy Council (Research and survey in nature conservation 10), Peterborough.

Kirby, K.J. (1993) Assessing nature conservation values in British woodland - a review of recent practice. *Arboricultural Journal*, **17,** 253-276.

Lister, J. and Whitbread, A.M. (1988) *Pembrokeshire Ancient Woodland Inventory*. Nature Conservancy Council, Peterborough.

Marren, P. (1990) *Woodland heritage*. David & Charles, Newton Abbot.

NCC (1989) *Guidelines for the selection of biological sites of special scientific interest*. Nature Conservancy Council, Peterborough.

Peterken, G.F. (1974) A method for assessing woodland flora for conservation using indicator species. *Biological Conservation*, **6**, 239-245.

Peterken, G.F. (1977a) Habitat conservation priorities in British and European woodlands. *Biological Conservation*, **11,** 223-236.

Peterken, G.F (1977b) *Woodland survey for nature conservation*. Nature Conservancy Council (CST note 2), Peterborough.

Peterken, G.F. (1981) *Woodland conservation and management*. Chapman & Hall, London.

Peterken, G.F. and Game, M. (1984) Historical factors affecting the number and distribution of vascular plant species in central Lincolnshire. *Journal of Ecology*, **72**, 155-182.

Pyatt, D.G. (1997) A site classification for Scottish native woodlands. *Botanical Journal of Scotland*, **49**, 455-467.

Pyatt, D.G. and Suarez, J.C. (1997) *An ecological site classification for forestry in Great Britain*. Forestry Commission (Technical Paper 20), Edinburgh.

Rackham, O. (1980) *Ancient woodland.* Edward Arnold, London.

Ratcliffe, D.A. (1977) *A nature conservation review*. Cambridge University Press, Cambridge.

Rodwell, J. (1991a) *British plant communities. I woodland and scrub*. Cambridge University Press, Cambridge.

Rodwell, J. (1991b) *British plant communities. II mires and heaths*. Cambridge University Press, Cambridge.

Rodwell, J. (1992) *British plant communities. III grasslands and montane communities*. Cambridge University Press, Cambridge.

Rodwell, J. (1995) *British plant communities. IV aquatic communities, swamps and tall-herb fens*. Cambridge University Press, Cambridge.

Rose, F. (1999) Indicators of ancient woodland. *British Wildlife*, **10,** 241-251.

Spencer, J.W. and Kirby, K.J. (1992) An inventory of ancient woodland for England and Wales. *Biological Conservation*, **62,** 77-94

Tidswell, R. (1990) *A test study on primary woodland indicator plants in Angus District*. Nature Conservancy Council, Edinburgh.

Verheyen, K., Honnay, O., Motzkin, G., Hermy, M. and Foster, D.R. (2003) Response of forest plant species to land-use change: a life-history approach. *Journal of Ecology*, **91**, 563-577.

Appendix 1.

Species suggested as possible ancient woodland indicators and included as woodland specialists in this analysis. Species ordered by number of lists in which included.

Key to Lists (areas)
1 Peak District; 2 Lincolnshire; 3 East England; 4 S.E England; 5 S. England;
6 S.W. England; 7 Carmarthen; 8. N.Yorkshire; 9 Dorset; 10 Somerset;
11 Worcestershire; 12 Angus.

Species	List												Number of Lists
	1	2	3	4	5	6	7	8	9	10	11	12	
Galium odoratum	1	1	1	1	1	1	1	1	1	1	1	1	12
Luzula pilosa	1	1	1	1	1	1	1	1	1	1	1	0	11
Melica uniflora	1	1	1	1	1	1	1	1	1	1	1	0	11
Paris quadrifolia	1	1	1	1	1	1	1	1	1	1	1	0	11
Anemone nemorosa	1	1	1	1	1	1	0	0	1	1	1	1	10
Chrysosplenium oppositifolium	1	1	1	1	1	1	0	1	1	1	0	1	10
Lamiastrum galeobdolon	1	1	1	1	1	1	0	1	1	1	1	0	10
Lathraea squamaria	1	1	0	1	1	1	1	1	1	1	1	0	10
Luzula sylvatica	1	1	1	1	1	1	0	1	1	1	1	0	10
Milium effusum	1	1	1	1	1	1	1	0	1	1	1	0	10
Veronica montana	1	1	1	1	1	1	1	1	1	1	0	0	10
Viola reichenbachiana	1	1	1	1	1	1	1	1	0	1	1	0	10
Adoxa moschatellina	1	1	0	1	1	1	1	1	1	1	0	0	9
Carex laevigata	1	1	1	1	1	1	1	0	1	1	0	0	9
Carex pallescens	1	1	1	1	1	1	0	0	1	1	0	1	9
Carex pendula	0	1	1	1	1	1	1	1	1	1	0	0	9
Carex remota	1	1	1	1	1	1	1	1	0	1	0	0	9
Carex strigosa	1	1	1	1	1	1	1	0	1	1	0	0	9
Carex sylvatica	1	1	0	1	1	1	1	1	1	1	0	0	9
Convallaria majalis	1	1	1	1	1	1	1	1	0	1	0	0	9
Lysimachia nemorum	1	1	1	1	1	1	0	0	1	1	0	1	9
Melampyrum pratense	1	1	1	1	1	1	1	0	0	1	0	1	9
Neottia nidus-avis	0	1	1	1	1	1	1	0	1	1	1	0	9
Vicia sylvatica	1	1	1	1	1	1	0	1	1	1	0	0	9
Allium ursinum	1	1	1	1	1	1	1	0	0	1	0	0	8

Species	List												Number of Lists
	1	2	3	4	5	6	7	8	9	10	11	12	
Aquilegia vulgaris	1	1	0	1	1	1	0	1	1	1	0	0	8
Euphorbia amygdaloides	0	0	1	1	1	1	1	0	1	1	1	0	8
Orchis mascula	1	1	1	1	1	1	0	1	0	1	0	0	8
Oxalis acetosella	1	1	1	1	1	0	0	1	1	1	0	0	8
Primula vulgaris	1	1	1	1	1	1	0	0	0	1	0	1	8
Ranunculus auricomus	1	1	1	1	1	1	0	0	0	1	1	0	8
Campanula trachelium	1	1	1	1	1	1	0	0	0	1	0	0	7
Conopodium majus	1	1	1	1	1	1	0	0	0	0	0	1	7
Epipactis helleborine	1	0	1	1	1	1	0	0	1	1	0	0	7
Equisetum sylvaticum	1	1	1	1	1	1	0	0	0	1	0	0	7
Geum rivale	1	1	1	0	1	1	0	1	0	1	0	0	7
Hyacinthoides non-scripta	1	1	1	1	1	1	0	0	0	1	0	0	7
Lathyrus linifolius	0	1	1	1	1	1	0	0	1	1	0	0	7
Polystichum aculeatum	1	0	0	1	1	1	0	0	0	1	1	1	7
Bromopsis ramosa	1	0	0	1	1	1	1	0	0	1	0	0	6
Dipsacus pilosus	1	1	0	1	1	1	0	0	0	1	0	0	6
Dryopteris affinis	1	0	1	1	1	1	0	0	0	1	0	0	6
Elymus caninus	1	1	0	1	1	1	0	0	0	1	0	0	6
Helleborus viridis	1	0	1	1	1	1	0	0	0	1	0	0	6
Hypericum pulchrum	1	0	0	1	1	1	0	0	0	1	0	1	6
Lathyrus sylvestris	1	0	0	1	1	1	0	0	1	1	0	0	6
Narcissus pseudonarcissus	1	0	1	1	1	1	0	0	0	1	0	0	6
Platanthera chlorantha	0	1	1	1	1	1	0	0	0	1	0	0	6
Poa nemoralis	0	0	0	1	1	1	0	0	1	1	0	1	6
Polygonatum multiflorum	1	0	0	1	1	1	0	0	1	0	1	0	6
Sanicula europaea	1	0	0	1	1	1	1	0	0	1	0	0	6
Scirpus sylvaticus	1	0	0	1	1	1	1	0	0	1	0	0	6
Calamagrostis epigejos	0	1	0	1	1	1	0	0	1	1	0	0	5
Chrysosplenium alternifolium	1	0	0	0	0	0	1	1	0	1	1	0	5
Daphne laureola	1	0	0	1	1	1	0	0	0	1	0	0	5
Dryopteris carthusiana	1	0	0	1	1	1	0	0	0	1	0	0	5
Epipactis purpurata	0	0	1	1	1	0	0	0	1	1	0	0	5
Hypericum androsaemum	0	0	0	1	1	1	0	0	0	1	1	0	5
Luzula forsteri	0	0	0	1	1	1	0	0	1	1	0	0	5

Species	List												Number of Lists
	1	2	3	4	5	6	7	8	9	10	11	12	
Mercurialis perennis	1	1	1	0	0	0	0	0	0	1	0	1	5
Moehringia trinervia	0	0	1	1	1	1	1	0	0	0	0	0	5
Myosotis sylvatica	1	1	1	0	0	0	0	0	0	1	0	1	5
Oreopteris limbosperma	1	0	0	1	1	1	0	0	0	1	0	0	5
Phyllitis scolopendrium	1	0	0	1	1	1	0	0	0	1	0	0	5
Potentilla sterilis	0	1	0	1	1	1	0	0	0	0	0	1	5
Ribes rubrum	0	0	0	1	1	1	0	0	0	0	1	1	5
Sedum telephium	0	0	0	1	1	1	1	0	0	1	0	0	5
Solidago virgaurea	1	0	0	1	1	1	0	0	0	1	0	0	5
Stachys officinalis	1	0	0	1	1	1	0	0	0	1	0	0	5
Vicia sepium	1	0	0	1	1	1	0	0	0	0	0	1	5
Blechnum spicant	0	0	1	1	1	0	0	0	0	1	0	0	4
Campanula latifolia	1	1	0	0	0	0	0	1	0	1	0	0	4
Ceratocapnos claviculata	0	1	1	0	1	1	0	0	0	0	0	0	4
Colchicum autumnale	0	0	0	0	1	1	0	0	0	1	1	0	4
Festuca gigantea	0	0	0	1	1	1	1	0	0	0	0	0	4
Hordelymus europaeus	1	0	1	0	1	0	0	1	0	0	0	0	4
Iris foetidissima	0	0	0	1	1	1	0	0	0	1	0	0	4
Polypodium vulgare	1	0	0	1	1	1	0	0	0	0	0	0	4
Ribes nigrum	0	0	0	1	1	1	0	0	0	0	0	1	4
Rosa arvensis	1	0	0	1	1	1	0	0	0	0	0	0	4
Ruscus aculeatus	0	0	1	1	1	1	0	0	0	0	0	0	4
Tamus communis	1	0	0	1	1	1	0	0	0	0	0	0	4
Vaccinium myrtillus	0	0	0	1	1	1	0	0	0	1	0	0	4
Cardamine amara	1	0	0	1	1	0	0	0	0	0	0	0	3
Dryopteris aemula	0	0	0	1	0	1	1	0	0	0	0	0	3
Gagea lutea	1	0	0	0	0	0	0	1	0	1	0	0	3
Holcus mollis	0	0	0	1	1	1	0	0	0	0	0	0	3
Melittis melissophyllum	0	0	0	0	0	1	1	0	1	0	0	0	3
Stellaria holostea	1	1	0	0	0	0	0	0	0	1	0	0	3
Viola odorata	0	0	0	1	1	1	0	0	0	0	0	0	3
Aconitum napellus	0	0	0	0	1	0	0	0	1	0	0	0	2
Athyrium filix-femina	0	0	0	0	0	0	0	0	0	1	0	1	2
Calamagrostis canescens	0	1	1	0	0	0	0	0	0	0	0	0	2
Cardamine impatiens	1	0	0	0	0	0	0	0	0	1	0	0	2

Species	List												Number of Lists
	1	2	3	4	5	6	7	8	9	10	11	12	
Cephalanthera damasonium	0	0	0	0	0	0	0	0	1	1	0	0	2
Cephalanthera longifolia	0	0	0	0	1	0	0	0	0	1	0	0	2
Epipactis leptochila	0	0	0	0	1	0	0	0	1	0	0	0	2
Festuca altissima	1	0	0	0	0	0	0	0	0	1	0	0	2
Geranium sanguineum	1	0	0	0	0	0	0	0	0	1	0	0	2
Gymnocarpium dryopteris	0	0	0	0	0	0	1	0	0	1	0	0	2
Hymenophyllum tunbrigense	0	0	0	0	0	1	1	0	0	0	0	0	2
Hypericum hirsutum	0	1	1	0	0	0	0	0	0	0	0	0	2
Listera ovata	0	0	0	0	0	0	0	0	0	1	0	1	2
Maianthemum bifolium	0	1	1	0	0	0	0	0	0	0	0	0	2
Melica nutans	1	0	0	0	0	0	0	0	0	1	0	0	2
Monotropa hypopitys	0	0	0	0	0	0	0	0	1	1	0	0	2
Phegopteris connectilis	0	0	0	0	0	1	0	0	0	0	0	1	2
Pimpinella major	0	0	0	1	0	0	0	0	0	1	0	0	2
Polystichum setiferum	1	0	0	0	0	0	0	0	0	1	0	0	2
Pulmonaria longifolia	0	0	0	0	1	1	0	0	0	0	0	0	2
Serratula tinctoria	0	0	1	1	0	0	0	0	0	0	0	0	2
Stellaria nemorum	1	0	0	0	0	0	0	1	0	0	0	0	2
Viola riviniana	0	1	0	0	0	0	0	0	0	1	0	0	2
Wahlenbergia hederacea	0	0	0	1	0	1	0	0	0	0	0	0	2
Alchemilla filicaulis	0	0	1	0	0	0	0	0	0	0	0	0	1
Brachypodium sylvaticum	1	0	0	0	0	0	0	0	0	0	0	0	1
Bromopsis benekenii	0	0	0	0	0	0	0	1	0	0	0	0	1
Campanula patula	0	0	0	0	0	0	0	0	0	1	0	0	1
Carex acutiformis	0	1	0	0	0	0	0	0	0	0	0	0	1
Carex digitata	1	0	0	0	0	0	0	0	0	0	0	0	1
Carex elongata	0	0	0	0	0	0	0	0	0	1	0	0	1
Carex montana	0	0	0	0	0	0	0	0	0	1	0	0	1
Circaea x intermedia	1	0	0	0	0	0	0	0	0	0	0	0	1
Cirsium heterophyllum	1	0	0	0	0	0	0	0	0	0	0	0	1
Daphne mezereum	1	0	0	0	0	0	0	0	0	0	0	0	1
Epipactis phyllanthes	0	0	0	0	0	0	0	0	1	0	0	0	1
Equisetum telmateia	0	0	0	0	0	0	0	0	0	1	0	0	1

Species	List												Number of Lists
	1	2	3	4	5	6	7	8	9	10	11	12	
Fragaria vesca	0	1	0	0	0	0	0	0	0	0	0	0	1
Galanthus nivalis	0	0	0	0	0	0	0	0	0	0	1	0	1
Geranium robertianum	0	0	0	0	0	0	0	0	0	0	0	1	1
Geranium sylvaticum	0	0	0	0	0	0	0	0	0	1	0	0	1
Gnaphalium sylvaticum	0	0	0	0	0	0	0	0	0	1	0	0	1
Helleborus foetidus	0	0	0	0	0	0	0	0	0	1	0	0	1
Hymenophyllum wilsonii	0	0	0	0	0	0	1	0	0	0	0	0	1
Hypericum tetrapterum	0	1	0	0	0	0	0	0	0	0	0	0	1
Lonicera periclymenum	1	0	0	0	0	0	0	0	0	0	0	0	1
Lysimachia vulgaris	0	0	0	0	0	0	0	0	0	1	0	0	1
Lythrum portula	0	0	1	0	0	0	0	0	0	0	0	0	1
Melampyrum sylvaticum	0	0	0	0	0	0	0	1	0	0	0	0	1
Ophioglossum vulgatum	0	0	1	0	0	0	0	0	0	0	0	0	1
Ophrys insectifera	0	0	0	0	0	0	0	0	1	0	0	0	1
Orchis purpurea	0	0	0	1	0	0	0	0	0	0	0	0	1
Orobanche hederae	0	0	0	0	0	0	0	0	0	1	0	0	1
Polygonatum odoratum	1	0	0	0	0	0	0	0	0	0	0	0	1
Primula elatior	0	0	1	0	0	0	0	0	0	0	0	0	1
Pyrola minor	1	0	0	0	0	0	0	0	0	0	0	0	1
Radiola linoides	0	0	0	1	0	0	0	0	0	0	0	0	1
Rubus caesius	1	0	0	0	0	0	0	0	0	0	0	0	1
Rubus saxatilis	1	0	0	0	0	0	0	0	0	0	0	0	1
Scrophularia nodosa	0	1	0	0	0	0	0	0	0	0	0	0	1
Scutellaria minor	0	0	0	1	0	0	0	0	0	0	0	0	1
Sibthorpia europaea	0	0	0	0	0	1	0	0	0	0	0	0	1
Silene dioica	0	0	0	0	0	0	0	0	0	0	0	1	1
Stachys sylvatica	0	0	0	0	0	0	0	0	0	0	1	0	1
Stellaria neglecta	1	0	0	0	0	0	0	0	0	0	0	0	1
Trollius europaeus	1	0	0	0	0	0	0	0	0	0	0	0	1
Valeriana officinalis	0	1	0	0	0	0	0	0	0	0	0	0	1
Viola palustris	1	0	0	0	0	0	0	0	0	0	0	0	1
Total	83	57	59	96	96	96	36	26	38	25	107	23	

English Woodlands: Historical Landscapes and Archaeology
Della Hooke

Abstract

Regions that were well wooded in historical times developed particular characteristics that are still recognisable today – notably in settlement and communication patterns. The use of woodland resources can be traced back in history but wood-pasture was a prime usage in early medieval England. Woodland remained a valued commodity in later periods, on one hand as a source of timber and as areas set aside for hunting, on the other as an industrial resource. Archaeological features of all kinds have often managed to survive in patches of woodland but wooded regions that supported industry are especially rich in archaeological remains. The role of woodland in the development of the Ironbridge and Coalbrookdale region of Shropshire is discussed.

Historical regions

Looking at the present-day landscape, it is still clear which regions were well wooded in early historical times, for settlement patterns, routeways, even administrative divisions, were influenced by the way that resources were used in the past. In a paper published in 2000 (Hooke, 2000), I noted how, from a vantage point on the Clent Hills in north Worcestershire, the surrounding countryside to the north-west was, despite its varied geology, one of mainly dispersed settlements – small early manorial nuclei, outlying farms and hamlets – set within a pattern of scattered woodland and small hedged fields. Today this is a heavily farmed landscape but the settlement framework was established when this was a well-wooded region, much of which was subsequently put under forest law (Figure 1). Ancient woodland landscapes can be recognised across the country, even when most of the woods have themselves vanished. This is a characteristic that has, of course, been well documented and recorded since at least the sixteenth century in the writings of Leland and Camden and which formed the basis of the studies of the French and English *pays* in the 1930s and '40s (Bloch, 1931; Homans, 1942). It has been recognised most recently in the work of Brian Roberts and Stuart Wrathmell (2000, 2002).

There is now, following the work of Rackham (1998) and Vera (2000), much more of a consensus about the nature of early woodland, although the balance that existed between true woodland cover and more open land with scatters of trees and shrubs is still a matter for debate (Kirby, 2003). With a main usage of wooded regions in early times as wood-pasture, much of the woodland was essentially of an open character, although individual small woods could be enclosed, at least temporarily, to facilitate regrowth or protect timber (wood being the main source of building materials) (Wager 1998). It is still uncertain how much woodland survived in England through prehistoric times and arguments have been presented that some regions that were obviously wood-pasture regions in the pre-Conquest period, such as the Weald, were much more open and more intensively cultivated before this. It can certainly be shown that woodland regeneration took place in some areas (like northern Hampshire) later in the early medieval period, probably when woods were given greater protection by later Anglo-Saxon rulers manifesting an increasing interest in hunting. In this, they were in part following cultural developments on the Continent, where Frankish kings were establishing legally protected forests as hunting reserves by the seventh century (Gilbert, 1979, 5; Hooke, 1989).

Trees in early medieval England

As a diversion within my own studies on the early medieval period, I have been plotting every record of individual tree species noted in pre-Conquest documents and literary sources, wherever the trees can be located (Hooke, in progress). This is not always quite as straightforward as might be expected: there can be problems with the identification of

Figure 1. Medieval forests, chases and parks in the west midland region.

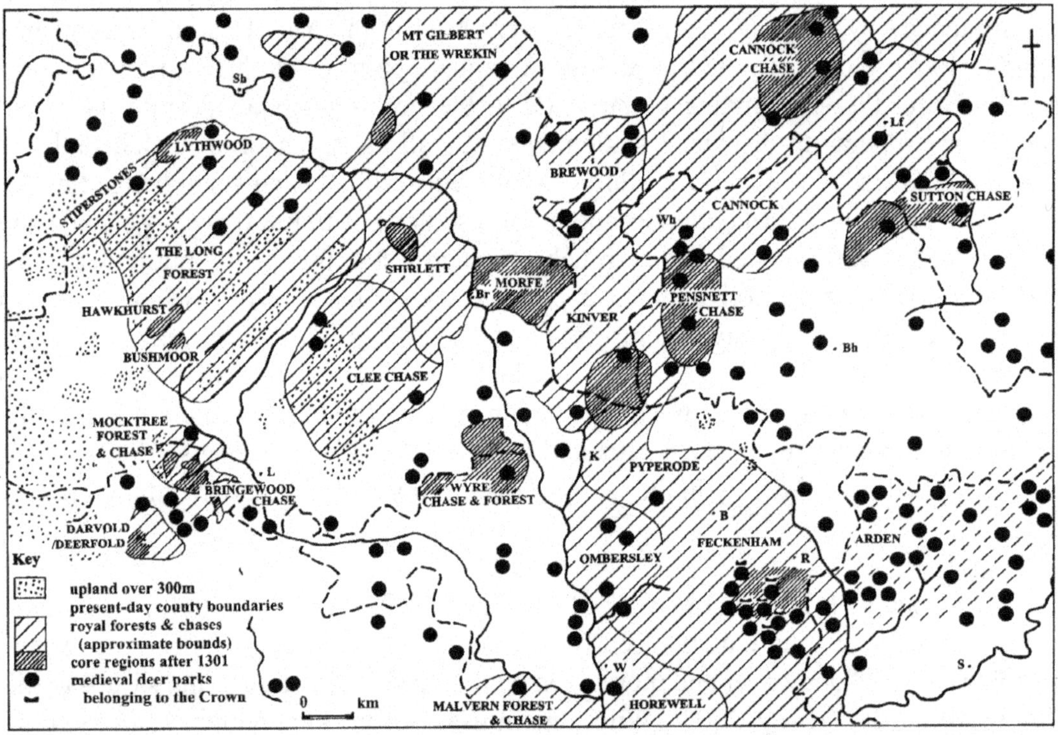

some species and with the virtual absence of others from the documentary record. Many references are found in place-names, but even more useful sources are the boundary clauses of charters, for these enable locations to be more precisely located. Some species are poorly represented or have not been correctly identified, such as the sweet chestnut, *Castanea sativa*, known on Roman sites in southern England, the black poplar, *Populus nigra*, and the hornbeam, *Carpinus betulus*, although an unidentifed *elebeam* is found in the charter-bounds of southern England. Detailed study suggests that the *cwicbeam* was usually a reference to the rowan, *Sorbus aucuparia*. Some species have restricted distributions: the box, *Buxus sempervirens*, is virtually confined to the calcareous soils of southern England, and the beech, *Fagus sylvatica*, is commonest in Hampshire charters. The lime or linden, *Tilia cordata*, shows concentrations in its regional distribution: in Worcestershire, it occurs in wood-pasture regions like the north-east of the county, the Malvern area and on the margins of Wyre; in the Weald it is found in areas of seasonal pasture and in the New Forest of Hampshire. Although Rackham (1990, 150, 174) has shown how, in Cambridgeshire, limes declined in wood-pasture regions, here the opposite seems to have been the case, for the species is still found in many of these regions today.

Figure 2. The distribution of oak and ash in pre-Conquest place-names and charters in south-central England.

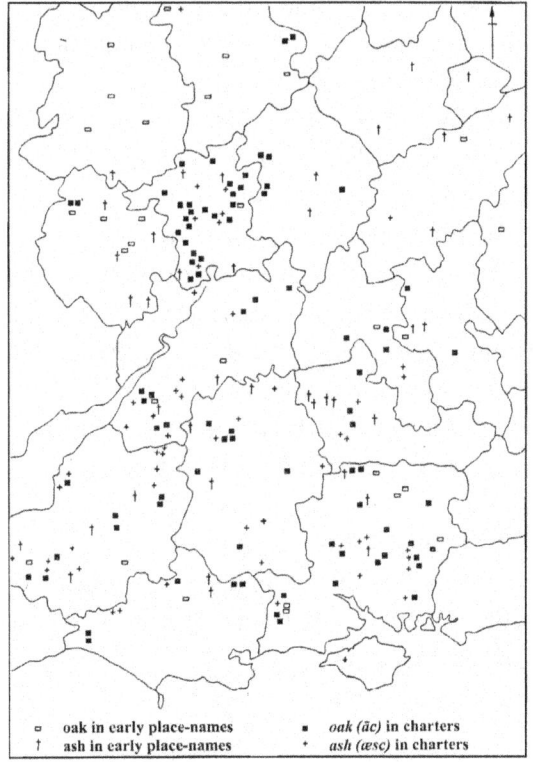

Figure 3. Regions of *leah* place-names in south-central England.

It is, however, the distribution of the oak and the ash which correlates most closely with the well-wooded regions of early medieval England and with the place-name term *leah*, indicative of an early woodland presence (Figures 2 and 3). These were the characteristic trees of wood-pasture and of the subsequent forests, and the concentration in the place-names and charters of Worcestershire fits well with this having been some forty percent wooded at the time of the Domesday survey (Rackham 1996, 50-1). Charter distribution is not ubiquitous and place-names help to extend the distribution further, beyond the range of the charters – into Herefordshire, for instance. It is interesting to relate this distribution to the maps prepared by Roberts and Wrathmell that depict regions of dispersed settlement (Roberts & Wrathmell, 2000, 2002). Many of our veteran oaks and ashes also survive in the same regions, occasionally on forest boundaries but more often as ancient pollards managed within medieval deer-parks (Figure 4). Some, indeed, bear witness to former parks not found in the documentary record or hint at emparkment preceding that of a later designed parkland landscape, as at Cothelstone, Somerset. Ancient trees deserve registration and protection as much as any archaeological site.

The generalised distribution of the *leah* term may be compared to the area of the chalk and limestone escarpments (shown hachured on Figure 3). Where the term occurs in large concentrations over the chalk, clay-with-flint or drift soils are often present, as in parts of Hampshire and Northamptonshire.

In addition to woodland being valued as a source of timber, or as a land use offering a habitat suitable for game that could be taken in the hunt, it was already in early medieval times a valuable industrial resource. Timber was taken in enormous quantities to the saltworks at Droitwich in Worcestershire, used as a fuel for the evaporation vats. Charcoal fired the bloomeries of early ironworks in many places and in the Weald many have been dated back as far as the Roman period, one certainly, two possibly, to the Iron Age (Cleere and Crossley, 1985, 282-3), and coppicing may have been in use by Roman times using any available species of timber readily available (Cleere, 1976; Rackham, 1980, 108-9).

Figure 4 Ancient oak pollard in Moccas Park, Herefordshire.

Archaeological features

A tree that serves as a link between the 'archaeology' of trees and more conventional archaeology has to be the yew, probably Britain's longest living tree. This is a tree whose role was apparently accepted into British Christianity when the pre-Christian associations of other trees were vigorously opposed. Not a few churchyard yews, like that at Much Marcle, Herefordshire, are likely to pre-date the churches beside which they stand and several, like the many-limbed yew (or yews) at Llanerfyl, Powys, or the yew at Claverley, Shrops, are associated with Roman or post-Roman burials. Yew has, indeed, been found accompanying Bronze Age barrow burials and may have been associated with the concept of rebirth from a very early date (Henderson, 1959–60).

Turning to more conventional archaeological features, some sites are not related directly to woodland land use, although wooded regions were often frontier regions and there may thus have been an indirect association. Linear dykes found within Wychwood in Oxfordshire and at Blunt's Green in the Warwickshire Arden may represent Iron Age enclosures constructed close to frontiers, in this case along the boundary of the Anglo-Saxon Hwiccan kingdom, a territory that may derive from that of the Iron Age Dobunni (Hooke, 1885, 16-18). Woods have grown up over many abandoned Iron Age hillforts in the Welsh Borderland and at Welshbury hillfort, in the Forest of Dean, the limes may be growing from a rootstock as ancient as the earthworks themselves. Some woods on the hillforts of the Welsh Border are modern plantations but many of these have replaced earlier woods and parkland trees. In some cases, as in some places in the southern chalklands, the presence of a patch of woodland has ensured the survival of earthworks that would otherwise have been destroyed by the ploughing-up campaigns of the 1950s and '60s. In northern Hampshire, in the woods of Faccombe and Crux Easton, it still possible to trace the so-called 'Celtic' field systems that were in use in late Iron Age and Roman times but abandoned at the end of the Roman period. The lynchets remain clear in the woodland that was regenerating in later Anglo-Saxon times as this became primarily an area of hunting (Hooke, 1988). Trees soon move in if fields or buildings are neglected, as wild nature regains control: thorns colonise abandoned fields and pastures and trees sprout on crumbling walls – at Sudeley in the north Gloucestershire Cotswolds a Roman villa lay by the eleventh century within the woodlands of Hawling (Hooke, 1985, 166).

Many archaeological features are directly associated with woodland usage: especially the wood banks that marked off stands of trees and woodland that needed to be protected from grazing. Sutton Park in the West Midlands was a chase of the Earl of Warwick in the thirteenth century but was granted to Bishop Vesey by Henry VIII, passing to Sutton Corporation. The coppices were enclosed, and the park turned over to pasture, but the rest of the timber was decimated. Some of the old holly coppices, however, survived within their banks as the holly was widely used to provide fodder for sheep and deer. The frequency with which holly occurs in the medieval place-names of the West Riding of Yorkshire may reflect the value attached to it as a fodder tree in hilly districts. The tree is common in the New Forest and Epping Forest and in other areas of wood-pasture, encountered, indeed, according to Rackham in 'every Forest and wooded common' (Rackham, 1980, 347). There are still scatters of ancient hollies in what used to be the Stiperstones Forest of Shropshire, especially at Lords Hill on the north side of the Stiperstones above Snailbeach, although many are now in an advanced state of decay, contorted with age – perhaps survivors from the edge of a once extensive oakwood (Morton , 1986, 74, 76) (Figure 5). Much of our ancient woodland has survived in parklands and the pales of medieval parks, together with the remains of fishponds, warrens and warreners' lodges are often to be found within or close to woodland. Trees anciently associated with a particular region, like the small-leaved lime, may also have managed to survive in such protected surroundings.

Figure 5 Ancient hollies on Lord's Hill near Snailbeach, Shropshire

Woodlands had, of course, their own associated industries. Since coal measure rocks are usually infertile, these have often remained wooded. In the Forest of Dean, in Gloucestershire, the coal measures overlie iron ore beds that supported ironworking by late Iron Age times. This is therefore one of the areas with relics of iron mining and ironworking, charcoal burning and coal digging. Iron mining, often from shallow outcrops, tends to give rise to heavily disturbed ground. The value of the timber trees in the Forest increased as the value of hunting declined, but they were little protected until their importance to the navy was recognised in the seventeenth century. It is interesting to note, however, that two of the best surviving midland forests are those of Dean, including the adjacent area of the Wye valley, and Wyre, both intensively used as an industrial resource, i.e. for charcoal. In Wyre, holly and beech are said to have been preferred by the charcoal burners and beech was planted amongst oak 'nurse' trees in some areas (Hickin, 1971, 11), but oak was a major source for the bark used by the tanneries of Bewdley, the residue used as poles for fencing. Cleft oak was also woven into skeps or scuttles (and probably earlier for the Severn coracles) and oak twigs were used in vinegar making.

Birch trees produced twigs for besoms – whisks of green stripped birch twigs were used by the Kidderminster carpet manufacturers, although softer heather was preferred in the Stourbridge glass houses (Rolt, 1949, 226-9).

Iron ore was generally roasted prior to smelting, to remove moisture and impurities, and was then refined by further heating in a bloomery that was fired with charcoal. It has been suggested that a medieval Wealden bloomery required about two acres of wood annually for each ton of iron produced (Cleere & Crossley, 1985, 100). The charcoal-fired blast furnace replaced the bloomery as continental technology was introduced into England in the mid-fifteenth century. In the mid-seventeenth century, Dean had the greatest concentration of ironworks in the country with twenty blast furnaces in the region (Riden, 1993), although it was not until 1795 that coke-fired furnaces were introduced at the Cinderford Ironworks, so plentiful were the supplies of charcoal.

Charcoal-burning areas are usually revealed by earthen platforms, still often floored with soil containing pieces of charcoal, that are often connected by systems of trackways. The industrial features located close to these supplies of charcoal – the bloomeries, blast furnaces and forges – have, in many regions, left significant archaeological remains. These include hammer ponds or their dams and leats, wheel-pits, masonry and quantities of slag and cinder, although only too often there are no surface remains, and the locations of such features are known only from documentary evidence. Coal mining has given rise to both early bell-pits in some woodlands, or to later features associated with shaft mining. Built by people who frequently combined mining with small-scale farming, cottages were often built around the edges of woodland commons in the post-medieval period to give rise to straggling hamlets or isolated settlements, some now long abandoned, others greatly altered.

The woodlands of Ironbridge and Coalbrookdale

A few years ago, I reviewed the role of woodland in the history of one of England's premier industrial areas: the Ironbridge/Coalbrookdale region, often regarded as 'the cradle of the Industrial Revolution' (Hooke, 1998).

The Coalbrookdale-Ironbridge Gorge area was well wooded at the beginning of the medieval period. In early medieval times, it had been a frontier region between the kingdom of the Magonsæte and a tribe known as the Wreocensæte. At that date woodland was the dominant feature of the region. The woods offered seasonal pasture to distant estate foci, most of those in the immediate region belonging to St Mildburg's monastery at Much Wenlock, a monastery established *c*. AD 680 but rededicated as a priory to its first abbess, St Mildburg, by Earl Roger after the Norman Conquest. The woodlands held by the priory at Madeley possessed woodland sufficient for fattening 400 pigs in 1086 (one of the largest woodland tracts in the county), those at Little Wenlock woodland sufficient to fatten 300 pigs (Thorn & Thorn, 1986). The pigs fed on oak mast in the late summer and autumn and because this was wood-pasture, it is likely to have been open woodland interspersed with many glades rather than dense woodland. Hunting was also carried out in the area and two enclosures for the capture of deer are recorded at Little Wenlock in Domesday Book. There was also an eyrie for the hawks used in the capture of game. In the period of forest expansion, under the Norman kings, Long Forest extended as far north as the Severn to the west of Much Wenlock and the area within the bend of the river fell within the forest of Shirlett, the original 'shire forest' (Figure 1). This forest provided grazing and other rights for the whole county (Rowley, 1986, 152). Land on the northern and north-eastern bank was included within Wrekin Forest, usually known as the Forest of Mount Gilbert.

Figure 6. Medieval woodland clearance in the Ironbridge region.

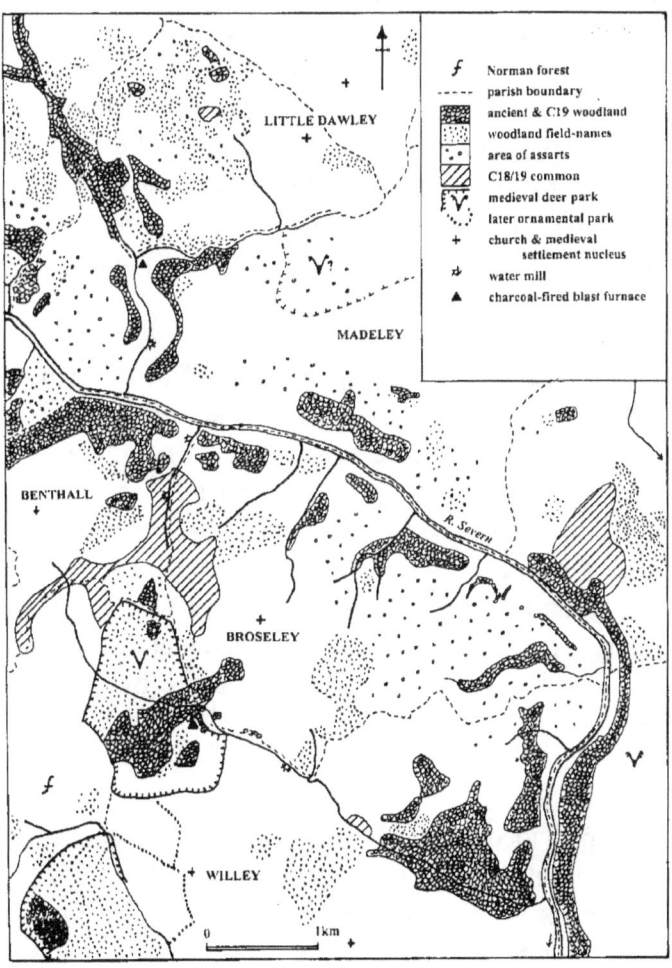

The medieval period was one of considerable assarting, much of it illegally carried out in the forests without licence. Parklands were also enclosed, like that of the Prior of Wenlock in the wood of Madeley in 1283. When Long Forest was disafforested, it was immediately replaced by a string of deerparks. Much of the clearance was, however, for farming, and field-names reveal just how much the wooded area diminished in extent (Figure 6): many of the newly established farms bore names indicative of assarting (Ridding, Woodhouse, etc) but studies of field-names suggest that large parts of parish areas remained well wooded until the twelfth, thirteenth or fourteenth centuries.

Woodland also provided the basis for local industry before the Industrial Revolution and was a factor in establishing the economic base from which future industrial expansion would take place. The monasteries established at Buildwas and Wenlock were actively involved in the mining of minerals but probably on a small scale. Wenlock Priory was digging for coal at Brockholes between Ironbridge and Madeley Wood in 1322 but mining is recorded at Benthall in 1250 (Rowley, 1972, 222; *VCH Shropshire X* 1998, 252). The priory had coalmines in Little Wenlock and Broseley (insetts within Ladywood) at the time of the Dissolution. In 1540, it was also working two iron foundries as well as ironstone quarries in Shirlett Forest and the monks of Buildwas had a small iron forge on their demesne in the sixteenth century (Rowley, 1972, 216). Large-scale development of mineral resources, however, was only to take place after the Dissolution, when land passed into private ownership. The extraction of coal from simple bell pits probably continued alongside the larger scale development that took place on the new landed estates.

Charcoal-fired blast furnaces were being introduced at the end of the fifteenth century and by the seventeenth century at least five had been established in the area between Wombridge and Willey with more to the south. In Coalbrookdale itself, the 'Old' or 'Upper' furnace was to be leased to Abraham Darby in 1708 when he moved here from Bristol. The use of branch wood was replaced by coppicing, with many new coppices established from the sixteenth century onwards that required active woodland management and conservation (Figure 7) – even so, there was insufficient cord wood available locally to supply the needs of the early eighteenth-century iron masters. A further use for estate woodland was for shooting and the frequency of field-names including 'Cockshut' – found in Sutton Maddock, Broseley and Madeley – refer to the shooting of woodcock.

The woodlands also provided a backcloth to the developing industry of the region as it expanded in the eighteenth century, and to the associated housing. Coal mining was expanding by the end of the sixteenth century as a summer activity when the water-table was low, the coal to be transported by river in winter when water levels were high, at first exported out from riverside wharves. By the mid-eighteenth century, however, much of it was destined to be used as coke for the new blast furnaces, of which there were eight in Coalbrookdale, supplying the nine forges in the dale. Some twenty miles of rails had been laid to convey the coal. The focus of industry moved from Willey to Coalbrookdale and Ironbridge. Limestone in vast quantities was taken from Benthall Edge, to be used as a flux in the ironworks. Until this date the area had been essentially rural, with Broseley, the centre of mining, the only urban centre, but after massive investment in industry by Abraham Darby and others (to the point where Darby himself was virtually bankrupt) settlement and industry were expanding rapidly. By the end of the eighteenth century it is said that *'The number of blast furnaces for iron between Ketley and Willey, about seven miles distant, exceed any within the same space in the kingdom'* (Plymley, 1813, 340). To

Figure 7 Coppiced woodland and industry in the Ironbridge region, Shropshire: the landscape of the Industrial Revolution.

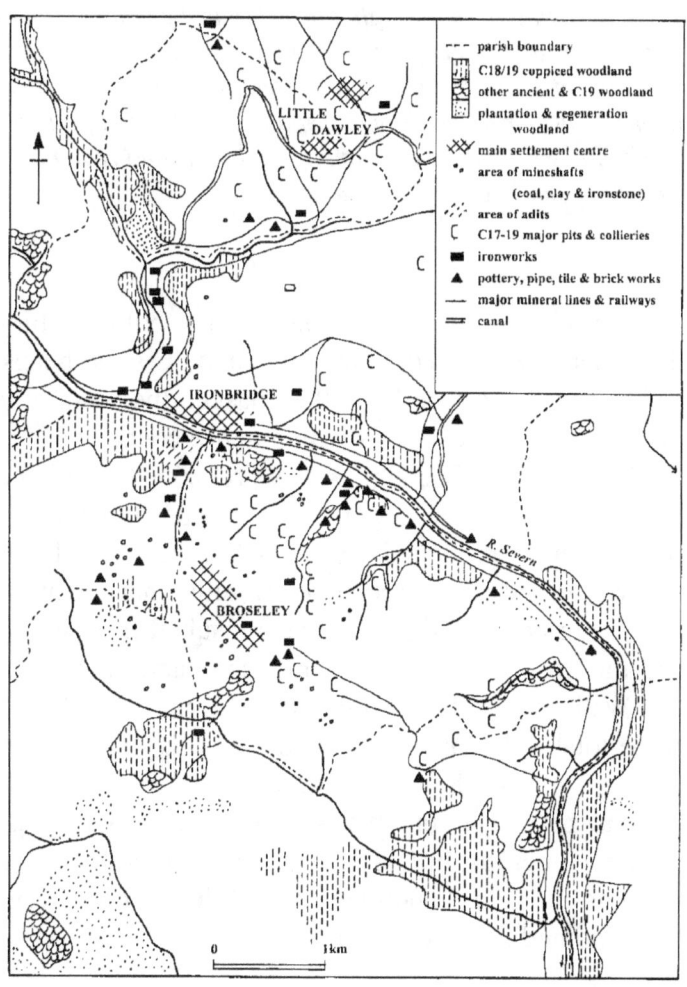

this, must be added clay extraction for brick and tile making and for the manufacture of clay pipes and porcelain – there were thirteen brick- and tile-works in the Gorge *c.* 1840. In spite of this expansion, the woods were part and parcel of the character of the area, surrounding mines and forges and reclaiming any abandoned land.

The woodlands as places for relaxation were valued by employers: in the late eighteenth century, Richard Reynolds established the 'Sabbath Walks' on the eastern slopes of Coalbrookdale for his workers' enjoyment and relaxation (and to discourage them from frequenting public-houses on Sundays). Woodlands were much appreciated in the later eighteenth century as renewed interest was being shown in the English countryside. Young, visiting the area *c.*1768 comments:

Walked by Benthall hall to a steep over the river called Benthall Edge. It is a very fine woody bank which rises very steep from the Severn; you look down an immense declivity on a beautiful winding valley two miles over, cut into rich enclosures, and broken by tufts of wood, the steep on which you stand waving from the right line exhibits the noblest slopes of hanging wood; in one place forming a fine round hill covered with wood, called Tick wood. In front the Wreekin [sic], three miles off, its sides cut by inclosures three parts up, and along the vale the river meanders to Shrewsbury. Further to the right at a spot called Agar's Spout, a most romantic view down a steep slope of wood with the Severn coming in a very bold reach full against it, winding away to the town in a most bending fanciful course

(Young, 1768, 150).

As industrial activity waned in the later nineteenth century, large areas of industrial wasteland became clothed with woodland. Cinder heaps and coal waste eventually reverted to scrub and woodland that masked the scars of past dumping and environmentally damaging activity. Areas with a dense concentration of early bell pits, such as Deerleap, Caughley and The Mines, have remained woodland because surface soil rendered them unsuitable for agriculture. The deeper nineteenth-century shafts of coal mining at Broseley have produced great standing pit mounds – those at Stocking and Barnetts Leasow now appear as tree-covered 'hills' that are attractive additions to the natural landscape. Surface landslips have also resulted from injudicious mining – a church at Jackfield in Broseley had to be demolished and, as a result of a major slip associated with the Wallace pit where mining dated from the 1760s, the community of Salthouses had to be totally demolished; only a temporary road crosses the site today. There are old adits in the Broseley woods where the coal was mined from outcrops near the river, old coal shafts, clay pits that supplied the former brick kilns, the sites of ironstone and limestone outcrops, limekilns and old quarries. Indeed, secondary growth on abandoned workings after the economic slump of the later nineteenth century has led to the extension of woodland in the whole area.

Although, in some areas, slag and pottery waste have been dumped indiscriminately, and some areas of dumping have provided sites for later industrial buildings, the region is today characterised by its sylvan setting and a former industrial landscape has once again been turned into a pleasant semi-rural environment. The woodlands, however, also contain abundant evidence of former minor industrial activity where this has been destroyed in many other regions by building, farming, or later industry. Many restored industrial buildings now form the core of a new tourist industry: Coalbrookdale and the Ironbridge Gorge area has been recognised as a World Heritage Site. However, this does not necessarily include the former industrial sites now dispersed through the woodland. An understanding of the area's development must take in the whole picture and include the *setting* of individual sites within the surrounding countryside.

This regional study shows how conservation must go much further than the protection of the individual built sites of the region, which currently attract the greatest attention, whether these are of former industrial or domestic usage, and several practical objectives were suggested for future woodland management:

(i) Areas of ancient woodland require active management if they are to be protected in the environment of a built-up area close to a busy and growing conurbation. Here various kinds of access stiles have been tried out, for instance, including entrances that make it difficult for wheeled transport to gain access.

(ii) Woodland provided the setting for former industry and still enhances the features of the industrial heritage – management cannot only improve the state of individual woods, but also use them to mask unsightly objects; views can be opened up in appropriate places. Again, this has been done, especially providing vistas over the famous iron bridge built by Abraham Darby in 1779–80 (Figure 8).

Figure 8. Abraham Darby's bridge across the River Severn at Ironbridge.

(iii) Within areas of woodland regeneration, there are many industrial features of interest. These can be protected by good management: access can be discouraged where necessary or sites may be deliberately featured through information boards or leaflets.

There is still scope for a more detailed study to be made of the potential, for educational benefit, of the features within such areas. The laying out of woodland trails, in particular, can provide information to visitors and extend their knowledge and experience of the character of the region; these can also relieve the pressure on 'honey-pot' sites.

This is not to say, however, that the woods themselves are not of historical interest – the species they contain and the way that the trees have been managed. Woods have a major role to play as major landscape features in countryside characterisation and we should be sorely deprived without them. This has, of course, been recognised in the planning and planting of new 'forests' like that which links the old Charnwood Forest in Leicestershire with that of Needwood in Staffordshire (Wade *et al.*, 1998). This helps to restore, to a certain extent, historical features of the landscape while planting woodland that is in step with modern requirements, in this area incidentally also helping to heal the scars of former coal mining. But we have to ensure that individual features are not all 'tidied away' in the name of landscape enhancement and the first priority, archaeologically, is to make sure such features are fully recorded.

Bibliography

Bloch, M. (1931) *Les Caractères Originaux de l'histoire Rurale Francaise*. Marc Léopold Benjamin, Oslo.

Cleere, H.F. (1976) Some operating parameters for Roman ironworks. *Institute of Archaeology Bulletin*, **13**, 233-46.

Cleere, H. and Crossley, D. (1985) *The Iron Industry of the Weald*. Leicester University Press, Leicester.

Gilbert, J.M. (1979) *Hunting and Hunting Reserves in Medieval Scotland*. John Donald Publishers, Edinburgh.

Henderson, A. H. (repr. 1959-60), 'The excavation of a barrow remnant at Lodge Moor, Sheffield, 1956–1957. *Hunter Archaeological Society Proceedings*, 331-6.

Hooke, D. (1985) *The Anglo-Saxon Landscape, the kingdom of the Hwicce*. Manchester University Press, Manchester.

Hooke, D. (1988) Regional variation in southern and central England in the Anglo-Saxon period and its relationship to land units and settlement. In: Hooke, D (ed.) (1988) *Anglo-Saxon Settlements*. Basil Blackwell, Oxford. 123-52.

Hooke, D. (1989) Pre-Conquest woodland: its distribution and usage, *Agricultural History Review*, **37**, 113-29.

Hooke, D. (1998) *The Historic Land Use and Cultural Landscape of the Ironbridge and Coalbrookdale Area*. Unpublished study for the Severn Gorge Countryside Trust.

Hooke, D. (2000) The appreciation of landscape history. In Hooke, D. (ed.) (2000) *Landscape, The Richest Historical Record*. Society for Landscape Studies supplementary series, **1**, 143-55.

Hooke, D. (in progress) *Trees in Early Medieval England: landscape, literature and legend*.

Homans, G. C. (1942) *English Villagers of the Thirteenth Century*. George Caspar, Cambridge, Mass.

Kirby, K. (2003) What might a British forest-landscape driven by large herbivores look like? *English Nature Research Report* No 530.

Morton, A. (1986) *The Trees of Shropshire*. Airlife Publishing, Shrewsbury.

Plymley, J. (1813) *General View of the Agriculture of Shropshire*. Board of Agriculture Report. London.

Rackham, O. (1980) *Ancient Woodland: its History, Vegetation and Uses in England*. Edward Arnold, London.

Rackham, O. (1996) *Trees and Woodland in the British Landscape*. Phoenix, London.

Rackham, O. (1998) Savanna in Europe. In Kirby, K. J. and Watkins, C. (eds.) (1998) *The Ecological History of European Forests*. CAB International, Wallingford. 1-24.

Riden, P. (1993) *A Gazetteer of Charcoal-fired Blast Furnaces in Great Britain in Use since 1660.* Merton Priory Press, Cardiff.

Roberts, B.K. and Wrathmell, S. (2000) *An Atlas of Rural Settlement in England.* English Heritage, London.

Roberts, B.K. and Wrathmell, S. (2002) *Region and Place, a study of English rural settlement.* English Heritage, London.

Rolt, L.T.C. (1949) *Worcestershire.* Robert Hale, London.

Rowley, T. (1972) *The Shropshire Landscape.* Hodder and Stoughton, London.

Rowley, T. (1986) *The Landscape of the Welsh Marches.* Michael Joseph, London.

Thorn, F. and Thorn, C. (1986) *Domesday Book, 25, Shropshire.* Phillimore, Chichester.

Vera, F. (2000) *Grazing Ecology and Forest History.* CABI Publishing, Wallingford.

VCH Shropshire X. The Victoria History of the County of Shropshire, Vol. X, (ed.) G. C. Baugh, University of London Institute of Historical Research, London.

Wade, P.M. Sheail, J. and Child, L. (eds.) (1998) *The National Forest: from Vision to Reality. East Midland Geographer* **21, Part 1**.

Wager, S.J. (1998) *Woods, Wolds and Groves. The woodland of medieval Warwickshire.* British Archaeological Reports, British series 269, Oxford.

Young, A. (1768) (1932 repr). *Tours in England and Wales.* London School of Economics and Political Science, London.

'Therapy of the Green Leaf': the development of forest and woodland recreation in twentieth century Britain

Robert A. Lambert
University of Nottingham

Introduction

"I know that in this wood at all seasons I felt an influence that lifted me out of my merely material self and brought to me comfort and healing through channels at other times sealed and unsuspected. I would enter it with nerves jangled by the strain of seemingly hopeless and unsuccessful effort, depressed and ready to retire from the struggle, and gradually the depression would lift, new life and hope would surge through me and I would return with spirit renewed and strengthened to face the world once more with a brave front." (Eaton, 1935).

This was John Eaton writing a personal appreciation of his local ancient woodland in the magazine *The Deeside Field* in 1935. Eaton thanked the wood that he had known for over forty years for all the recreational pleasure it had given him. When walking in this wood he felt a real sense of spiritual ownership, an intimate sense of place.

His words came just one year before the Forestry Commission (FC) established the first National Forest Park in Britain in Argyll, but many of us would still identify with these sentiments at the start of the twenty-first century. Our enjoyment of woodlands for recreation has a long history. Too often, I think, we imagine recreation to have sprung on the scene as a rural landuse post-1960. In fact, private woodlands have been absorbing visitors back to the second half of the eighteenth century at least. The first real wave of tourists descended on the ancient pinewoods of Rothiemurchus (near Aviemore) in the 1880s, full of admiration for the Highland sylvan scene. Back in 1832, the laird had granted the Duchess of Bedford permission to construct a carriage road through the woods to make her recreational excursions more pleasurable. Now, around 370,000 people visit the woods of Rothiemurchus for pleasure each year, walking around picturesque Loch an Eilein on that same carriage road (Lambert, 2001; Smout and Lambert, 1999).

State Provision

It was with the state provision of National Forest Parks (NFP) in the twentieth century that woodland and forest recreation developed apace. The Forestry Commission were warming to organised recreation as early as the late 1920s, particularly to better control the growing number of people seeking to enjoy the newly opened forests, and overcome the associated threat of fire. There were 400 incidents of fire in 1929, costing the Forestry Commission around £46,000 (Lambert, 2001). The Forestry Commission also wanted to make use of any surplus and unplantable land, and of course, make money from domestic holidaymakers (Mackay, 1995). Argyll emerged in 1935 as the first candidate for a National Forest Park, and an Advisory Committee was hastily assembled to investigate, tour and report on the potential site. Argyll NFP, comprising the unplantable areas of Ardgarten, Glenfinart, Benmore and Glenbranter, was born in 1936 with a donation of £5,000 from the Treasury. The establishment of this first National Forest Park is central to an understanding of later events in state forests across the UK after the Second World War. It had to be seen by the Forestry Commission and other participating access and amenity bodies as a public success, and the tactic of appointing an Advisory Committee had to be seen to have worked on both the regional and national scale as a way of encouraging all interests to work together. Person nights at Argyll NFP rose from 13,312 in 1936 to 32,080 in 1941. Criticism over the Forestry Commission's utilitarian planting schemes in the Lake District in the 1920s and 1930s meant that there was a necessary and obvious public image angle to the whole National Forest Park ideal (Sheail, 1976).

By 1938, the much expanded Argyll Advisory Committee was acting as the leading forum for the wider extension of the National Forest Park (NFP) scheme. They urged that a report should be produced for each potential National Forest Park site (for example: Forestry Commission, 1938; Forestry Commission, 1945). The Forest of Dean NFP was declared in 1939 with the blessing of National Parks campaigner Rt. Hon Viscount Bledisloe GCMG KBE, as Senior Verderer of the Forest. Snowdonia NFP was declared in 1940, Glentrool NFP in 1948, and Glenmore NFP in the Cairngorms in 1948. Then came Queen Elizabeth NFP in 1953, and a Border NFP in 1956 (Stamp, 1974). In addition, the Forestry Commission allowed camping under permit in the New Forest, issuing 83,000 permits in 1956, this rising to 300,000 permits in 1969. In the late 1940s, a Forestry Commission committee that included representatives from the Council for the Protection of Rural England (CPRE) and Winchester College, investigated some of the complex access and landuse issues that could arise with the anticipated post-war development of tourism and recreation in the New Forest, and presented their findings to the Minister of Agriculture and Fisheries (Forestry Commission, 1947). My own research into the history of Glenmore National Forest Park has shown how its popularity with visitors developed steadily from 1948-1964 [see Figure 1], and offers actual statistical evidence of the growing demand for outdoor recreation resources, thus making clear a trend that had hitherto been largely hidden for the first half of the century (Simmons, 2001). In response to the many problems generated by growing visitor numbers the Forestry Commission introduced a spate of byelaws for each National Forest Park from 1948-1954, with national byelaws coming in during 1971 (Forestry Commission, 1971). It was estimated that 15 million day visits were paid to state forests in 1970, and that over one million camper-nights were spent at Forestry Commission sites by 1972 (Haines, 1973; see also Figure 2). The Forestry Commission also published an attractive (now rather collectable) visitor guide book for each National Forest Park property covering aspects of local social and cultural history, folklore, forestry and natural history. Some of these guide books have run to many editions, for example: Argyll NFP (first published 1938/39; then Walton, 1947; fifth edition Edlin, 1976) and Glenmore NFP (first published May 1949; then third edition Walton, 1960; fifth edition Woodburn, 1975).

Figure 1. Annual visitor totals ('person nights') for all parts of Glenmore National Forest Park, Cairngorms, 1948-1964.

	Public Camping Ground	Juvenile Camping Ground	Norwegian Huts	Total
1948	794	261	1,500	2,558
1949	1,050	472	1,650	3,172
1950	2,388	772	3,517	6,677
1951	2,673	1,707	3,720	8,100
1952	3,685	1,098	5,625	10,408
1953	5,175	1,172	5,551	11,898
1954	5,464	1,574	6,784	13,822
1955	13,950	446	7,085	21,481
1956	9,614	988	6,831	17,433
1957	9,868	3,622	5,148	18,638
1958	9,571	1,133	7,288	17,992
1959	16,283	2,402	6,509	25,194
1960	16,272	1,002	8,932	26,206
1961	14,468	1,043	8,870	24,381
1962	17,225	653	8,722	26,600
1963	35,751	2,858	8,208	46,817
1964	51,613	2,362	7,743	61,718

Source: Robert Lambert, *Contested Mountains* (2001), based on FC archives.

Figure 2. Overnight stays on all National Forest Park sites in the UK, 1948-1972.

1948	1949	1950	1951	1952	1953	1954
c.15,000	18,775	42,691	53,600	c.50,000	c.64,000	c.75,000

1960	1961	1963	1964	1969*	1970	1972
267,000	250,000	c.250,000	354,000	470,000	850,000	c.1,000,000

Source: Robert Lambert, *Contested Mountains* (2001), based on FC archives.

In 1943 the Forestry Commission felt confident that they could create a National Forest Park every year for the next decade at a cost of £50,000; or even better, make a special feature of the scheme, and offer an additional £100,000 to establish twenty National Forest Parks by 1955 (Forestry Commission, 1943). But, lest we forget, an internal Forestry Commission memo of 1967 reminded all site managers that although public recreation was now regarded as important, and a great money-spinner, it would always come second to growing timber. For a more complete history of the National Forest Park ideal across the UK, see work based on primary archival research by John Sheail (1981; 2002) and Robert Lambert (2001), and a useful commissioned report by R.D. Watson (1993).

Other Providers

We should at this juncture acknowledge and applaud the important role played by the Royal Society for the Protection of Birds (RSPB), numerous county wildlife trusts, National Trust, English Nature, Scottish Natural Heritage and the Countryside Council for Wales, and some enlightened private landowners, in providing greater opportunities for woodland recreation on their properties across the twentieth century. Sadly, it is almost impossible to chart changes in visitor numbers and perceptions over time for these hundreds of woods as there is little historical recreational evidence available. From its birth in 1972, the Woodland Trust has pursued a wise and generous policy of both protecting woodlands and opening them up to wider public enjoyment. In 2002, the Trust in conjunction with publishers Harper Collins produced a number of attractive guidebooks in a series called 'Exploring Woodland', each containing 101 beautiful woods to visit and an introduction by 'woodland enthusiast' and TV comedian Alistair McGowan (for example: Woodland Trust, 2002). All these initiatives have allowed millions of visitors to soak up what Warwick Deal (1976) called, 'the therapy of the green leaf'.

Forest recreation surveys

George Haines (1973) reproduced the findings of the first pilot national recreation survey in 1965 conducted by the British Travel Association and the University of Keele, which was seen as a source of information for the new wave of rural recreational planners. The results suggested that hiking, cycling and camping were actually becoming less popular forms of outdoor recreation in Britain; quite a large proportion of the people questioned had partaken of them in the past (early 1960s), but the numbers who had actually engaged in them in the year in question (1965) were rather small. Haines concluded that British people in the late 1960s were already starting to look to foreign holidays and less traditional forms of outdoor recreation for excitement and pleasure. However, visiting friends, leisure shopping and Sunday drives in the countryside were by far the most popular weekend activities (Haines, 1973). Haines also reported on an early Forestry Commission recreation survey of four forest properties (Cannock, Allerston, Glenmore and Loch Lomond and the Trossachs) in 1964. At three of the forests, picnicking and pleasure driving were the most popular reasons for visiting, with rambling a distant third. Even at Glenmore, hillwalking came second to pleasure driving, with camping in third place. The results were, of course, affected by the differing localities and facilities of each of the forests, but as Haines concluded, 'these results are especially significant because the people questioned had chosen to go to the rural peace of the forestry plantations and would therefore be expected to be weighted in favour of walking, nature study and other similar pursuits'. He added, 'a significant fact is the large percentage of those going for pleasure drives who had no other activity in mind' (Haines, 1973).

In 1968 Bill Mutch published the results of his own investigations into public recreational habits in state forests. He identified two distinct types of visitors: the first group wanted only the basic facilities provided, so as not to impinge on the wild quality of the forest; the second group demanded toilets, car-parks and children's play areas as a visible sign of their needs being catered for. This second group were less keen on venturing out onto waymarked trails or paths, and did not stray far from the car: rather, they sought the sanctuary of a visitor centre, tea-room or picnic site (Mutch, 1968).

Over this period the Forestry Commission never really undertook any intensive internal visitor recreation surveys on their National Forest Park (NFP) properties. A university geography student did the first comprehensive visitor survey at Glenmore in the summer of 1979, concluding that the Forestry Commission should charge a toll to enter the National Forest Park, and then plough the money obtained back into developing a proper visitor management strategy (Ruddock, 1980). Remember, they did not appoint Recreational Planning Officers to most regional offices until 1974, despite having appointed a landscape consultant (with half an eye on public opinion) in 1964. In 1980, the Forestry Commission launched a long overdue (some would say, very late) public information policy and procedure booklet on *Recreation*, including a shift of emphasis in the provision of facilities away from the holidaymaker to the day tripper: 'those who want to spend a day in the country...they come mainly from towns, usually by car, and their principal requirement is for somewhere to park, to picnic and to walk for fairly short distances' (Forestry Commission, 1980). The recreational development remit of the 1980s would focus on these visitors, and the further provision of car-parks, picnic places, viewpoints and shorter forest walks. Indeed, one gets the sense from the archives that up to the mid-1970s the Forestry Commission were always genuinely surprised by the enduring popularity of the National Forest Park scheme, and were, therefore, unprepared to deal with such large numbers of visitors.

Some interesting evidence we have comes from survey work done by a team of university psychologists working with the Forestry Commission over 2001/2. The report *Perceptions, Attitudes and Preferences in Forests and Woodlands* (2002) may lead to significant changes in forest design throughout the UK. The research found that many people admitted to feeling vulnerable in forests; over fifty percent of women and thrity-three of men felt lost and frightened. Many perceived the forest environment as dense, dark and dangerous. A third of visitors feared they might be accused of trespassing, and many had experienced forest claustrophobia. Maybe 'fear' and 'therapy' go hand in hand? Psychologist Terence Lee traced these forest fears back to our evolutionary history, the power of memory, folklore, fairy tales and horror films. In another part of the study 1,500 people were interviewed as they entered forests and asked to pick landscapes they preferred from a series of photographs. Researchers found that water features including lakes, streams and waterfalls were by far the most popular. As Lee reported 'water features seem to hold the greatest aesthetic value, rather than the actual trees'. The *Sunday Times* reported this story under the headline 'Fear factor cuts back forests' (Adams, 2002).

These research findings made me think of that wonderful observation by the Chairman of the Forestry Commission in London during January 1944 when they were formulating a response to a first draft of the Dower Report on National Parks. The Chairman, Sir Roy Lister Robinson, felt that any National Parks would make it impossible for the Forestry Commission to conduct their timber operations, and (speaking for the populace) concluded that John Dower had 'entirely missed the point that there was much more of interest in walking through a wood than over a bare hillside' (Lambert, 2001; Smout, 2000; Smout, 1993). This came at a time when the Forestry Commission (with the connivance of the Treasury) was vying to be the UK National Park authority themselves.

Woodland and Forest visits

We go into woodlands and forests for a variety of reasons. Birds have been a particular draw, both in the past and present. The Loch Garten RSPB Osprey Centre sits in the heart of their Abernethy Forest reserve, and since it opened in 1959 has attracted two million visitors, and seen seventy-four young ospreys Pandion haliaetus leave the nest [see Figure 3]. It stands as a wonderful example of how to balance the sometimes competing demands of nature conservation and outdoor recreation, and provides considerable economic benefits to local communities (Lambert, 2001; Page and Dowling, 2002; Harley and Hanley, 1989; Brown and Waterston, 1962). Indeed, the countryside writer, Richard Mabey, has argued that rural recreation should be seen as both a 'fully fledged rural landuse in its own right', and a 'logical and potentially profitable' new use for 'obsolete landscape features'. Unplantable land adjacent to upland forests falls into this category. Mabey suggests that the landuses of nature conservation and outdoor recreation should form an important part of 'the alternative rural economy' (Mabey, 1993).

Figure 3. Annual visitor numbers to RSPB Loch Garten Osprey Centre, Abernethy Forest, Cairngorms, 1959-1999. .

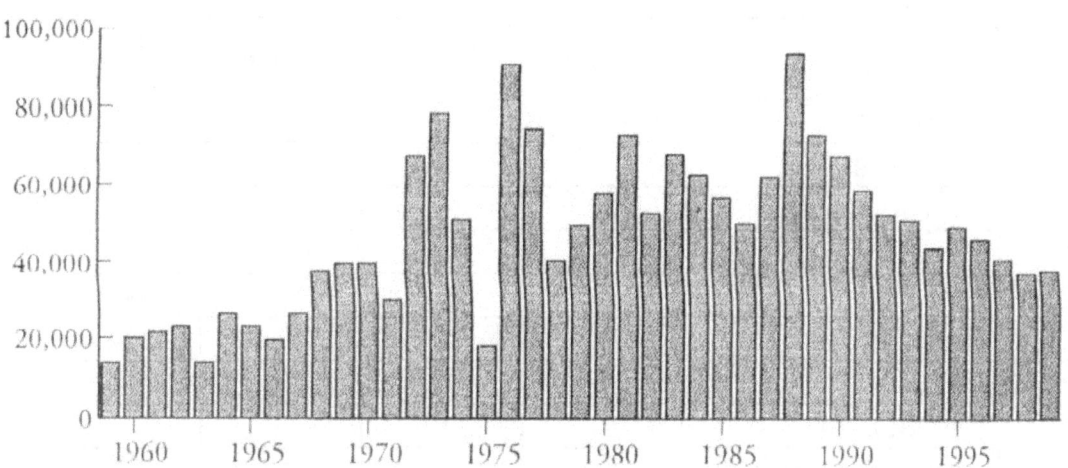

Source: Robert Lambert, *Contested Mountains* (2001), based on RSPB archives.

The Red Kite Centre at Fineshade Wood, Rockingham Forest, Northamptonshire, builds on this tradition. Opened in 2001 in a converted barn, it welcomed 2,443 visitors in thirteen weeks of that summer, and 12,300 visitors in 2002. Seventy-seven of the 5,500 visitors who signed the visitors' book in 2002 came from within fifty miles of the Centre. There were 20,000 hits on the RSPB/FC/English Nature red kite *Milvus milvus* reintroduction project website in summer 2002 (Juliette Kerr, Project Officer, *pers.com*). The Symonds Yat peregrines *Falco peregrinus* in the Forest of Dean, Gloucestershire, have a similar popular appeal.

The geographer Ian Simmons (2001) has suggested that rural Britain post-1950 experienced a 'leisure explosion', driven by increasing free time and new technology. As the amount of disposable income in the population increased, developments in engine and cycle technology meant that 'traditional' low-intensity countryside leisure users had to compete for space with a group that Simmons has identified as, a 'hi-tech spectrum' of users. Many forests now reflect this diverse nature of outdoor recreation in the modern age, and are complex experiments in the multiple use of land. There has to be room for botanists and birdwatchers, ramblers, campers and caravaners, school groups, and activities such as orienteering, mountain biking, dog sled racing, horse riding, rally driving, skiing, water sports, angling, adventure playgrounds, music concerts, and wood sculpture trails. Some popular state forests have lake or coastal beaches well away from busy seaside resorts (Glenmore in the Cairngorms, Roseisle in Moray, Tentsmuir in Fife, and Newborough on Anglesey). For more information on the full range of recreational

Figure 4. Forest Enterprise recreational facilities, as of 31 March 2001.

	England	Wales	Scotland	Great Britain
Forest Walks	233	53	361	647
Cycle Trails	84	12	94	190
Horse Riding Routes	32	3	55	90
Forest Drives	6	1	5	12
Car Parks	356	89	236	681
Picnic Sites	209	50	110	369
Toilets	57	12	25	94
Play Areas	27	9	2	38
Orienteering Courses	35	15	14	64
Visitor Centres	20	5	9	34
Wildlife Hides	13	2	7	22
Forest Classrooms	23	3	3	29
Viewpoints	0	0	32	32
X-Country Ski Routes	0	0	7	7

Source: *Forestry Commission Facts and Figures* (October 2001)

options available to both day-trippers and holidaymakers in state forests look at back issues of the Forestry Commission's own glossy free publication Forest Life, now published twice a year. Figure 4 is a stock take of state forest recreational provision as of March 2001. We have come a very long way since 1936.

Recreational Forests

Should we redesign existing forests or create recreational forests to be in tune with public demands? Yes, according to Lars Kardell, Professor of Environmental Forestry at Uppsala, writing in the journal *Ambio* in 1985. He saw planned recreation forests as a new silviculture concept. It was too difficult, he believed, to balance the demands of nature, tourism and recreation, and timber production, so certain forests (those close to urban areas) should be set aside as places for just recreation. He suggested that foresters managing popular forests should avoid clear-felling as 'to walk through such a desert is not a cherished experience'. Rotation periods should be increased from ninety years to at least 150 years to produce old open stands which are greatly appreciated by the public. Broad-leaved species should not cover more than thirty percent of the woodland, as although they played an important visual role in spring and autumn they were less attractive in the winter, when conifers became 'more pleasant companions'. But, he warned, 'I believe it is important to let the forest remain forest, rather than to urbanize or civilize it'. Bright and ambitious architects and urban planners had to be kept away, so that the forests did not turn into some sort of garish and vulgar Disneyland (Kardell, 1985).

On that note, a recent CenterParcs glossy magazine advert sold their forest health and beauty aqua saunas under the banner: 'Turkish Bath, Indian Blossom Steam Room, Japanese Zen Garden, English Woodland' (CenterParcs, 2003). This formerly Dutch owned company now has thirteen huge holiday centres across Europe: in France, the Netherlands, Belgium and the UK. The first development in the UK opened in 1987 at Sherwood Forest. In 1998 they attracted 650,000 visitors to their three UK sites. Oasis recently entered the forest holiday market with centres in Cumbria and Kent (Williams, 2003). Is this the future for some forests?

Let us return to the psychologists' report. The Forestry Commission response has been to start to re-design some woodlands. Landscaping work at Grizedale Forest in the Lake District aims to create wider paths, provide more information boards and clear large areas of trees to create more open spaces. Similar work in the Forest of Dean led to the felling of fifteen percent of its trees much to the consternation of local conservationists who saw the action as a cull to please public opinion. The Forest of Dean was also given a man-made lake. Money is being spent clearing areas in the Queen Elizabeth NFP in

Stirlingshire to make it 'less intimidating'. James Swabey of the Forestry Commission was reported in the *Sunday Times* as saying that some forests in the UK would be 'transformed' in line with public needs and demands; 'we have started developing forests where people can feel safe, with dappled shade and open areas'. This article also spoke of how, with these new makeover initiatives, the Forestry Commission was trying to cater more for the needs of working class urban visitors, and less for their more traditional clientele, the middle class ramblers and naturalists (Adams, 2002).

All this conjures up horrible images of a wave of *Ground Force* inspired forest makeovers (perhaps televised!) each completed with one of those obligatory Charlie Dimmock water features. But there is a serious point here. In an age when environmental NGOs and government agencies are becoming more people-led, or dare I say it, customer-led, then the future for some of our most popular forests may well be one of restaurants, CCTV cameras, concrete paths, lampposts, large retail outlets and bigger and better holiday camps. In the forests of the future there will be no surprises. If people are the winners, then will biodiversity be the loser?

This has certainly already happened at Glenmore Forest in Scotland. Here the National Forest Park has undoubtedly given a great deal of enjoyment to people since 1948 in organised recreational provision, but this has been at a cost to the area's flora and fauna, quite apart from the damage to the native pinewood. Over the 1920s, the greenshank *Tringa nebularia* had its largest breeding density in Strathspey on the shores of Loch Morlich at Glenmore. As the shoreline there filled with holidaymakers, the greenshank population fell to four pairs in 1951, and to just one pair in 1963. By the 1970s they were gone. The archives suggest that the Forestry Commission did not even notice this (Lambert, 2001; Nethersole-Thompson and Watson, 1981).

Trees and People

We must not forget that our forests and woodlands are places of beauty, tranquillity and biodiversity. They are also important for our health and well-being. Just after the Second World War, the Department of Health in Scotland investigated the 'pleasant and beneficial effects' of bringing the colour green to the people, by planting more trees in urban and suburban areas. Their report urged Local Authorities to introduce new trees and protect existing trees, as 'to the city dweller they afford a record of the changing seasons and serve to remind him of the open country which lies beyond the confines of his urban dwelling' (Department of Health for Scotland, 1948). The twentieth century has shown that there has to be room for people in the woods, but to let much of our woodland heritage now fall under the over-eager eyes of makeover artistes, developers, design consultants and PR agencies would be a great shame. Indeed, should we even be contemplating further provision, knowing that Michael Dower's 'Fourth Wave' of leisure broke across the face of the British countryside in the 1960s and 1970s (Dower, 1965), and that current tourism research suggests a stabilisation through the 1980s and 1990s of the proportion of the population that visit the countryside, from a national high in 1977. This suggests that continuing growth owes more to the increasing frequency with which a minority of users visit (for exercise or dog walking), rather than widening participation within the population at large. It also reflects a shift in leisure lifestyles towards more home-centred activities (Williams, 2003).

The Forestry Commission's Ancient Woodland Project in the East Midlands, launched in 2000, encourages community groups, parish councils and individual users to have a say in how local woodlands are managed. The project newsletter, *Ancient Woodland*, has reported on how foresters were surprised when forest users insisted on keeping Second World War concrete runways in place at Twyford Wood near Colsterworth in Lincolnshire. The runways were valued as an interesting aspect of local military history, as providing open glade-like habitat for butterflies, and because they formed a network of all-weather walks. Dave Solly, FC Recreation Ranger, felt that the consultation process with local people had 'highlighted local concerns about getting the right balance between increasing recreation facilities and keeping the woods looking as natural as possible' (Forest Enterprise, 2001). In 2001, the consultation process allowed people the opportunity to comment on management plans for thirty-four sites including Maulden Woods in Bedfordshire, Salcey Forest in Northamptonshire, and Bourne Woods in Lincolnshire. The project newsletter reported that people had asked for more mapboards, waymarked trails and benches, and that these requests would mean the creation of more 'public open space' in the woods (Forest Enterprise, 2003).

Public opinion is important, and yes, an artificial water feature or open glade can make a forest even more beautiful. But, it is surely all about striking a balance between the sometimes competing demands of both Nature and People. Forest managers in the twenty-first century will have to protect our ancient woodlands and their associated flora and fauna, whilst also providing opportunities for many people to come and visit and use them as places of recreation. The practitioners (and the imperatives) of ecological science, nature conservation, forestry and leisure may well have to forge a better relationship with public opinion (be it local, regional or national), but should not become a slave to it. After all, there is more at stake here, something altogether bigger and less tangible than public opinion, as Chris Smout captured in his introduction to a 1987 collection of photographs of National Nature Reserves (NNR) in Scotland:

'To walk through the oakwoods of Ardnamurchan on a spring morning, or among the ancient pines of Rothiemurchus when they are lit with the flames of autumn birches, is to feel the spirit lifted by the perfection of the place…the wildness, the sense of peace, the feeling of belonging to a greater, natural world which we all experience amid such beauty' (Baxter, 1988).

We have returned full circle to that 'sense of place', and the 'therapy of the green leaf'.

References

Adams, L. (2002) Fear factor cuts back forests. *The Sunday Times*, March 31.

Baxter, C. (1988) *Scotland - The Nature of the Land: Photographs of National Nature Reserves in Scotland*. Colin Baxter Photography/NCC, Biggar.

Brown, P. and Waterston, G. (1962) *The Return of the Osprey*. Collins, London.

CenterParcs. (2003) Because time is precious. *Country Living*, February, **206**, 46-47.

Deal, W. (1976) *A Guide to Forest Holidays in Great Britain and Ireland*. David and Charles, Newton Abbot.

Department of Health for Scotland (1948) *Memorandum on Tree-planting in Urban and Suburban Areas*. HMSO, Edinburgh.

Dower, M. (1965) *The Fourth Wave: the challenge of Leisure*. Civic Trust, London.

Eaton, J. (1935) In a Pine Wood. *Deeside Field*, **7**, 21-25.

Edlin, H.L. (ed.) (1976) *Argyll Forest Park – Forestry Commission Guide*. HMSO, Edinburgh.

Forest Enterprise (2001) *Ancient Woodland*, Project News, Issue 2.

Forest Enterprise (2003) *Ancient Woodland*, Project News, Issue 4.

Forestry Commission (1938) *Report of the National Forest Park Committee (Forest of Dean)1938*. HMSO, London.

Forestry Commission (1943) *Post-War Forest Policy – Report by HM Forestry Commissioners Cmd 6447*. HMSO, London.

Forestry Commission (1945) *Report of the National Forest Park Committee (Glentrool) 1943*. HMSO, London.

Forestry Commission (1947) *Report of the New Forest Committee Cmd. 7245* HMSO, London.

Forestry Commission. (1971) *Forestry Commission Byelaws 1971, No.997* HMSO, London.

Forestry Commission. (1980) *The Forestry Commission and Recreation: Policy and Procedure Paper No. 2*. FC, Edinburgh.

Haines, G.H. (1973) *Whose Countryside?*. Aldine/J.M. Dent, London.

Harley, D.C. and Hanley, N.D. (1989) *Economic Benefit Estimates for Nature Reserves: methods and results*. Discussion Paper in Economics 89/6, University of Stirling.

Kardell, L. (1985) Recreation Forests – a new silviculture concept? *Ambio*, **14**, 3, 139-147.

Lambert, R.A. (2001) *Contested Mountains: Nature, Development and Environment in the Cairngorms Region of Scotland, 1880-1980*. White Horse Press, Cambridge.

Mabey, R. (1993) *The Common Ground: the history, evolution and future of Britain's countryside*. J.M. Dent, London.

Mackay, D. (1995) *Scotland's Rural Land Use Agencies: the history and effectiveness in Scotland of the Forestry Commission, Nature Conservancy Council and Countryside Commission*. Scottish Cultural Press, Aberdeen.

Mutch, W.E.S. (1968) *Public Recreation in National Forests: A Factual Survey*. HMSO, London.

Nethersole-Thompson, D. and Watson, A. (1981) *The Cairngorms - Their Natural History and Scenery*. Melven Press, Perth.

Page, S.J. and Dowling, R.K. (2002) *Ecotourism*. Pearson Education, Harlow.

Ruddock, C. (1980) *Visitors and Visitor Management in Glen More Forest Park*. Unpublished MA (Hons) dissertation, No. 334, Department of Geography, University of St. Andrews.

Sheail, J. (1976) *Nature in Trust: the History of Nature Conservation in Britain*. Blackie, London.

Sheail, J. (1981) *Rural Conservation in Inter-war Britain*. Clarendon Press, Oxford.

Sheail, J. (2002) *An Environmental History of Twentieth-Century Britain*. Palgrave, Basingstoke.

Simmons, I.G. (2001) *An Environmental History of Great Britain: from 10,000 years ago to the present*. Edinburgh University Press, Edinburgh.

Smout, T.C. (1993) *The Highlands and the Roots of Green Consciousness, 1750-1990*. Occasional Paper No.1, SNH, Battleby.

Smout, T.C. and Lambert, R.A. (eds.) (1999) *Rothiemurchus: Nature and People on a Highland Estate, 1500-2000*. Scottish Cultural Press, Dalkeith.

Smout, T.C. (2000) *Nature Contested: environmental history in Scotland and Northern England since 1600*. Edinburgh University Press, Edinburgh.

Stamp, D. (1974) *Nature Conservation in Britain*. Collins, London.

Walton, J. (ed.) (1947) *Argyll – Scottish National Forest Park Guides, No. 1*. HMSO, London.

Walton, J. (ed.) (1960) *Glen More – Cairngorms, National Forest Park Guide*. HMSO, Edinburgh.

Watson, R.D. (1993) *The History and Development of the Glenmore National Forest Park*. Landwise Scotland/Save the Cairngorms Campaign, Inverness.

Williams, S. (2003) *Tourism and Recreation*. Pearson Education, Harlow.

Woodburn, D.A. (ed.) (1975) *Glen More Forest Park - Cairngorms*. HMSO, Edinburgh.

Woodland Trust (2002) *Exploring Woodland – East Anglia and North Thames*. Collins, London.

Woodland Trust (2002) *Exploring Woodland - Peak District and Central England*. Collins, London.

Figure 1.   Walking in Longshaw near Sheffield.

The Ghosts at the Ends of the Earth: Tree-Land in Four Hemispheres
Oliver Rackham
University of Cambridge

In 1996, Jennifer Moody and I published *The Making of the Cretan Landscape*. A review in *Antiquity* claimed we were wrong to apply to a different country the methods of landscape archaeology, which the two reviewers called 'quintessentially British — or even just English', suited to an 'intimate landscape of fields and enclosures, old pastures and rough grazings, ancient woods and conserved parklands' (Fleming and Hamilakis,1997). They asked 'How well does English-style archaeology travel?' (They had not noticed that one of the authors isn't English.)

This an amazing comment, which would hardly be taken seriously except that one of the reviewers is a distinguished English landscape historian and the other an eminent Greek social anthropologist. I can only reply with further questions: Can any discipline be peculiar to one country? Could botany be confined to Sweden? Is climatology quintessentially Italian? Each country has its strengths and weaknesses in different types of evidence, but are the principles not international? Do they not apply to the intimate landscapes of England and the large-scale landscapes of Texas and the ultra-intimate landscapes of Crete?

Six years later, other speakers at the 2003 *Working and Walking in the Footsteps of Ghosts* conference have shown that landscape archaeology does apply in many parts of Europe. It falls to me to show how some of the methods apply to the ancient tree-lands of other continents, with other species, genera, and families of trees, and other human civilizations. This is not a small field — there are well-established Forest History Societies in North America and Australia — and I can deal only with a sample of aspects.

Tree-lands

There is a tendency, which I regret to see even in this volume, for European and American ecologists to talk about forest and woodland as if these were interchangeable and were the normal habitat of trees: to forget about the wood-pastures and non-woodland trees of our own continents, and to foist the forest ethos on other continents too. Travellers to the Mediterranean have a tradition of reproaching southern Europe for not being crowded with tall straight upright trees standing close together, destined by a beneficent Providence for the north European timber trade.

My term *tree-land* covers at least five situations:
- Forest (where the trees are close together and the ground vegetation, if any, is shade-bearing);
- Savanna (grassland or heath with trees, where the ground vegetation is not shade-bearing, Figure 1.);

Figure 1. Savanna of the 'classic' tropical kind. The trees are several species and ages of eucalyptus; the hard, fireproof mounds are built by the termites that recycle wood. Laura, Cape York Peninsula.

- Coppice (Figure 2.), periodically cut at short enough intervals for non-shade-bearing plants to flower after each felling;
- Farmland trees;

Figure 2. Mixed coppice-wood of about 15 years' growth. Ogawa, Kitabaiuki, Japan.

- Maquis (trees reduced to the status of shrubs by browsing and burning (Figure 3) — the approximate Australian equivalent is *mallee*).

Figure 3. Maquis in an extreme form. The low green bushes are *Quercus coccifera*, which is palatable to goats. If allowed to grow only a little bigger than this they will produce pollen and acorns. If browsing ceases they will grow up into big oak-trees.

Some years ago I challenged palynologists to come up with a means of discriminating between these on pollen evidence. They have not responded, and even now articles are published on the basis that tree pollen is by itself evidence for forest.

Woodland History: Some International and Intercontinental Aspects

Giant coppice stools and the origin of coppicing

Woodland history resides not only in written records but in features like giant coppice stools. Most European species of tree sprout from the stump if cut down; repeated felling and sprouting produces a stool which enlarges a little at each cycle. Stools two metres or more in diameter are independent evidence of centuries of coppicing (Figure 4). Ancient coppice stools of *Fraxinus, Quercus, Carpinus, Tilia, Fagus, Ulmus glabra*, etc. are the stuff of woodland history in England (Rackham, 1990), France, Italy, Norway, Hungary (Szabó, this volume), Corsica, Greece (Figure 5) and Crete (Rackham and Moody, 1996), among many other countries. Some trees which refuse to coppice are clonal, growing from root suckers in ever-enlarging circular patches; most other species of *Ulmus* and some of *Populus* and *Prunus* do this.

Figure 4. Ancient coppice stool of ash (*Fraxinus excelsior*), Bradfield Woods, Suffolk, England.

Figure 5. Ancient coppice stool of chestnut (*Castanea sativa*). Mount Athos, north Greece.

Such features of ancient woodland do not always survive. At this conference the field trip to the Derwent Valley illustrated how it is possible for almost all historic features, including old trees, ancient coppice stools, and diagnostic plants, to be wiped out of an ancient-woodland site by management unsympathetic to ancient woodland. In in this case it was by a combination of early-twentieth-century estate forestry, tree-planting, and sheep.

Ancient coppice stools are also the stuff of woodland history in Japan (Figure 6). In that country the trees are different species mostly of the same genera as in Europe, with much the same distribution of coppicing and suckering behaviour among genera. An unrelated human civilization has independently invented traditions of woodmanship, wood-pasture, and plantation forestry, which are separate from each other, as in Europe. Japanese coppice-woods have much in common with English, especially the mixtures of tree species, but there are differences of detail; for instance the Japanese have learnt to

Figure 6. Ancient coppice stool of oak (*Quercus serrata*). Asunaro, Kamikawa, Japan.

distinguish *Quercus acutissima* from other deciduous oaks and cut it as a pollard, not a stool, even within woodland. (Europeans, in contrast, failed to distinguish *Q. robur* from *petræa* until the seventeenth century (Rackham, 2003 p.283).)

Australia, however, is in effect another planet. The trees are utterly different. The recycling job that fungi do in Europe or Japan is done in Australia by fire — except in the small area of Australian rain-forest — and termites. However, coppicing behaviour is present both among fire-adapted eucalypts and in rain-forest trees. Many species of *Eucalyptus* possess a permanent woody lignotuber, formed by the young tree, from which it can sprout if the above-ground stem is killed by a hot fire. In areas with a history of hot fires the lignotuber can grow into a structure very like an ancient coppice stool (Figure 7). This too has its human component: throughout the Holocene, Australian Aborigines have profoundly affected the continent's ecology by altering the fire frequency. As in Europe and Japan, some Australian trees are killed by felling, and others are clonal: Tasmania has circular clonal patches both of the native *Melaleuca* (Figure 8) and of the introduced *Populus alba.* (Nevard and Rackham, 2001).

Figure 7. Coppice-like stools of jarrah (*Eucalyptus marginata*) in fire-adapted woodland. Avon Valley National Park, S.W. Australia.

Figure 8. Clonal tree, *Melaleuca ericoides*. Stanley, Tasmania.

In temperate North America, which is a different continent but not another planet, there are coppicing and suckering trees of much the same genera as in the Old World, although all the species are different. There are three types of coppice stool. European-style coppicing has been going on for some 350 years and has had time to produce only modest-sized stools. Big stools of a lignotuber character, however, can be produced by fire: for example in middle Texas, which has had European settlement for only 150 years, but previously had Native Americans managing the landscape by burning (Figure 9).

Figure 9. Ancient stools of *Quercus texana*, presumably resulting from repeated fires in aboriginal times, when prairie reached up to this spot. Near Valley Mills, middle Texas.

The third type of American coppice stool results from self-coppicing. When *Tilia americana* reaches a certain age it sends up a ring of shoots from around the base of the trunk. The old trunk rots at the base and falls down, leaving the shoots to fill the gap without needing to start again from seed. After a few cycles the result irresistably recalls a giant stool of European lime. This behaviour is shared by *T. japonica* and *T. maximowiczii* in Japan, and presumably *T. cordata* once did this too. Self-coppicing is a property of *Castanea dentata* in North America, and of several American and Japanese species of *Magnolia*. Among beeches, European *Fagus sylvatica* coppices, American *F. grandifolia* is clonal, and Japanese *F. japonica* self-coppices but not *F. crenata*.

This raises the question: How did coppicing originate? What did trees do with this property before people invented axes? It may come in useful as a reaction to fire, but it is not a fire-adaptation: many of the species having it, such as those just mentioned, are incombustible, whereas many fire-promoting trees, especially pines, lack this property.

Building timbers

A kind of evidence not much cited in this conference is the species, sizes, ages, and shapes of the trees that went into early buildings or the first permanent houses built by settlers. As I have long pointed out, most medieval buildings in England, from cathedrals to lower-class houses, are built from small or smallish trees — each tree producing just one beam. The great majority of timbers are oak, although this is partly an effect of survival: less durable timbers presumably formed a larger proportion of the original stock of structures. It is very clear that medieval woods and hedges were managed to produce a rapid turnover of young oaks, which were used in their hundreds of thousands annually (Rackham, 2003 pp. 145—7, 457—62). The ecology of oak was different from what it is now: today oak behaves as a pioneer tree and seldom regenerates in existing woods. Wattle-and-daub provides similar information about coppicing and the underwood produced by it: for example there is a surprisingly large proportion of aspen (*Populus tremula*), despite its lack of durability.

The same can be seen in ancient and vernacular buildings in many other countries in Europe, and in Japan; and in settlers' architecture in European America, European Tasmania (Figure 10), and even in tropical Colombia and Queensland. In most cultures, the carpenter went into the woods and chose the smallest tree that would make the beam or plank required. Even if he were a slave, he avoided wasting time and energy in felling and subdividing big trees. Tree-lands were managed to produce a succession of conveniently small timber trees. Cutting up forest giants was a job that was generally left until the invention of steam-engines and sawmills and power tools. Medieval England generally imported boards — now called 'Baltic oak' — from specialist suppliers in eastern Europe who did have a supply of very big, slow-grown trees and the means of converting them.

Figure 10. Log building of the first settlers, *c*.1830, made of *Callitris* •••. The pioneers evidently found a large number of evenly-matched stems of this rare tree. Little Swanport, E. Tasmania.

Pictures

Early photographs are a most valuable source of information, including — perhaps especially — those in which trees and woods are the background incidental to some other activity. Aerial photographs might be expected to go back almost to the beginnings of photography (which is younger than ballooning), but for some reason they are not an important source until well into the twentieth century (Rackham, 1992).

Paintings and drawings are another matter. Landscape paintings go back to the Bronze Age Ægean (excavations on Santorini), but only a few European artists have been capable of drawing a convincing tree. The famous picture of a coppice-wood by the late-medieval Fleming, Simon Benninck, shows recognisable lime, oak, aspen, and elm trees, areas of underwood of different years' growth, and even coppicing plants,[1] but is somewhat exceptional. Most artists, even those specialising in landscape, show trees as bland and generic; it is surprising how seldom it is possible to say what kind of tree is represented. (Is this because all paintings of big trees are simplified abstractions — life is too short to draw a naturalistic tree — and few artists appreciate what are the distinctive features?)

European artists have a strong preference for single-stemmed trees, even in situations where it is known that most trees were multi-stemmed. They often prefer dead trees to living, perhaps because dead trees are easier to draw. From Dürer onwards artists have been fascinated by pollards and veteran trees, especially in eighteenth- and nineteenth-century England where artists such as Strutt specialised in portraits of ancient trees.

---

[1] British Library: Add. 18855 f.108v.; Rackham (2003), frontispiece.

Conversely, the painters of the Barbizon School in nineteenth-century France usually drew bland and unconvincing trees, paying little attention to the dramatic ancient oaks then abundant in the Forêt de Fontainebleau on the edge of Barbizon.

In Japan, pictures are much more informative. Japanese artists possess the supreme skill of indicating the 'jizz' of a recognisable tree with a few flicks of the brush. From the fourteenth century onwards, landscape paintings contain trees of a dozen recognisable species, including conifers; often they are of specific scenes and can be compared with what is there now, illustrating (for example) the drastic decline of pine.

Europeans improved when taken out of the art-school tradition and transported to Australia (e.g. for forgery). Euro-Australian artists became observant and convincing at the difficult task of painting recognisable eucalyptuses, getting right the diagnostic details of bark; they picked up the distinctive conical bases with a blackened hollow at one side, the effect of recurrrent fire damage and compensatory growth.

Savanna and Wood-Pasture History

In 1996, I spoke on 'Savanna in Europe', the opening lecture in the British Ecological Society's conference on the Ecological History of European Forests, in which I sought to show that forests were not the only possible habitat for trees. Wood-pasture, trees scattered in grassland or other non-shade-bearing vegetation, was a historically extensive class of vegetation in Europe (several articles in Kirby and Watkins, 1998) and had antecedents in wildwood (the vegetation that existed before the coming of significant human activity). It was an extension of the savanna vegetation of Asia, Africa, North and South America, and Australia (Rackham, 1998).

The theme has been developed at this conference by Franciscus Vera. This is not the place to criticise or review the details of his thesis (see Rackham, 2003 chapter 32), but he emphasises that there was more to wildwood than just trees and trees and trees. He finds a place in wildwood for large herbivores, animals that graze and browse but cannot climb and therefore need low-growing vegetation (Vera, 2000).

Savanna is vegetation at the transition between grassland and forest, in environments where some limiting factor allows trees to grow but not forests. The limitation most easily understood is moisture, but it may be cold or fire or browsing animals (Figure 11). It used to be thought that wood-pastures in Europe were maintained solely by human activities, whereas savannas in lower latitudes were 'natural' and existed without human intervention, but this distinction is no longer tenable. Grassland with trees has a complicated history of interactions between drought, cold, grazing, and burning, which often involves human land management as well as the natural behaviour of trees and plants. For example, hundreds of thousands of square km of West African forest are not primaeval wildwood but are ex-savanna: the people who kept the savanna were murdered or carried off by slavers, and their habitat infilled into forest (Fairhead and Leach, 1998).

Figure 11. Savanna: moist enough for trees (junipers and live-oaks) but too dry for forests. Davis Mountains, west Texas.

Fire, grazing, and weather play a part in the complex dynamics of Davis Mountain savannas. The junipers (*Juniperus deppeana*), are older than the oaks (*Quercus grisea*) and pines (*Pinus cembroides*), and some of them go back far beyond European settlement.

Pollards and ancient trees

If ancient coppice stools are the stuff of historic managed woodland, pollards are the stuff of wood-pasture. Pollarding has been done in various styles and for different purposes, especially to produce leaves on which to feed domestic livestock. As a means of producing wood it is more laborious than coppicing, but puts the new growth out of reach of browsing domestic livestock or wild beasts.

Pollards turn into veteran trees much as coppicing produces ancient stools.[2] Ancient pollards are the stuff of wood-pasture history: pollard oaks and beeches in England, pollard oaks in Hungary (Szabó, this volume), pollard elms and ashes in Norway (Austad, 1988), pollard evergreen oaks in Spain and Crete, pollard deciduous oaks in Sardinia and the Balkans (Grove and Rackham, 2001, especially chapter 12). Even Japan has the remains of savannas with pollard horse chestnuts, elms, oaks, and yews, surprisingly for such a northerly and wet country with a history of not keeping many animals for meat.

Ancient trees occur in almost any situation, but are typical of wood-pasture and are not typical of ancient woodland. Ancient woods contain ancient coppice stools, but seldom contain upstanding ancient trees except on boundary banks. This is partly because most ancient woods have been managed to produce timber trees small enough to be handleable, but also because the competition of neighbouring trees is a powerful factor shortening a tree's life. Where ancient trees are now in woodland, this is almost always a sign that the tree came first and the wood grew up round it.

---

[2]The reader is reminded that by convention ancient coppice stools do not count as veteran trees.

In the last 200 years there has been a tendency for the world's forests to get denser, and for savanna to infill and turn into forest. This is a result of decline in traditional land-uses — the slave trade being an extreme cause — and the spread of the forestry ethos. If drought is a limiting factor the result may be a forest of small, slow-gowing, drought bitten trees (Grove and Rackham, p. 193f).

It is easy to forget that most ancient trees were not originally forest trees: if they occur in forest now, the forest has grown up around them (Figure 12). Veteran trees are not relics of wildwood: they tend to go with savanna and to have a human element in their history. Often they are threatened by infilling by younger trees which shade the veterans and compete with them for water. Burnham Beeches and Staverton Thicks (Figure 13) are well-known examples of infilled wood-pastures in England. Others can be found all over southern Europe. The Mount Athos peninsula in north Greece is a sacred mountain which for a thousand years has been inhabited only by monks, and its forests have been held up as an example of primaeval wildwood. In reality they contain scattered ancient oaks and giant pollard planes whose spreading habit demonstrates that they began as free-standing trees (Rackham, 2002).

Figure 12. Veteran tree at odds with its present surroundings. The Major Oak, Sherwood Forest, a nineteenth century postcard. The artist visualised it as a free-standing, wide-spreading tree (medieval Sherwood Forest was largely heathland) around which a wood of tall crowded trees has grown up: a common fate for wood-pasture trees around the world. (I am indebted to Ian Rotherham for this illustration.)

Figure 13 A wood of immense hollies, infilled into a wood-pasture of ancient pollard oaks. About 1800 the hollies sprang up between the great oaks, and by 1900 had overtopped and killed many of them. Staverton Thicks, Suffolk, England.

Savannas in North America and Australia

North America largely escaped the pollarding tradition (but I have seen pollards in Costa Rica). Its extensive savannas are strongly influenced by the behaviour of the trees as well as by human cultures. The 'oak openings' of Michigan were the effect of Native American burning, which resulted in grassland scattered with multi-stemmed lignotubers ('grubs') of deciduous oak. When burning was suppressed they infilled into ordinary forest (Peters, 1978).

In middle Texas, however, the common savanna trees, *Quercus fusiformis* and *Ulmus crassifolia,* are clonal. The unit of tree growth and longevity is the *mott,* a clonal patch of oak or elm stems typically ten to thirty metres in diameter (Figure 14). Individual stems appear to be 50—200 years old, but the mott, like a lignotuber, is several centuries old and was already there when settlers came in the 1840s. This is certainly a cultural savanna, maintained by browsing animals and formerly by burning. If browsing and burning both cease, it infills with *Juniperus ashei* and turns into forest. The infrastructure, however, probably dates from pre-Columbian times and has lived through four successive human cultures, two Native American and two European-style.

Figure 14. Savanna by motts: a clonal patch of *Quercus fusiformis* among grassland. Near Pidcoke, middle Texas.

In Australia, savannas cover more than half an entire continent. They are, in part, a cultural landscape inherited from the Aborigines. This may even involve pollarding, either with axes or as a result of fire; the Western Australian marri and jarrah eucalypts can be turned by a fierce fire into a pillar of charcoal, which sprouts and grows a new top (Figures 15 and 16). In the Cape York Peninsula the eucalyptus savanna is affected by changes in the fire regime and by the spread of flammable exotic grasses. If deprived of fire, the savanna may infill with fire-sensitive rainforest trees (Figure 17). (In a similar way the ancient oaks of Staverton Thicks have been infilled with holly, the European equivalent of a rainforest tree (Figure 13).)

Figure 15. .Ancient pollard-like jarrah (*Eucalyptus marginata*), hollowed out by many fires. Near Toodjay, S.W. Australia.

Figure 16. Rainforest trees growing up between the big eucalypts of former savanna, the effect of fire suppression. Note the blackened bases of the eucalypts. Kurunda, Queensland.

Figure 17. Pollarding by fire: a marri (*Eucalyptus calophylla*). Avon Valley National Park, S.W. Australia.

Artificially large numbers of deer

In much of England, as several other papers in this volume show, densities of deer at present are higher now than they have ever been in the historic, maybe even in the prehistoric, past. There are unquestionably more species than ever before. Most deer are not really forest animals: in continuous shade they soon exhaust the leafage within reach, creating a browse-line, and then starve or move on. They soon destroy most of the shade-bearing woodland vegetation, which is not adapted to resist browsing. They are creatures of the boundary between forest and grassland, and flourish especially where woods interdigitate with farmland. The twentieth century, with increasingly warm winters and the fashion for autumn-sown crops, provided deer with a more-than-ideal habitat.

Perhaps the greatest unsolved questions in prehistoric ecology are: How many animals were there in wildwood times? How much grassland or heath was needed to feed them? I leave this question to Vera or his successors.

Excessive numbers of deer are not peculiar to England. In much of North America there are now more deer, usually of native species, than at the time of European contact; this has to do with the extermination of carnivores, break-up of large extents of inhospitable continuous forest, and with a very active hunting movement. In Japan the native deer have gone so far as to destroy the forest in certain areas (Figure 18). Introduced Eurasian deer have wrought havoc among the unadapted vegetation of New Zealand and Australia.

Figure 18. Stand of *Abies homolepis* killed by deer eating the bark. Mount Odaigahara, Japan.

Historical Ecology as an Intercontinental Discipline

Landscape history does work in other continents. Some of the conservation issues dependent on it are intercontinental, such as the multiplication and homogenisation of the world's deer, the infilling of savanna and the decline of ancient trees.

I have dealt with certain aspects that emphasise the unifying features, but I should avoid the impression of too much unity. Trees are wildlife and not environment. They are not passive recipients of whatever destiny mankind chooses to inflict on them: each species has its own agenda in life. Environmental factors also vary: outside England the investigator has to understand fire and fire-promoting vegetation. There may also be utterly different plants. Japan is not a different planet, but it has one 'extra-terrestrial' feature, giant bamboos, *Phyllostachys bambusoides* and *Ph. heterocycla.* These clonal grasses, said to have been introduced from China as human food, are quite capable of overtopping and killing a big tree (Figure 19). They form thickets on abandoned cultivation terraces at the base of the mountains, spreading upwards and taking over the mountain forest. They have come to be an important substitute for timber and to play a part in Japanese culture.

The investigator has to begin by discovering the properties of each country's particular trees and plants: which species coppice? which are clonal? which are edible? which are combustible? The answers are unlikely to be printed in forestry textbooks: the student has to go out and look.

Figure 19. *Phyllostachys pubescens*: the introduced grass that overtops big trees and reduuces the historian to the stature of an ant. Near Osaka, Japan.

For 150 years, since the time of John Muir in America, many conservationists have been obsessed with wildwood supposedly unaffected by human actions. Preserving wildwood and re-creating wildwood are probably still the most commonly cited motives for conservation. But the idea of wildwood has been steadily receding, as archaeological study shows how early and how widespread human influence has been. Except on oceanic islands, people of various cultures have been using and manipulating tree-lands for thousands of years, and have been capable of acting at a distance. It is arguable that the profoundest effect of humanity on the world's forests was the extermination by Palæolithic peoples of the super-elephants of previous interglacials: the withdrawal of animals capable of breaking down a big tree can hardly fail to have had momentous consequences. One begins to ask whether there has been extensive wildwood at all in this interglacial, except in Madagascar and New Zealand which apparently had no human presence before *c.*1500 AD.

Trees and woodland are normally the product of human cultures acting in combination with the environment and with the natural behaviour of animals and plants. It makes little sense to study the biological aspects in isolation, or to divorce biological conservation from other kinds of conservation.

An example: the ghosts at the ends of the earth

Tasmania has many landscapes, and most of them are haunted. They are haunted by ghosts of black people with firesticks, burning the button-grass plains and spearing fat juicy pademelons in the savannas. These have left majestic savannas of great trees in the mountains and stolen savannas in the lowlands. Savanna trees survive in settlers' farmland; their charred hollow bases are the marks of the Aboriginal culture that died 180 years ago (Figure 20). Present Tasmanians, who love these scattered eucalypts, are distressed that they gradually die and no research has discovered how to bring on a new generation of eucalypts in pasture.

Figure 20. Savanna trees (*Eucalyptus obliqua*), now in farmland. The conical, hollow, charred bases indicate a fire history, although the surroundings will not now burn. Bruny Island, Tasmania.

Other ghosts with greyish-pink faces clank around Port Arthur, the scene of a famous experiment in penal reform. Under a great spreading savanna tree sits a ghost dreaming of a ticket-of-leave; the tree is now in the midst of a wood, hemmed in by its children (Figure 21).

Figure 21. Old tree at odds with its present surroundings. A eucalypt (*Eucalyptus obliqua*), once free-standing in savanna, now hemmed in by its children. The branches, originally horizontal, have turned upwards as competition increased. Port Arthur, Tasmania.

Tasmania, unlike most of Australia and North America, is a land of pollards: pollard European trees (especially elm), pollard eucalypts, and even pollard rainforest trees (*Nothofagus*). Aboriginal and European landscapes are intertwined. Thousands of the great pre-settlement eucalypts on farmland are pollards (Figure 22). Was it a black or a white hand that started the pollarding?

Figure 22. Savanna eucalypts near Longford, Tasmania. Who undertook the immense labour of pollarding these iron-hard trees, and why?

Acknowledgements

Among many friends and colleagues in other countries I am especially indebted, for introductions to sites mentioned here, to the following: in southern Europe to Dick Grove, Jennifer Moody, Philip Oswald, and Duncan Poore; in America to Bill Allen, Susan Bratton, Wick Dossett, and Jennifer Moody; in Japan to Katsue Fukamachi, Tomohiko Kamitani, Jun-ichi Ogura, Toru Nakashizuka, Hiroshi Tanaka, and Toshiya Yoshida; in Australia to David Currie, Daniel Lunney, Jenny Mills, and Tim Nevard.

References

Austad, I. (1988) *Tree pollarding in western Norway.* In: Birks, H.H. and others (eds.) *The Cultural Landscape — Past, Present and Future* Cambridge University Press, Cambridge.

Fairhead, J. and Leach, M. (1998) *Reframing Deforestation: global analysis and local realities: studies in West Africa.* Routledge, London.

Fleming, A. and Hamilakis, Y. (1997) Peopling the landscape. *Antiquity*, **71,** 75—7.

Grove, A.T. and Rackham, O. (2001) *The Nature of Mediterranean Europe: an ecological history.* Yale University Press, Yale.

Kirby, K.J. and Watkins, C. (eds.) *The Ecological History of European Forests.* CAB International, Wallingford.

Nevard, T. and Rackham, O. (2001) *Cultural Landscapes [of Tasmania].* Tasmanian Heritage Council.

Peters, B.C. (1978) Michigan's Oak Openings: pioneer perceptions of a vegetative landscape. *Journal of Forest History,* Jan. 1978, 19—23.

Rackham, O. (1998) *Savanna in Europe.* In: Kirby and Watkins, above.

Rackham, O. (1990) *Trees and Woodland in the British Landscape,* 2nd ed. Dent, London.

Rackham, O. (1992) Woodland ecology in recent and historic aerial photographs. *Photogrammetric Record,* **14,** 227—39.

Rackham, O. (2002) The Holy Mountain. *Plant Talk,* **27,** 19—23.

Rackham, O. (2003) *Ancient Woodland: its history, vegetation and uses in England,* 2nd ed. Castlepoint Press, Colvend.

Rackham, O. and Moody, J. (1996) *The Making of the Cretan Landscape.* Manchester University Press, Manchester.

Vera, F.W.M. (2000) *Grazing Ecology and Forest History.* CAB International, Wallingford.

Historical Diversity in the Woods of the Lower Wye Valley
George F. Peterken

Summary

The diverse history of individual woods in and around the Lower Wye Valley is illustrated by three individual woods. These indicate the diversity of former coppice treatments and the uncertainty of the distinction between coppice and wood-pasture in space and time. During the nineteenth and twentieth centuries, traditional management was replaced by a new diversity of neglect, conversion to high forest, replacement by conifer plantations, and growth of secondary woodland on heaths and fields, but the woods retained several historical features. Traditional treatments cannot be restored, except on a small scale, but understanding of past management can inform future management strategies and treatments.

Introduction

Ever since the *Historical Ecology Discussion Group* was active at Monks Wood in the 1970s, we have tried to understand semi-natural ecosystems in terms of their pasts, and then apply this understanding to management for conservation. As far as woodland was concerned, this meant giving priority to ancient woods, and resuming coppicing or wood-pasturage wherever possible. Now, however, the application of historical understandings in woodland management seems far less straightforward.

At about the same time, woodland historians became used to drawing a distinction between two kinds of traditional management, wood-pasturage and coppice. The early, well-researched sites, the New Forest (Hants) (Tubbs, 1968), Staverton Park (Peterken, 1969) and Hayley Wood (Cambs) (Rackham, 1975), became type examples. Here, too, however, further experience revealed numerous complications. The clear distinction was necessary as a basis for study, but we came to recognise that history on the ground did not fall into clear and unambiguous categories. For example, the ancient Highland pine-birch woods (Steven and Carlisle, 1959) were different in many ways, some New Forest wood-pastures were once coppices, and Hayley Wood has certainly seen some pasturage in the past.

In this paper I describe three woods in the Lower Wye Valley. All three are mixtures of beech, small-leaved lime, sessile oak, hazel, yew and holly, with irregular contributions from ash, wych elm, large-leaved lime, pedunculate oak, alder and other species, a composition that is characteristic of the dry and well-drained slopes of the Lower Wye, but which is rare elsewhere. Collectively, they illustrate variation in woodland histories within a district, and the difficulties of applying historical understandings to management.

Lady Park Wood

This is now well-known as a long-established minimum-intervention reserve with a detailed record of stand development, but until 1870 it was a coppice-with-standards woodland cut on a large-scale (Peterken and Jones, 1987). Historically, the reserve was part of the very large Hadnock Wood, itself a peripheral part of the Forest of Dean. King John (1199-1216) granted it to John of Monmouth to form a park about 1200 and by 1381 it was waste of the Duchy of Lancaster. Iron was mined in Lady Park coppice from at least the sixteenth century until the early twentieth century, but not elsewhere in Hadnock Wood. The wood was leased then sold about 1600, and remained part of the estate attached to Highmeadow House until 1817, when the whole area was bought back by the Crown to fill a gap in the age-class distribution of the Forest of Dean oaks.

Hadnock Wood was divided into five named parts, one of which – Lady Parke – includes the modern reserve. A survey carried out in 1608 (Table 1) showed that Hadnock Wood extended to 762 acres; that the whole area had been coppiced in four successive winters from 1600-1603; and that the wood as a whole contained many 'timber trees' (presumably oaks) and 'great trees' (presumably large oaks) as well as some 'decayed trees' and 'beeches'. Whereas the other four coppices had an average of eight to ten trees per acre, Lady Parke was conspicuous by its low density of trees (0.4 trees per acre); the high proportion of beeches; and the low value (half or less of the value in other coppices) placed on all categories of tree. The distinct character of Lady Parke as a vigorous coppice with relatively few, low-value trees is presumably explained by the mining.

In 1817, the oldest trees in Highmeadow Woods were said to be just sixty years old, and most were much younger. This is probably true, for no navy timber was cut in Highmeadow Woods until 1850-1864. In 1849, William Downes said that 'there are some very fine young oaks on the High Meadow Woods, very thrifty and handsome' (House of Commons Journal, 1851, p.205). In 1851 sixty-two oak timber trees and 160 cords of 'oak miners' timber' cut in Lady Park Wood were offered for sale (Hart 1966, p.220). Ring counts of trees felled in 1941 confirmed that the oaks originated mainly from 1800-1810 and the mid-nineteenth century, indicating periods of heavy felling.

Table 1. Hadnock Woods in 1608, as recorded in Matthewe Nesson's survey (PRO MPC 108)

	Lady Parke	Skirrette	Cowvall quarter	Buckholde	Prishette
Area (acres)	**106**	183	140	141	192
Number of trees					
Timber trees	**2**	1000	844	951	1118
Great trees	**18**	637	498	240	373
Decayed trees		55	12	52	18
Beeches	**18**	200	35	5	13
Value of each tree (sh.)					
Timber trees	**5**	10	13.3	10	10
Great trees	**2.5**	5	6.7	5	5
Decayed trees		1	1	1	1
Beeches	**2**	2	2	2	2
Underwood					
Age in 1608 (yrs growth)	**4**	7	6	6	5
Value per acre at 20 yrs growth (sh.)	**33.3**	20	20	20	20

The last coppicing took place in 1870. In 1897 Lady Park Wood was described as "*coppice of beech, ash, lime, hazel, and some oak thirty to thirty-five feet high; maple, service tree, aspen, willow and wych elm all represented. Good growth. Vigorous standards of oak comparatively thinly scattered of medium size. No medium aged standards.*" (Hill, 1897). On Hill's recommendation, a decision was taken in 1897 to thin towards beech high forest. After thinning in 1902 and again in the 1930s, then partial felling in 1942, the Forestry Commission set aside some of the original Lady Park coppice as a research reserve in 1944.

The present wood still clearly shows its history as coppice-with-standards. A few individuals were cut as stubs, but most appear to have been cut close to the ground. Huge lime stool clusters indicate considerable antiquity of coppicing.

Cadora and Bigsweir Woods

This is the collective name by which the Woodland Trust knows the woods between Redbrook and Bigsweir, most of which they own. The woods form a belt of woodland running continuously for 4 km along the Gloucestershire bank of the Lower Wye. They are just one of several large, linear woodlands on the steep upper slopes of the valleys around Redbrook, most of which are ancient with a long history of coppicing. Significantly, Redbrook became one of the centres of iron production in the early seventeenth century, the first furnace being built by William Hall of Highmeadow, the lessee of Lady Park Wood (Thomas, 2000).

Historically, Cadora Woods is an amalgam of many separate small woods in Newland and St Briavels parishes, each with its own name and history, one of which was named Cadora Grove: these are shown clearly on the Tithe maps for Newland (1840) and St Briavels (1842), held by Gloucester Record Office (GRO PC1812). With minor peripheral exceptions, all the woodland is ancient, though some may be ancient secondary woodland. Offa's Dyke runs close to the top edge of the southern half: it may have been constructed in open ground, and must have caused some disruption to any woodland when it was built. Small, rectilinear parcels defined by rows of stone apparently show where the fields above the wood once extended into the upper margins of the present woodland, and one parcel, Caleys Grove, contains an ancient clearance cairn. Fragments of secondary woodland also exist on the lower margins following the nineteenth century straightening of the track that once ran through the upper edges of the Wye floodplain meadows

Detailed records of management have survived from the eighteenth century, notably the Bond family woodland management records of 1709-1738 (GRO D2026 A2-3). These show that the various named coppices were cut on a nine to fourteen (but mostly ten to twelve) year rotation, that appears to have been co-ordinated with cutting in the nearby Highbury and other woods to produce a continuous supply of wood. Much of this wood was converted to charcoal on site - charcoal hearths remain a conspicuous feature today – and used in the Redbrook and other local furnaces. Coppices were cut as a whole and usually protected from browsing by a hedge and/or a bank, remnants of which can also be seen, though in 1720 the Little Ruffett below Church Wood 'was not before inclosed by which reason there was no hoops and the other wood [was] much spoilt and damaged'. Costs were incurred for cutting, marking, hedging, rinding and carriage to both Redbrook and Bristol. Income was received from the sale of hoops (including 'rind hoops' and 'smart hoops'), cordwood, backwood, great and small faggots, bast (often 'without the wood'), white rods, bark and stub wood. The last refers to stub trees, which were mentioned in several descriptions of individual coppices. Thus, in 1720 there was a memo 'to cut the stubs next cutting' of Church Wood. In Hembridge Wood, also in 1720, 'the former cutting ... [unreadable] ... which way occasionally by the damage by the copsework and the height of the stubs by former ill cutting'. David's Grove in 1722 made more profit than at previous cuttings partly because 'the stub woods which I suppose were about £20, and partly [due to] the better management of the part of the upper [wood, which] was not cut the former cutting'.

Today, much of Cadora Woods is maturing conifer plantation, and this has eliminated much of the semi-natural coppice woodland. Fortunately, a line of deep millstone quarries along the upper ground acted as a restraint on planting, and the planters themselves spared marginal woodland and scattered trees within. From these patchy and attenuated remnants, it is clear that the coppice was dominated by small-leaved lime, but also included hazel, ash, wych elm, beech, both oak species, field maple, alder, holly, *etc*. Coppicing was carried out in an extremely irregular manner. Stools were cut at any height from the soil surface to 3m, thereby generating an array of coppice stools, stubs, stub-pollards and true pollards. The majority of those that survive are small-leaved limes, but all species were treated in this manner. Most of the stubs and pollards are associated with stony ground, but the association is not absolute, and no obvious explanation for the long-established and enduring practice of variable cutting height has ever been produced. In addition, Cadora Woods contains some monumentally large lime pollards, all of which are definitely or probably associated with internal boundaries.

Figure 1 shows the distribution of 'notable trees' marked for the Woodland Trust, i.e., the still-living stubs, pollards and large stools. The original density of these forms is indicated at the northern end, where Causeway Grove has remained unaffected by plantation forestry. The southern end, where Bigsweir Wood was converted from coppice to oak high forest in the 1870s, is mixed deciduous high forest dominated by maiden oak, but it still shows clear traces of a coppice history, albeit with few remaining high-cut coppice, stubs and small pollards. In the main Cadora Woods in between, the living stubs and pollards have been much reduced by shade from the conifers, but lines associated with old boundaries are still detectable, and throughout the wood dead and dying limes and other species show that stubs, large coppice and small pollards were abundant within the management units, as well as on the margins.

Hudnalls

This was - and still is in part - a large wooded common in the parishes of St Briavels and Hewelsfield. Its history can be divided into three periods:
(i) before about 1780 it was a large, undivided wooded common of about 1,250 acres (506 ha), forming an outlying part of the Forest of Dean;
(ii) a transition period from about 1780 to 1810 during which it was colonised by squatters, and
(iii) a modern period mostly as a landscape of minute fields and scattered houses, with

Figure 1. Map of Cadora Woods with notable trees superimposed.

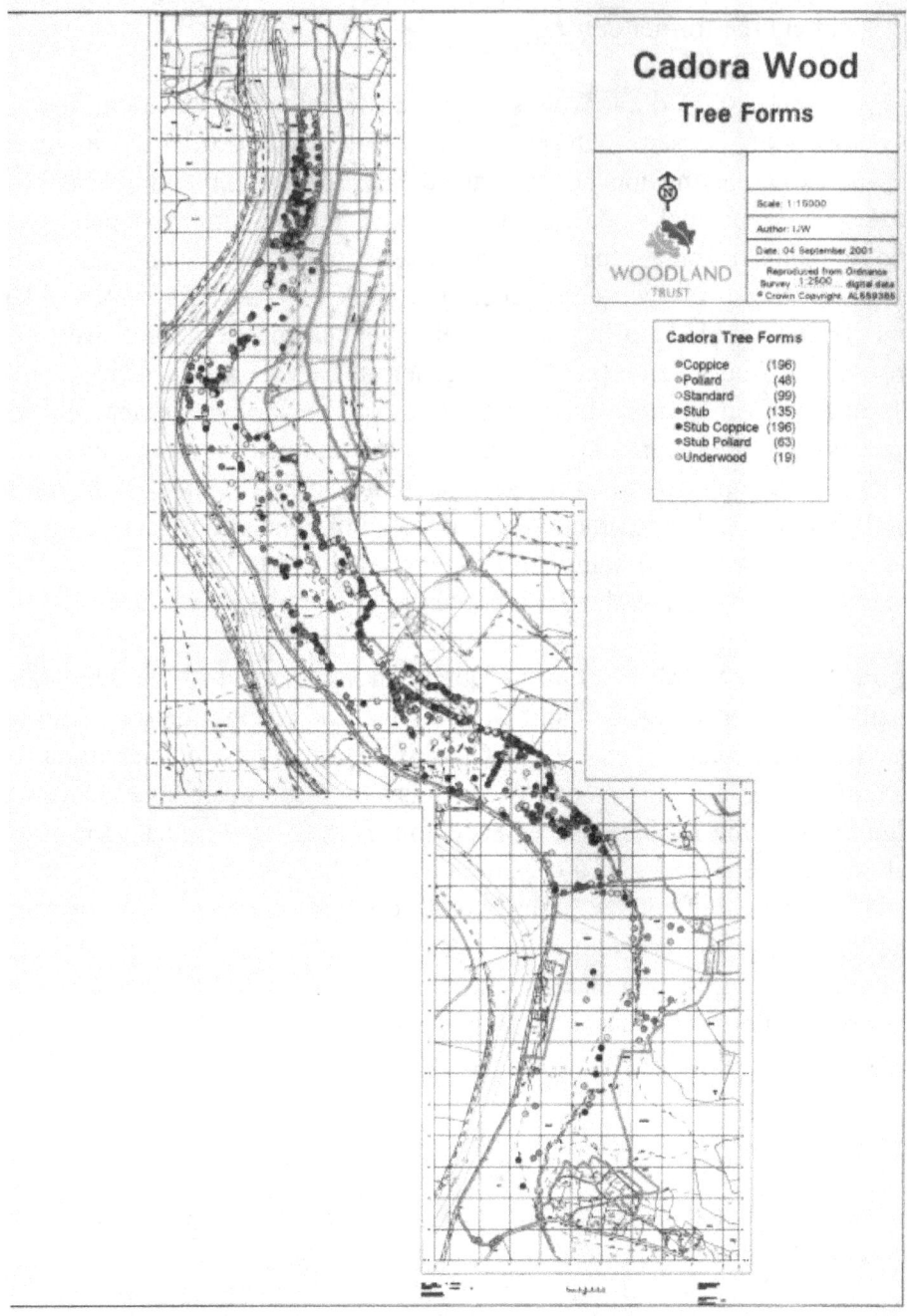

The distribution of 'notable trees' in Cadora Woods in 2001. The maps shows the location of large and old trees that were tagged as an aid to management by the Woodland Trust. With only a few exceptions, these included most of the living pollards, stubs and large coppice stools, as well as the largest standard trees. In addition (not show) numerous dead coppice stools were present beneath the conifer plantations in the core of the wood. Reproduced from a map prepared by the Woodland Trust.

woodland and common rights remaining on parts of the steep slopes overlooking the Wye.

The history of the local landscape has been documented by the Victoria County History (Herbert, 1996) and Austyn Williams (2003), a lifelong resident. Domesday Book records extensive woodland in the general area in 1086, and there was a forge at Harthill in 1141, but the earliest mention of the 'Hodenhales' itself (1282) records that: 'The Hudnalls wood is a desmesne wood of the Lord King and is cut down by the men of Saint Briavels, who claim the liberty of taking from there at will and have always taken from there in this way', i.e. it had then long been a common. Harthill Wood, a peripheral portion of the common, had a woodward in the late thirteenth century and was mentioned in a perambulation of 1300, but by the seventeenth century it had evidently lost its woodland and was known as 'Harthill Common'. Sixteenth century records of cattle and sheep in the Hudnalls and of hedged fields along the Mere Brook – the parish boundary within the Hudnalls – confirm continuing common pasturage and early assarting. In 1608 a detailed map confirms it as a wooded common with some open areas on the higher ground, totally lacking any enclosures, but crossed by one lane. The woodland is shown as a low-density scatter of large trees, quite distinct from nearby private woods, which suggests it was an open wood-pasture. Surveys from 1638 and 1641 describe it as rough, woody ground containing about 700 acres of underwood and approaching 500 acres of open ground. A further survey of 1662 again describes it as a coppice of underwood, and Isaac Taylor's map of 1777 shows that much of the St Briavels portion was still wooded. Perhaps the best description of the traditional state comes from Heath's Wye Tour Guide (Heath, 1806). *"The wood, from being open to a number of families, does not arrive at any growth to render it of any much value. The poor who cut it, and to whom the right belongs, make it up into small faggots, and send them by water to Bristol, where it is purchased by the bakers ...."*. Describing the parts visible from the Welsh shore: *"... the oak pollards were as numerous as the beech* [on the Welsh side of the Wye] *but from the high price which has of late years been given for bark, they have been so destroyed, as not to leave a twig behind from which a pound of bark was to be obtained."*

Encroachments are recorded from the sixteenth century onwards, but they were evidently repelled until about 1780, when squatting was widespread. The earliest Ordnance Survey MS maps (MS of 1813, held by the British Library) show that woodland had been cleared back almost to its present boundaries, and the existing network of lanes on the common was virtually complete. Comparison with the first published one inch sheets (1831), which evidently included some survey revisions, show that the woodland boundary was pared back at the top edge after 1813. In 1813, Messrs. Driver recorded that Hudnalls land 'is in general of good quality, but so much encumbered with bushes and large stones that it would be very difficult to plant it and much more to protect it from depredations, otherwise it would produce good oak timber as the shoots from the stools now growing there are extremely vigorous'. The area was still covered in stones in 1825, but these were cleared by making a dense network of drystone walls and stone cairns, as described in William Creswick's (1996) memoirs. The speed of colonisation was such that many old trees were not cleared, but incorporated within the walls and hedges.

Since the early nineteenth century, the cleared land has been used as pasture, meadow, orchards and for cultivation, and the remaining woodland continued to be cut irregularly under the remaining common rights. The number of houses has increased: between 1921 and 2002 sixty-nine acres (twenty-eight hectares) changed from field to houses and gardens. Latterly, some fields reverted to woodland, leaving a complex mosaic of ancient and recent woodland (Figure 2). The ancient woods are still notable for the dense scatter of conglomerate rocks, as described in 1825, which once supported an industry manufacturing millstones. Currently, the average field size remains at 1.1 acres, and most fields still have semi-natural grassland used as pasture and meadow, surrounded by walls and/or hedges, both with mature trees. Common right usage was clearly in decline by 1885, but cattle were still being taken into the woods about 1940, where they were restrained from browsing stool regrowth by a cowherd. Historically, the district has much in common with New England, both in the sequence of events and its timing. Parts of the modern landscape, with broken walls and remains of small stone houses running through a mosaic of ancient and recent woodland, are pure Massachusetts.

Surviving boundary trees and woodland show that this was a wood-pasture composed equally of lopped beech, small-leaved lime, sessile oak and pedunculate oak, itself an unusual combination. Parts have an intimate mosaic of tiny meadow, scrub and ancient stubs and pollards, in which there is a strong association between lime trees and stones as both walls and cairns, a combination that is similar to Scandinavian wood-meadows. Much of the woodland is old-growth, with many ancient beeches, limes and oaks, but patches where common fuel rights were last exercised still have a coppice structure.

Diversity of traditional management

None of three woods described is unique within the Lower Wye Valley. There were, for example, six other wooded commons in the parishes of St Briavels and Hewelsfield, all with similar structures, though only the Hudnalls contains areas of informal wood-meadow. Taken together, they illustrate the historical diversity within ecologically similar woods of a small district. They also illustrate diversity between districts: comparisons

Figure 2   **Map of Coed Ithel-weir showing ancient and recent woodland.**

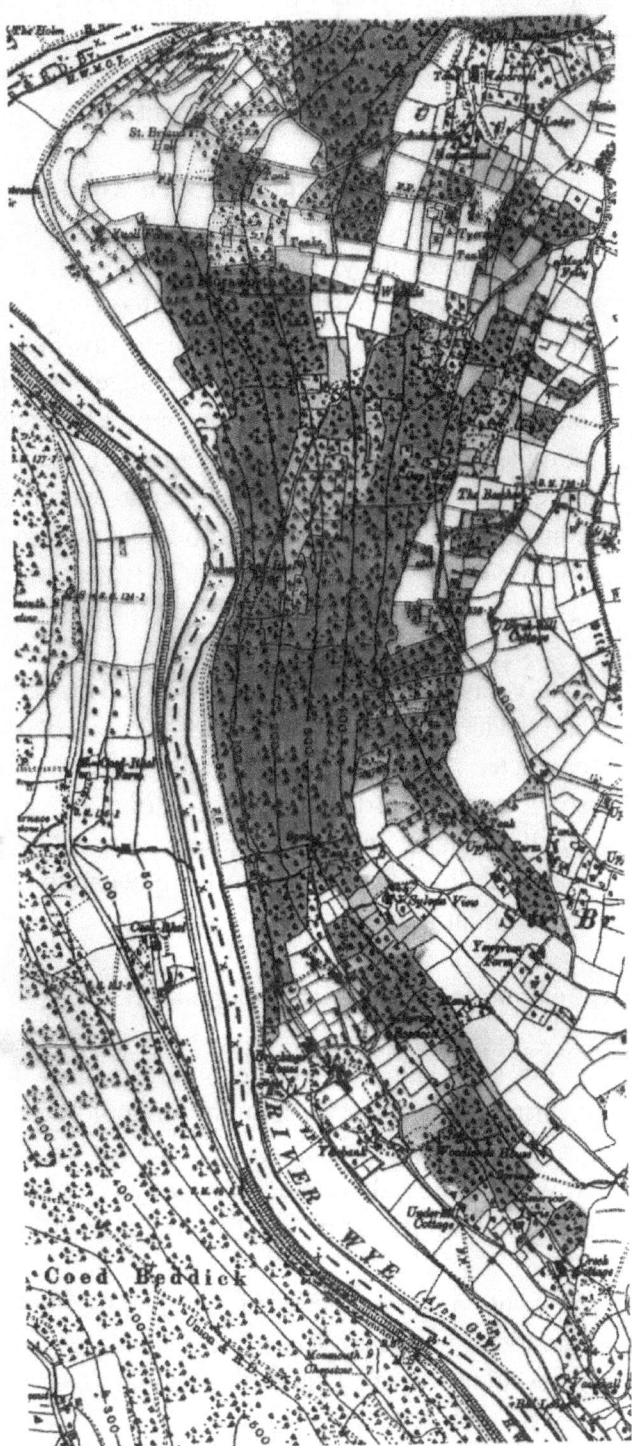

The distribution of ancient (blue/ dark) and recent (orange/ pale) woodland in the western part of the Hudnalls. The main block of ancient woodland is still subject to common rights. The late nineteenth century Ordnance Survey map used as a base shows the pattern of early nineteenth century enclosure and settlement.

with the coppices of eastern England (Rackham, 1980) suggest that rotations were closer to those of Cadora Woods than Hadnock Woods, but without the same variation in coppicing height.

Two features of traditional management impress:

- **The uncertain distinction between wood-pasture and coppice in space and time**. Lady Park Wood may have changed from parkland to coppice before the seventeenth century. The Hudnalls contained both coppice and wood-pasture with no obvious barriers between the two, and the remaining woodland still shows this mixture. Elsewhere, Chepstow Park Wood appears to have changed from park to coppice. The Dowards were wooded commons, but Lords Wood on the Great Doward became a coppice and parts of the Little Doward became both beech high forest and a deer park in the mid-nineteenth century. The huge Wyeswood Common was described as woodland in 1581, and appears to have contained both coppice and wood-pasture in earlier centuries, but when it was enclosed in 1810 it was heathland, except on the slopes overlooking the Wye (Bradney, 1913).

- **The variety of coppice treatments.** The contrast between Lady Park Wood and Cadora Woods illustrates this. Long-rotation coppice seems to have been characteristic of the Crown Woods and large estates. Short-rotation coppice with stubs, mini-pollards and high-cut stools appears to have been widespread in the smaller woods. In addition, there were many alder woods along streamsides and flush lines that appear to have been cut as simple coppice, probably with intermittent grazing.

Historical elements in current management.

Can we use our knowledge of historic management to inform modern management? We can give priority to ancient woods, but how should these woods be managed?

First, we have already come a long way from traditional management, which has been transformed with Inclosure and twentieth century modernisation:

- Inclosure of most wooded commons generated a landscape of small fields with numerous boundary trees that eventually became a bastion of semi-natural grassland survival. This small-field landscape is widespread in the Wye Valley and Dean fringes. Retention of boundary pollards in hedges, including numerous limes (mostly *Tilia cordata*), is characteristic of field boundaries close to ancient woods.

- Conversion of coppice to high forest of beech or oak, as in Bigsweir and Lady Park Woods, was a policy in Crown woods of Dean and Tintern from the 1890s and early twentieth century (Schlich, 1915), and the large estates, of which the Bigsweir Estate is the main one within the valley itself.

- Continued coppicing, then neglect, leading to development of a form of high forest. Most woods seem to have been coppiced until the early century, so we now have a widespread 80-100 year age class. The main exception is the Fiddlers Elbow woodlands, which were coppiced for pulpwood in about 1970 and again recently.

- Conversion of outcrown coppice to conifer high forest by felling and planting. This was the fate of much of Cadora Woods and parts of several other woods. Today, this conversion is being reversed by the Woodland Trust and the Forestry Commission.

- Emparking for deer, as on the Little Doward, was unusual, but in the last 50 years ever more woods have become *de facto* deer parks as fallow deer populations increase.

In addition, stand composition appears to be changing:

- Armitage (1914) remarked that ash was uncommon in the Wye Valley woods, and indeed it is localised as old coppice. Today, it is widespread as maiden trees, even in stands that did not include it as coppice. It is difficult to think of reasons why it should have been deliberately excluded from traditional coppice, and the factors behind its current surge may have a natural element.

- With the introduction of continuous cover forms of management, foresters are having to select species for retention. This is not entirely an innovation, for traditional managers selected for oak as timber, and early twentieth century foresters selected for beech in conversion to high forest, but the degree and perhaps diversity of selection has increased latterly. Selections are made against a background of advice that is given on a national basis: this external opinion is probably more influential now than outside influences were on traditional managers.

- The surge in populations of fallow deer and grey squirrels is forcing selectivity on managers. Deer have browsing preferences that control the composition of regeneration: in Lady Park Wood in the 1950s, the order of preference was oak > ash > beech > birch, with dogwood by far the most sought-after subsidiary species (Peterken and Jones, 1989). Grey squirrels damage beech, sycamore and to a lesser extent oak, which leaves ash and lime as the less vulnerable species.

Changing circumstances inevitably limit the practicability of restoring traditional treatments. In addition to the deer, which eat coppice regrowth, conifer reforestation and conversion to high forest eventually results in deterioration of historic features, as Cadora Woods demonstrates. Public sentiment is against clear-cuts, even though this was the traditional pattern of coppicing, and averse to deer culling, even though the woods fail to regenerate. Commoners have generally aged and gone up-market, so there is little prospect of remaining common woods being treated traditionally. Those that are still grazed are full of sheep, and lopping ceased eighty years ago.

Against this background, the scope for including historical elements in future management is limited. Past processes, such as coppicing, lopping and wood-pasturage, can be restored on a limited scale, but only with modifications (e.g. deer fences) and subsidy (e.g. ownership by Woodland Trust). We can preserve the physical features for a long time, but unmanaged pollards and old stools deteriorate within decades, and even wood banks and charcoal pits become obscured. We can preserve records of past management, and thus the memory of past management. There is value in restoring a few woods to facsimiles of traditional management, particularly for research and demonstration.

More productively, perhaps, we can use historical information to identify the habitat conditions that allowed wild species to thrive, and use this in designing conservation management. This would emphasise the need for sustained and locally substantial silvicultural interventions. We can evaluate ecological isolation and habitat continuity as factors in species distributions, and from this derive guidance on the design and implementation of forest habitat networks. This will demonstrate the importance of ancient woods and the need to build out from existing woodland. We can use historical data to identify tree populations that have not been altered by planting, which should be important in research on the genetics of native trees and the value of local genotypes. This would probably demonstrate the importance of common woods and underwood species in coppices. In short, we cannot revive historical forms of management on the original scale, but we can translate our knowledge of historical diversity into strategies and plans that help us to restore and sustain native woodland, and develop new forms of diversity.

Acknowledgements

Eustace Jones and Ian Standing helped to bring together the historical information on Lady Park Wood. At Cadora Woods, the historical account was built on work originally undertaken by David Thomas, and the tree survey was undertaken for the Woodland Trust. My neighbours in the Hudnalls helped in several ways, and some aspects of survey were assisted financially by the Countryside Agency.

References

Armitage, E. (1914) Vegetation of the Wye Gorge at Symonds Yat. *Journal of Ecology*, **2**, 98-109.

Bradney, J.A. (1913) *A history of Monmouthshire. II(2), The Hundred of Trellech.* Mitchell Hughes and Clarke, London. (Reprinted by Academy Books Ltd, london, 1992).

Creswick, W.G. (1996) *Where I was bred. The thoughts and reminiscences of William G. Creswick J.P.* Forest of Dean Newspapers, Coleford [written in the 1970s].

Hart, C.E. (1966) *Royal Forest. A history of Dean's Wood as producers of timber.* Clarendon Press, Oxford.

Heath, C. (1806) *Historical and descriptive accounts of the ancient and present state of Tintern Abbey .... and its neighbourhood.* Heath, Monmouth.

Herbert, N.M. (ed) (1996) *A history of the county of Gloucester, V. Bledisloe Hundred, St Briavels Hundred, The Forest of Dean.* Victoria County History. Oxford University Press, Oxford.

Hill, H.C. (1897) *Report on the Forest of Dean, with suggestions for its Management.* H.M.S.O., London.

Peterken, G.F. (1969) Development of vegetation in Staverton Park, Suffolk. *Field Studies*, **3**, 1-39.

Peterken, G.F. and Jones, E.W. (1987) Forty years of change in Lady Park Wood: the old-growth stands. *Journal of Ecology*, **75**, 477-512.

Peterken, G.F. and Jones, E.W. (1989) Forty years of change in Lady Park Wood: the young-growth stands. *Journal of Ecology*, **77**, 401-429.

Rackham, O. (1975) *Hayley Wood. Its history and ecology*. Cambridge and Isle of Ely Naturalists' Trust, Cambridge.

Rackham, O. (1980) *Ancient woodland*. Arnold, London.

Schlich, W. (1915) The Tintern Crown forests. *Quarterly Journal of Forestry*, **9**, 194-204.

Steven, H.M. and Carlisle, A. (1959) *The native pinewoods of Scotland*. Oliver and Boyd, Edinburgh and London.

Thomas, D. (2000) *Historical and archaeological report on Cadora Woods*. Unpublished report to Woodland Trust.

Tubbs, C.R. (1968) *The New Forest: an ecological history*. David and Charles, Newton Abbot.

Williams, A.J.P. (2002). *The history of the Hudnalls at St Briavels*, Gloucestershire. Privately published.

The Age of Wood
Francis T Evans
University of Sheffield

Despite the massive growth in the use of metals and then plastics since the Industrial Revolution, wood remains the commonest material. More than one and a half billion cubic metres of wood are produced annually, and an even greater amount is used as fuel. It has itself become an industrialised material, processed and manufactured into standardised forms to fit in with modern manufacturing and construction methods. Roof trusses are delivered ready made; the stores sell cheap kits to assemble at home, sometimes of pine but more often chipboard or some other reconstituted wood like MDF. Without touching on the aesthetics or economics of the business, it is clear that modern technology does not use wood in the same way that eighteenth- and nineteenth-century craftsmen did. It has been a broad change, involving a long spectrum of technical and social adjustments. In the process, a lot of knowledge has been lost, and this may be a good moment to remind ourselves of what it meant to employ a technology largely based on the use of wood. That earlier technology depended on wood, wind and water and it will require an act of imagination to try and understand how ingenious engineers and craftsmen were to achieve such mastery over the constraints imposed by the material they had to use. It may also help our understanding of woodlands if we have some grasp of the uses to which various kinds of timber were put.

Standard histories often refer to the growing shortage of timber from the seventeenth century onwards. In fact Britain has been an importer of wood since at least the middle ages and estrich boards (East Reich) and wainscotting came in greater quantity from the Baltic, as did naval supplies even during the Napoleonic Wars. It was said that Norwegian timber merchants warmed themselves comfortably by the Great Fire of London in 1666. Progressively, the Americas and then Asia, Australia and Africa supplied high quality timbers. By contrast, home grown supplies were neglected and over a long period reports appeared complaining at the unwillingness of English craftsmen to use the native product because it was not so well finished, not so convenient – even that English wood was too hard to work. The frustration caused by poor timber is expressed by the man in charge of vertical frame saws in a big railway waggon building works: " 'We like forest grown oak the best,' said the foreman, 'Hedgegrown is scrubby and full of rubbish – knots and stones, and nails sometimes two feet inside the wood. But they don't punish us as bad as they do the circulars.'"

It needed two World Wars to force this country to make more efficient and rational use of home grown timber. But this was a far cry from the great oak trees round Sheffield in the seventeenth century that John Evelyn described in his book on woodlands:

> *'For now Rivelin itself is totally destitute of that issue she once might have gloried in of Oaks.'*

The figures for production and consumption, however, can do little to deepen our understanding of how craftsmen designed and built in wood. As touching their uses, a thousand tons of balsa wood, of pine or of oak are totally different materials. Every job required a particular kind of timber, with only a limited range of possible alternatives. This was not hidebound traditionalism – it was a precondition of durability and effective working. Consider a simple cartwheel. The stock – the barrel shaped centre of the wheel - had to be elm and this is a very hard tough wood. It also has a very twisted grain, so it does not split willingly: this meant that the wheelwright could hammer the spokes into a tight fit in their holes without sundering the stock. The spokes, on the other hand, were made of oak because that is the hardwood which <u>can</u> split. A firm tap on a wedge will split the oak easily along the grain. Again, the grain is important because if the spoke is sawn instead of split, then the saw cut as like as not will run across the grain and weaken it. We have to remember that most woods are only strong along the grain and have only a very small fraction of the strength across it. Lastly, we come to the wheel rim, the felloe, which was usually made of ash. Ash is a very tough wood, and singularly resistant to shock. We can imagine the battering a cartwheel took as it supported a weight of a ton or so along a rough stony country road. Finally, there was the iron tyre, a continuous band of wrought iron forge- welded at the joint. Naturally the iron resisted wear better than the ash felloes, and it was cheaper to replace a tyre than to rebuild the wheel. But it had another function. The tyre was carefully made to an overtight fit, so it could only be put on the wheel after it had been heated red hot and expanded. It was cooled in water, and as it contracted it exerted a powerful squeezing force, tending to compress the wheel.

If we now look at the complete wheel, it is not flat – it is distinctly conical. Mounted on its axle, the cone points inward, toward the body of the waggon. In effect it is like an arch, for the thumping of the heavy waggon body against the wheel tends to tighten it. A flat wheel would simply become looser till it fell apart – it is a compression structure, and compression structures are tight like masonry arches. The distinction becomes clearer if we compare with a bicycle wheel whose thin steel spokes are in tension: in a cartwheel, the weight is carried down through the bottom spoke to the road; in the bicycle, your weight is hanging by the top spokes from the wheel rim. It is lighter than the compression wheel, but in the heyday of farm waggons, oak spokes were a very good solution to the problem.

Oak, elm and ash were the traditional English engineering hardwoods and their individual properties guided the craftsmen. Windsor chairs have elm seats because they withstand the hammering in of the pegs. The keels of the Royal Navy's sailing ships

Figure 1. Wooden framing of an eighteenth century ship.

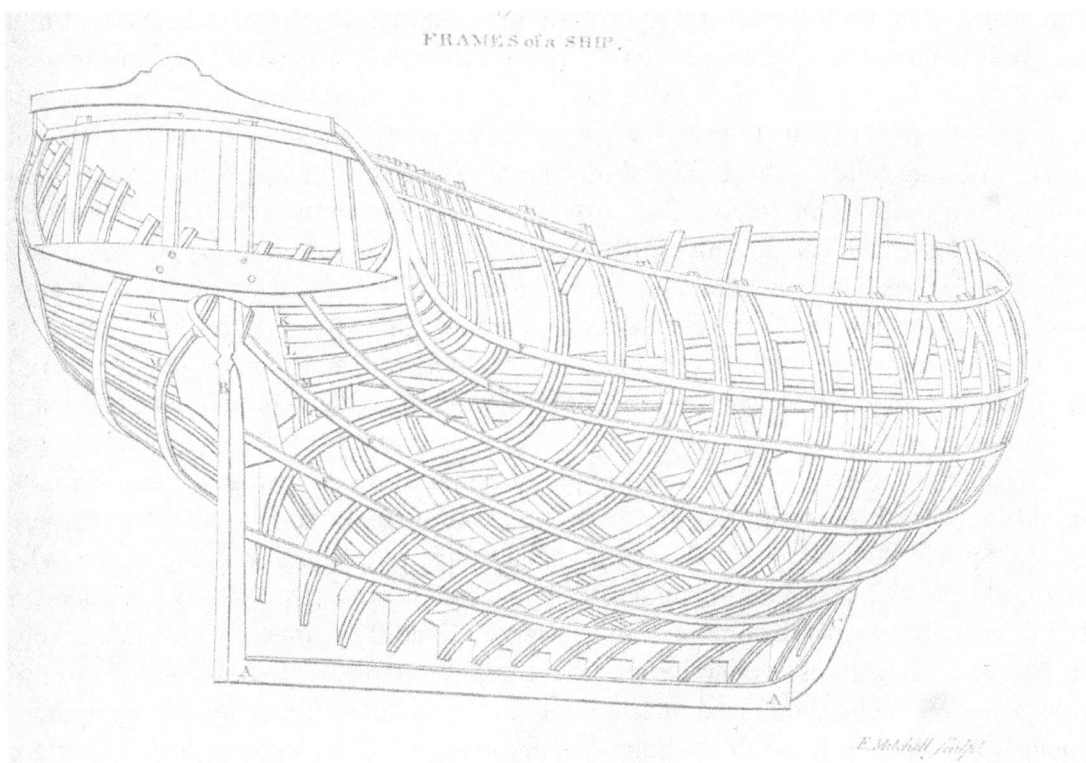

were elm too because it did not rot under water and, again, did not split when long bolts were driven into it to fix the frames and other timbers. Elm's curly grain and toughness resisted abrasion if the vessel scraped over submerged rocks. Oak was the predominant structural material because of its strength in building large frameworks, whether on land, for the roofs and ceilings of great churches and timber framed buildings, or at sea. Its splittability was a huge advantage. The ceiling beams of genuine old pubs often show that they were split and roughly shaped with an adze. It is hard to imagine the labour that was demanded in sawing a great oak trunk longwise into planks. Stone floors were colder than wooden ones but much cheaper. Another advantage of splitting oak was that it revealed the beautiful silver grain, the medullary rays, which we find in old cupboard doors and panelling. Ash too had its special uses. It made frames for machinery and for road carriages, including early automobiles. Its shock resistance established its use in hammer and other tool handles, and in billiard cues and lances as well. There were good reasons for choosing ash to make World War I aeroplane undercarriages. On the RE8 reconnaissance plane 'The undercarriage was definitely weak. It was composed of nothing more or less than faired gaspipes. At the Artillery Observation School in Egypt those undercarriages averaged two landings each, until someone had the brainwave of making some out of ash. None were broken after this except in definite crashes.' The same lessons had been learned by prehistoric man. Archaeologists have found that in a large well scattered sample, two thirds of prehistoric spear shafts were made of ash.

Fundamental explanations of the way wood behaves depend on its natural internal structure of long cellulose fibres bound together in a matrix of lignin. Within this general pattern, the variations are legion. Balsa wood has only one tenth of the density of water and floats high; whereas a number of other timbers like greenheart, *lignum vitae* and some kinds of oak have densities exceeding one gramme per cc and simply sink in water. *Lignum vitae*, incidentally, has exceptionally compact interwoven fibres and cannot be sawn but has to be machined. It contains a natural lubricant, and is an excellent material for bearings even today for ships' propeller shafts and, in earlier times, in clocks.

Generally, the strength of wood is proportional to its density and, astonishingly, weight for weight, most timbers are as strong as mild steel, though naturally they are bulkier. Spruce, for instance, will support 18,000 lbs. per square inch in tension. The hollow fibres which give most strength to the wood buckle more easily if they are loaded in compression, but even so a compression resistance of 5,000 lbs. makes it an impressively strong material. Stiffness is another excellent quality. A piece of chalk is stiff but not strong; a dog's rubber bone is strong but not stiff. Without stiffness and strength, there would be no wooden furniture, buildings or aeroplanes – often stiffness is as important as the ultimate strength of the material.

The common English timbers have general characteristics which dictate the way they behave and how they have to be used. As everyone knows, the growth of trees takes place by the annual addition of new rings of woody fibres and this living material is saturated with water. When the tree is felled and begins to dry, the water evaporates and shrinkage begins and so do problems because the shrinkage is not isotropic. The wood shrinks very little along the grain, remaining practically the same length. Radial shrinkage is more pronounced, and it reduces the diameter of the drying wood. More serious, the biggest shrinkage occurs tangentially – best imagined as a marked shortening of the annual rings – and this sets up substantial stresses. And so the wood splits, creating the familiar V shaped fissure we see in trunks felled in the woods and left to dry out. This tangential shrinkage is the bugbear of timber merchants and carpenters. A plank sawn from the side of a log will shrink more on the outside face where the tree ring is longer, and that face will warp to become slightly concave. If the sawing does not follow the grain, which can sometimes be twisted, then the plank will develop a rotated deformation or 'winding'. These movements of wood are not just academic problems as any visitor looking at Chesterfield Church spire will see.

The worker in wood had to live with its idiosyncrasies. In a panelled door, the grain of the frame follows parallel to the four edges. The small cross sections of wood in this frame will not move much if the wood is reasonably dry. The panels are much larger, however, and they will swell and shrink much more. If they were fixed firmly in the frame, they would split – so they are left loose; and the DIY enthusiast who thinks to glue them in place will soon find himself applying Polyfilla to the fissures. The elaborate mediaeval wood joints fixed with tenons and wedges are further attempts to control a material which has a mind of its own, and comes in inconvenient sizes. Iron was used sparingly and this was not only because of the cost. Compared with iron, wood is soft and flexible. There is nothing wrong with some flexibility – a plant that bends to the wind is less likely to be broken than something brittle that takes the full force until it suddenly breaks. A wooden structure held together with nails will suffer as the nails cut into the wood as it flexes. Whereas a wooden structure assembled using joints and wooden dowels is all of the same hardness and its components can work together with less wear. Amundsen's sledges were held together with leather thongs and they flexed; Captain Scott's sledges, with metal fixings, were stiffer and rode less easily over the snow. Wooden structures creak, groan and complain but this is because they are working.

It took time and skill to choose the right piece of timber and perhaps build it up into a more complex form, and from the point of view of industrial production, the various composites like chipboard board are more stable and come in the right sizes. They are easier to use in machine manufacture. It is a characteristic of the whole of recent technology that the skill is built into the machine or the artefact, and not into the user – a hands-on equivalent of the dumbing down process alleged against the media. Modern design makes it impossible for the individual to repair a microprocessor or even an electric toaster. Whether this is good or bad in some philosophical sense is not under discussion. It is necessary only to recognise that the direct and concrete relationship that a craftsman had with his materials and the creative understanding that he needed to use them have changed utterly. Along with this change, a multitude of skills have disappeared like extinct species of plant or animals. Old tools and artefacts may survive in museum collections, but they do not convey much understanding of the living skills they served. Old tools make little sense without knowledge of the hands that guided them.

Abbeydale Hamlet in Sheffield is a remarkable survivor from this period of technical history. Built largely in the eighteenth century, it was the work of millwrights not engineers. Modern production machinery is massive and is precisely designed to work as a totally constrained geometrical system resisting any deflecting forces by the rigidity of its castings and steel guideways. For its time, Abbeydale itself was massive, with power inputs to its wooden machinery of as much as ten or fifteen horsepower. The machinery is largely made from wood. The big axles of the waterwheels, the shaft driving the hammers, the twelve feet diameter cogwheel driving that shaft, the helves of the hammers – all wood. Most of the old fastenings are wood. Where a wheel has to be centred on its wooden shaft there are wedges, and delicate fitting and adjustment was achieved by the millwright hammering in wedges until the wheels ran true or the hammers struck their blow precisely upon the anvil. Of course wedges are only a primitive form of adjusting screw – geometrically speaking, a screw is a wedge wrapped round a cylinder. The fact remains that old carpenters and millwrights could attain precision using a simple piece of wood shaped by an axe. The fundamental soundness of the millwrighting approach to machinery is proved beyond dispute, for the Abbeydale hammers worked continuously from 1785 until 1930. On the other side of the Pennines, wood was equally common in the early textile machines like Spinning Jennies and Mules.

An engineer of 1830 would have known the properties of as many as 130 different timbers. There are woods which are not flammable, like jarrah and others that do not rot, like greenheart. Many of them are tropical, but Britain herself produces some interesting timbers.

The mediaeval long bow (a Welsh invention) was made of yew, a very resilient wood. It provides a striking example of how craftsmen used wood's properties. Boxes of well preserved longbows were found in the wreck of Henry VIII's Mary Rose. These were powerful weapons, with a draw weight of up to 200 lbs. As in most timbers, the yew heartwood tends to be stronger in compression and the sapwood in tension. All these bows had the heartwood on the face nearest the bowman, i.e. in compression, and the outer curved face – in tension – was sapwood. Its range of up to 350 yards was impressive. Cricket bats need another sort of resilience, absorbing the impact of the ball elastically, and then adding this stored energy to the power of the batsman's stroke. It seems that the air in cells of the willow are compressed giving a pneumatic spring to the process.

Walnut is a wood with beautiful complex grain, much prized in good furniture. The complex grain renders the wood less likely to shatter and so it was an excellent material for making gun butts. Furthermore, walnut wood secretes a sweet oil which does not corrode iron. It was used to make boxes for mathematical instruments, as well as non-corrosive furniture for guns. Oak, by contrast, contains tannin which does react with iron; hence it is not used for gun butts, and requires brass screws if it is likely to get wet. In some other British woods, the grain is almost imperceptible. Pear wood, for instance, can be carved easily in any direction and illustrators used it to make woodcuts. Pattern makers also use pear wood for the models which are used to make sand-casting moulds, because it is so stable and amenable. Lime-wood is softer than pear-wood, but again is easy to carve in any direction, so it has long been used by sculptors – Grinling Gibbons did his great works using lime. Birch's lack of grain allows the wood to be peeled into large thin sheets. These sheets make good quality plywood and also, being flexible, apothecaries' pill boxes and other containers for fish and cheese like Camembert. Sycamore is another wood without much grain. It makes excellent chopping boards because it is a sweet wood and does not splinter easily.

Beech is a hard attractive wood, much used in furniture but not building. It is a sweet wood and very attractive to beetles and woodworm. The hornbeam closely resembles the beech, but its wood is quite different, being exceptionally tough and fibrous. Millwrights preferred it when making the wooden cogs for gear wheels. If a piece of hornbeam is placed in a vice and hit with a hammer, it takes a very strong blow to break it.

Wood fuel

As a fuel, wood burns cleanly and leaves little ash. Its modern use is mostly in domestic heating, but in earlier times it was more carefully chosen for specific tasks. Beech, for instance, is chemically very pure and glass blowers used it when welding handles because there was no chemical reaction with the lead in the glass. (Sulphur in the fuel turned the glass black.) In iron making, whether in the bloomery making wrought iron, or the blast furnace producing cast iron, wood charcoal was the universal fuel. It is worth recalling that the charcoal not only produced heat, but also played an essential part in the chemical reactions resulting in iron separating from the ore. The carbon constituting charcoal had a strong chemical affinity for the oxygen locked up in the iron oxide of the ore. Burning charcoal produced highly reactive carbon monoxide gas which took the ore's oxygen away, leaving the metal free. Sheffield steel-makers preferred Swedish or Russian iron to convert into steel, probably because those countries still used charcoal whereas English iron picked up harmful phosphorous and sulphur from the coke used in smelting. The chemical process using charcoal was essentially the same in all early metal smelting, whether lead, copper or other metals were being produced. The demand for wood for iron-making was enormous. In 1824, the ironmaster David Mushet worked out that it needed 2,400 acres of woodland to maintain one blast furnace. Charcoal and the less familiar whitecoal for lead smelting were produced in Ecclesall Woods and many other sites in South Yorkshire. It may be worth mentioning that there is a high proportion of sweet chestnut trees in the Ecclesall woods and that, according to Mushet's experiments, chestnut gives a higher proportion of charcoal - 23.3 % by weight – than any other common English wood.

Charcoal was also one of the three essential ingredients of gunpowder. Willow and alder, two trees which flourish near water, were considered the best for powder making, perhaps because the saltpetre and sulphur entered into the microscopic pores more effectively as the powder was incorporated in the mill. One of the biggest powder producers was Faversham (originally Feversham) in Kentish marshy land.

Classics

In the course of human history there is a constant process of replacement, as one technology becomes obsolete and another takes its place. Many factors play a part. The new technology may be cheaper, or more powerful or more satisfying. In the recent past, we have seen electronic calculators replace wooden slide rules. There is no way back for the seventy-eight gramophone record, given the quality of music on CD; no way back for gas lighting where electric light is an alternative; no way a vintage Bentley could outperform a Ferrari. Yet despite the objective superiority in terms of cost or convenience or performance of a new over an old technology, there remains some quality in the best of the old which evokes respect. The old Bentley or Bugatti retains the quality of excellence, from its own time and milieu, which marks it as a classic. It is not a question of luxury: the VW Beetle, the Citroen traction avant, the Mini all have that spark of genius that marks the classic. Can one discern such classics from the age of wooden technology?

Leaving aside the expensive antique trade, there is the plain Windsor chair which seems to go on down the generations as one of the perfected artefacts in wood. A bodger in a forest with a simple treadle lathe could make one. A windmill – the whole elegant structure built of wooden parts, held together by wooden dowels.

One of Nelson's seventy-fours could stay at sea for many months in virtually any weather and withstand the recoil of firing its heavy guns. J.M.W Turner's painting captures the angst Englishmen felt as the black smoking steam tug towed the fighting Temeraire to its last berth. These great fighting ships were not scientifically designed, but three centuries of experiment and evolution had resulted in a vessel that combined all the virtues that could be demanded of it. The Victorian navy was still building wooden battleships in 1858. It was not shortages of timber that led to their demise but technical advances in gunnery. Even in great battles like Trafalgar, ships were rarely sunk by solid iron cannonballs. A ship was beaten when it had lost its power of manoeuvre by damage to masts and rigging, and the crew – after terrible casualties – could no longer serve the guns. A French artillerist, Colonel Paixhans, invented an exploding shell against which wooden ships were defenceless. Whereas the old solid shot had holed the hull, the new exploding projectiles shattered it. Iron framed and iron armoured ships were the only answer to the new weapons. HMS Warrior, still to be seen at Portsmouth, was the first in this new iron navy.

Clippers

Iron ships possessed other advantages. The vibration of steam engines was more damaging to wooden hulls. Surprisingly perhaps, the hull of iron ships formed a smaller proportion of their loaded weight because wooden ships had to be over-designed, owing to the duplication of timbers caused by joints. Even so, the old sailing ships could put up remarkable performances. The clipper *Melbourne* in 1876 sailed more than 300 miles on each of seventeen consecutive days, and *Cutty Sark* once ran 2,164 miles in six days. At sixteen and a half knots the *Cutty Sark* was developing 2,250 effective horsepower from the wind on its sails. A crew of twenty was enough to man the ship. It may be interesting to point out one of the great advantages which the wooden sailing ship had over the Mediterranean galley. It was generally reckoned that five men were needed to do the work of one horse. By this measure, a galley would have needed 11,000 men to match the Cutty Sark, and would have needed great stores to feed them. From this fact, galleys could never voyage far from land; while sailing ships could roam the great oceans.

Structures

The English language is not fussy about the use of the word carpenter. He is a man who works in wood. The French are more precise, because they associate *charpentier* with another word, *charpente*, meaning framework. Their carpenter is the man who builds the wooden framework of roofs, the tapering skeletons of church spires. In a similar way, the unfussy English accept the statement of writers like Nikolaus Pevsner that the Crystal Palace was a great triumph of glass and iron – 'the outstanding example of mid nineteenth century architecture was rather its enormous size ... the absence of any other materials, and an ingenious system of prefabrication for the iron and glass parts.' But in fact the biggest spans of the Crystal Palace were arched over in wood – seventy-two feet laminated arches of Memel fir. The 205 miles of wooden sash bar and thirty-four miles of wooden guttering were also essential to the 'glass and iron' palace's structural integrity. In 1850, the modern material, the fashion one might say, was iron – so wood was ignored. Isambard Kingdom Brunel had more sense than to follow fashion. Railway bridge collapses like the bridge over the River Dee near Chester convinced him that cast iron was a treacherous material. It was well enough in pure compression, but twisting and tension forces, especially if there were flaws in a casting, meant that it could go with a bang – it was brittle. Brunel said. *'Cast iron bridges are always giving trouble ... I never use cast iron myself if I can help it but in some cases it is necessary, and to meet these I*

Figure 2. Erecting the 72 feet wooden spans of the Crystal Palace.

have had girders cast of a particular mixture of iron. The number I have is few because as I have before said, I dislike them.' Many of Brunel's railway viaducts were timber - thirty-four of them between Truro and Plymouth alone. Even his great Saltash railway bridge was designed originally as a 250 ft wooden span flanked by six 100 ft spans also in wood.. Wood and wrought iron are more forgiving materials than cast iron. Brunel's wooden railway viaducts were neat economical structures, designed so that individual timbers could be replaced if need be. Some of them lasted into the 1930s. There were many other timber railway bridges elsewhere in Britain, economical and durable, with spans of up to 150 feet. Wooden bridges rarely exceeded this span, and when Brunel needed to exceed 400 feet at Saltash, he did turn to wrought iron as did Robert Stephenson for the Britannia Bridge at the Menai Straits between Wales and Anglesey. Great wooden bridges were erected elsewhere in the world, like the Grubermann brothers' 193 foot span at Schaffhausen or the British military engineers' 205 feet span across the Mahaweliganga completed in 1833.

Aircraft

Wooden aircraft are an ideal example to illustrate the transition from a craft to a scientific technology. All the successful and unsuccessful aircraft pioneers before the First World War used wood to build their machines. It was a cheap material, easily available, light, stiff and strong. It was furthermore the best material for a craftsman who was building one-off experiments. Apart from its engine, the Wright Flier could be built using just simple hand tools and – equally important – it was quick and easy to repair. It was literally a rather large powered kite. Like other kites, it derived its lift from air passing slowly over a large wing surface – in other words it had a low wing loading. During the Great War, nearly all aeroplanes were still built from wood - some 55,000 in Great Britain alone. It was not that aluminium and welded steel tube space frames had not been tested. 'Timber has held its own up to the end of the war as the best material for spars, struts, longerons and many other parts of aeroplanes, owing to its remarkable strength and lightness.'

We have to remember the general technical environment in which these aircraft were built. The engines were not powerful, reaching 200 h.p. towards the end of the war period. Therefore, the aircraft rarely exceeded speeds of 120 mph even at the end of the War; at the beginning , sixty mph was more typical. At these speeds air resistance was a secondary consideration. This affected the rest of the design. The strongest wing construction available was the biplane which resembled a bridge truss, deep and cross braced with struts between the wings and various steel wires helping to keep it rigid. At these speeds, too, the weight and complexity of a retractable undercarriage was not justifiable, so the wheels and axles stuck out at the bottom adding their considerable area to the air resistance. It is a fair generalisation that no biplanes flies at more than 250 mph. And as we have seen, low speeds mean low wing loading and therefore low stresses on the structure. So far, so good, for wood.

As engines became more powerful in the 1920s, aeroplanes flew faster, so they did not need such big wings – though there was greater loading on those wings. Greater speeds also mean sharply increasing air resistance. The biplane wing with its struts and wires, and the fixed undercarriage, became an unacceptable liability. The new generation of aircraft were metal monoplanes with retractable landing wheels. The Gladiator biplane which flew at 250 mph was replaced by the metal Spitfire monoplane, capable of 350 mph. In the same wave came the Douglas Dakota, the Messerschmitt 109 fighter, the Junkers fifty-two transports ….. obviously, it seemed, wood was finished.

Yet one of the most effective aircraft in the Second World War was the de Havilland Mosquito, built of wood. It was, however, designed by scientific technology using wood as virtually a new material. The early wood glues based on bone and gelatin softened and broke down easily. The Mosquito's structure was ply wood using new resins, and the sandwiching of balsa wood and birch veneer resulted in what was virtually a designer material. The Mosquito was small but its two Rolls Royce Merlins made it as fast as the contemporary German fighters, yet its bomb load was comparable with that of the four engined Flying Fortress. The new plywoods played further significant roles in the Bailey Bridges (designed by a Sheffield graduate), troop carrying gliders like the Horsa, and in high speed launches. During the war, Britain's annual production of aircraft grade plywood rose to some two square miles.

Figure 3. Mosquito High Speed Bomber.

A de Havilland Mosquito high-speed bomber.

The progress from craft material to advanced engineering material was not a simple jump, but a series of events which were unpredictable – as things are where the creative engineering mind is at work. Wood lost its place with mechanical engineers in the early nineteenth century because cast iron and wrought iron seemed more compatible with precision machinery. It is a fundamental fact about wood that it is a product of evolution. Wood makes good beams but it is not a good material for shafts transmitting high powers because nature does not know torsion, whether in bones or wood. In specific conditions, wood is never likely to perform as well as advanced steels, or nylon or Kevlar. Still, the Fat Lady has not yet delivered her aria. As Richard Dawkins says, evolution is blind; but we should add that 'Technology is mind.' Sailing ships, great wooden buildings, aeroplanes and longbows do not evolve – they are a product of human thought. Perhaps, even so, there is an atavistic inclination towards things made of wood. Wood has evolved, but so have human beings and they like handling wood. Blind people prefer the touch of wood to plastic. Over the millennia we have acquired a taste for cheeses, fish and bacon smoked over burning wood. Perhaps most of all, wood is still there in enormous quantities in a planet that for its own health needs to keep its forests.

Select Bibliography

Aeronautical Research Committee. (1920) *Report on Materials of Construction used in Aircraft and Aircraft Engines.* HMSO London.

Appleton, (1861) *Dictionary of Mechanics*, New York.

Evelyn, J. (1664) *Sylva,* London.

Gordon, J.E. (1968) *New Science of Strong Materials,* Penguin.

Rees, A. (1819) *Cyclopaedia,*

Sturt, G. (1963) *The Wheelwright's Shop*, Cambridge.

Tredgold, T. (1840) *Elementary Principles of Carpentry*, London.

For more detailed bibliography see: Evans, F.T. (1982) Wood since the Industrial Revolution: a Strategic Retreat?, *History of Technology Annual Volume,* **7**, pp. 37-55.

Surveying the wood for the trees: the archaeology of Sheffield's Heritage Woodlands.

Nick Sellwood[1] and Jim McNeill[2]

[1]Parks, Woodlands & Countryside, Sheffield City Council; [2]South Yorkshire Archaeology Service

Introduction

An archaeological survey of twenty-three ancient woodlands in Sheffield, covering over 250 hectares, was carried out under the auspices of the *'Fuelling a Revolution – the woods that founded the steel country'* project, an Heritage Lottery Fund (HLF) funded project co-ordinated by South Yorkshire Forest Partnership, but led on the ground by Sheffield City Council. The project began in 2000 and aims to facilitate the re-introduction of active management into woodlands that have been under-managed for much of the last 100 years.

The Trees and Woodlands Team, Sheffield City Council, co-ordinate management of the 1,500 hectares of woodland in the council's ownership, in what is the country's most wooded city. South Yorkshire Archaeology Service (SYAS) are the archaeological advisers to the local authorities of South Yorkshire. The service provides advice on all aspects of protection and conservation archaeological heritage. This includes agri-environment issues, such as Countryside Stewardship and forestry works, both to the local authorities and other organisations working within the county.

Fuelling a Revolution

The major aim of this project is the re-introduction of management to twenty-three ancient woodlands, through a combination of site management and infrastructure improvements closely linked to a programme of education and interpretation project work, under-pinned by detailed management plans for each site, community consultation and involvement.

The Project extends across the South Yorkshire Forest Project area to include ancient woodlands in Barnsley and Rotherham MBC, and within Wickersley Parish Council, Rotherham. Overall £1.5million has been awarded by the HLF across the Project area, which with match funding from the partners brings the total project costs to £2million (South Yorkshire Forest Partnership, 1997). As part of the Project, full archaeological surveys of all the sites in the South Yorkshire Forest Project area was proposed, including the twenty-three in Sheffield.

Archaeology of woodlands

Woodlands contain a wide variety of archaeological remains. These can be grouped into two basic types:

archaeology **of** woodlands - those features specifically related to woodlands. Examples might be historic woodland boundaries, charcoal burning kilns, managed tress (pollards, coppice). They exist because the wood exists; they are the physical remains of past woodland use.

and

archaeology **in** woodlands - includes prehistoric monuments, bell pits, sites that are contained by the woodland but only because of a co-incidence of location. They may even pre-date the woodland.

However, all monuments and features will be affected in some way by management and can affect the direction and manner in which woods are managed. Knowledge that significant archaeological features exist can be taken into account when planning management, such as tree felling and path improvement. This can then be done in a manner that minimises or removes threats to features.

Most of the woodlands within Sheffield had had little or no formal survey prior to the Project commencing, so our knowledge of such archaeological features was partial and mostly inadequate. However, the important pioneering work of Jones (1986, and 2003) in the 1980s demonstrated the archaeological potential of the woodlands (and ultimately helped in securing support from the HLF). Many woodlands had very few known remains: most had none. Therefore, the first step to protecting archaeological remains was in identifying their location and nature: this was the primary purpose of the survey.

Archaeological Survey: Aims and Objectives

The main aim of the survey was to provide good basic information that could feed into management planning and implementation. This was done by an initial review of sources, followed by archaeological field survey of the woodlands. The survey included both rapid walk-through survey and (where appropriate) more detailed measured survey.

Method

First stage – review and assessment

A desk-based assessment was prepared by a professional archaeological consultant to assess the present state of information about the woodlands. This reviewed all available sources, such as the Sites and Monuments Record; museum records and archive sources. The resulting report drew together and summarised this information, identifying known and likely sites within each woodland (Coutts, 1996).

Second stage - field survey undertaken in 2000 and 2001

Using information from the desk-based assessment, professional archaeological surveyors carried out a rapid walk-through survey of each woodland. They recorded all remains from all periods – an abandoned early twentieth century industrial building, for example in a former quarry – is no less important at this survey stage than prehistoric earthworks nearby. The surveyors also recorded areas or individual examples of previous woodland management, such as pollards or coppice stools. Finally, the surveyors were required to record any areas of damage or potential threat that was observed. Findspots were noted in desk-based assessment but were generally not included in the results of survey as they are unlikely to have visible traces on ground.

The survey was made by archaeologists walking in transects, at regular spacings through each compartment in turn. As features were identified, they were marked and rapidly recorded. A survey recording form was completed and the feature sketch-plotted. A brief text description was made and any relationship to other features noted.

The location of each feature was determined by GPS. For this, the survey team were provided with digital mapping data loaded into the GPS. Following each day of survey, the GPS data was downloaded into a database and plotted directly onto a computer mapping system. After completion of the survey, the field data was transferred to a database, collated and analysed, and a report prepared.

Report

For most features, this is all the survey that will be made, so it was important that the report was as comprehensive as possible. The report (Northern Archaeological Associates, 2001a) describes the results of the walk-through survey by compartment, describing features or groups of features.

Some analysis of archaeological feature types was made, discussing the possible nature and period where possible. Importantly, observed damage and possible threats to features was also described. An assessment was also made of the level of importance of each feature, using the methodology developed by Keen and Carreck (1987). This aimed to assess whether the features were of national, regional or local importance and suggest an appropriate level of management.

Following this, the initial report highlighted areas that were appropriate for more detailed measured survey. This applied mainly to particularly significant features that had been identified. As such, measured survey was undertaken on a number of features within various woodlands and an associated additional report produced.

To summarise, all of every available part of woodland was surveyed by walk-through survey. Selected parts of some woods had further detailed measured survey. However, some small parts were not surveyed because they were not accessible, mainly because of a dense understorey. The boundaries of these areas were also recorded, since it is important to know that these areas were not surveyed, and to build this into management planning, etc.

Results

This is clearly the most extensive woodland survey yet carried out in the county. By the time the whole HLF Project is completed, four woods in Barnsley, four in Rotherham and twenty-three in Sheffield will have been surveyed, a total area of over 400 hectares.

A total of 255 hectares of woodland was surveyed in Sheffield. The review of sources in the desk-based assessment identified forty-one sites. By the end of the survey, 584 archaeological features had been identified, a more than ten-fold increase.

Only three monuments were assessed as Level I in importance - these being the woodland boundary bank in Rollestone Wood, Gleadless Valley, South Sheffield; the Romano-British field settlement in Wheata Wood, north Sheffield and the late prehistoric hill fort of Wincobank Wood, north east Sheffield. The latter two are already Scheduled Ancient Monuments. The majority of the others were given level II status.

Monument Period and Type
There is a difficulty in assessing monuments by period from an initial survey. Various banks and linear ditched features were recorded whose age is as yet undetermined. However, it would appear that the majority of the features are post-mediaeval in date.

Woodland-related features, such as charcoal platforms and Q-pits were recorded. Charcoal was produced as a fuel for the iron industry and charcoal platforms were found in Buck, Glen Howe Park, Wheata and Wincobank woods. One particularly well-preserved example in Buck Wood (Figure 1) was selected for more detailed survey.

Q-pits were for the production of "whitecoal", dried wood used in lead smelting, and are common in some woods in the west side of Sheffield. Examples were recorded in Buck Wood and Carr, Ashes and Coneygree Woods, all in the Gleadless Valley. An example from Ashes Wood (Figure 2) was subject to a detailed measured survey.

The majority of features identified relate to extractive industries, principally mining and quarrying of coal, ironstone and sandstone. Pits for coal and ironstone, probably related to extraction on the Duke of Norfolk's estates from the seventeenth century

Figure 1. Charcoal Platform in Buck Wood, Gleadless Valley.

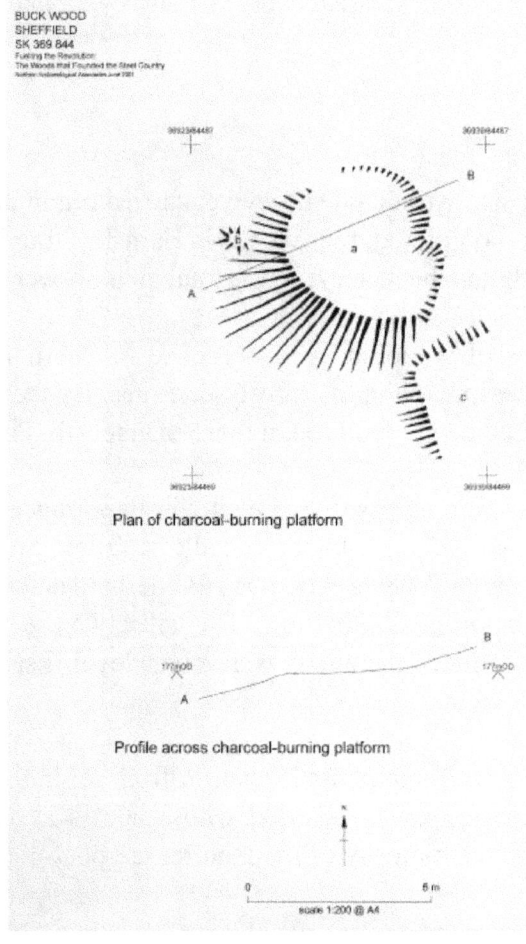

onwards, were recorded on Wincobank (Figure 3). Extensive complexes of mounds, bell-pits, and other earthworks (Figure 4) were recorded at Thorncliffe Wood, part of a much larger industrial landscape outside the wood linked to the former Thorncliffe drift colliery, north east Sheffield .

Virtually all of the woodlands had irregular pits interpreted as quarry pits. Probably many of these were for stone for nearby drystone walls. However, formal quarries for quarrying of sandstone were also recorded in a number of woodlands as well.

Figure 2. Detailed Survey of Chaarcoal Platform in Ashes Wood, Gleadless Valley.

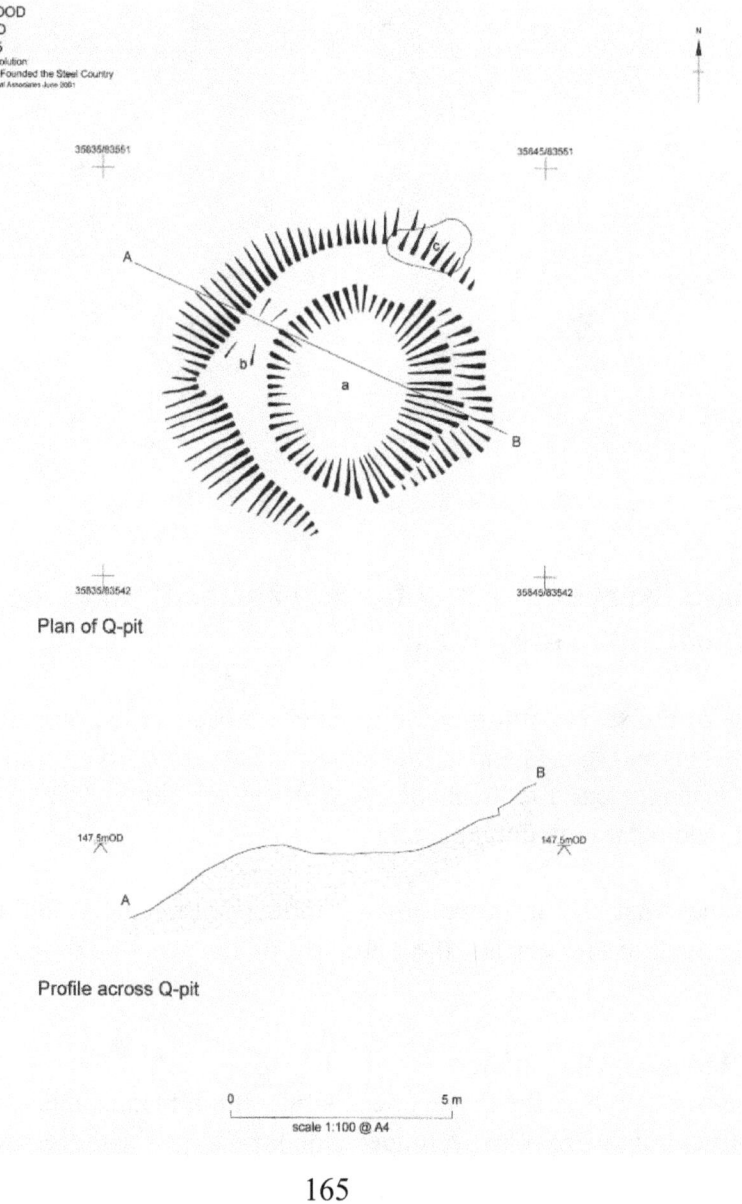

Figure 3. Coal Pits in Wincobank Wood.

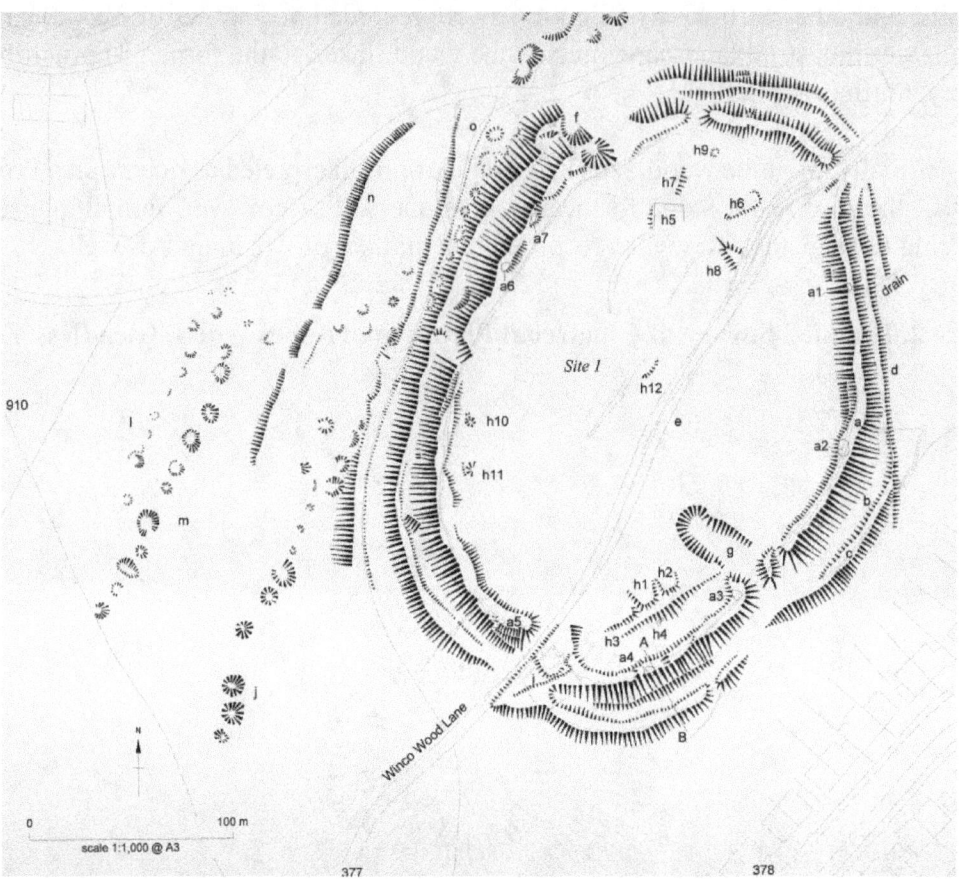

Archaeological survey as a tool for management planning and multi-purpose woodland management

The main use of the survey information to date has been in the preparation of detailed management plans and subsequent implementation for each of the woodlands, attempting to integrate management for archaeological interests with nature conservation, tree management, and recreation amongst other things.

Key issues that the information has influenced include, felling and thinning operations; recreation and access; the antiquity of the woodlands; and education and interpretation.

Felling and Thinning Operations
Nearly all the woodlands in the Project need silvicultural management. For example, to increase structural diversity in even-aged stands or to gradually restore sites planted

Figure 4. Complex of Features at Thorncliffe Wood.

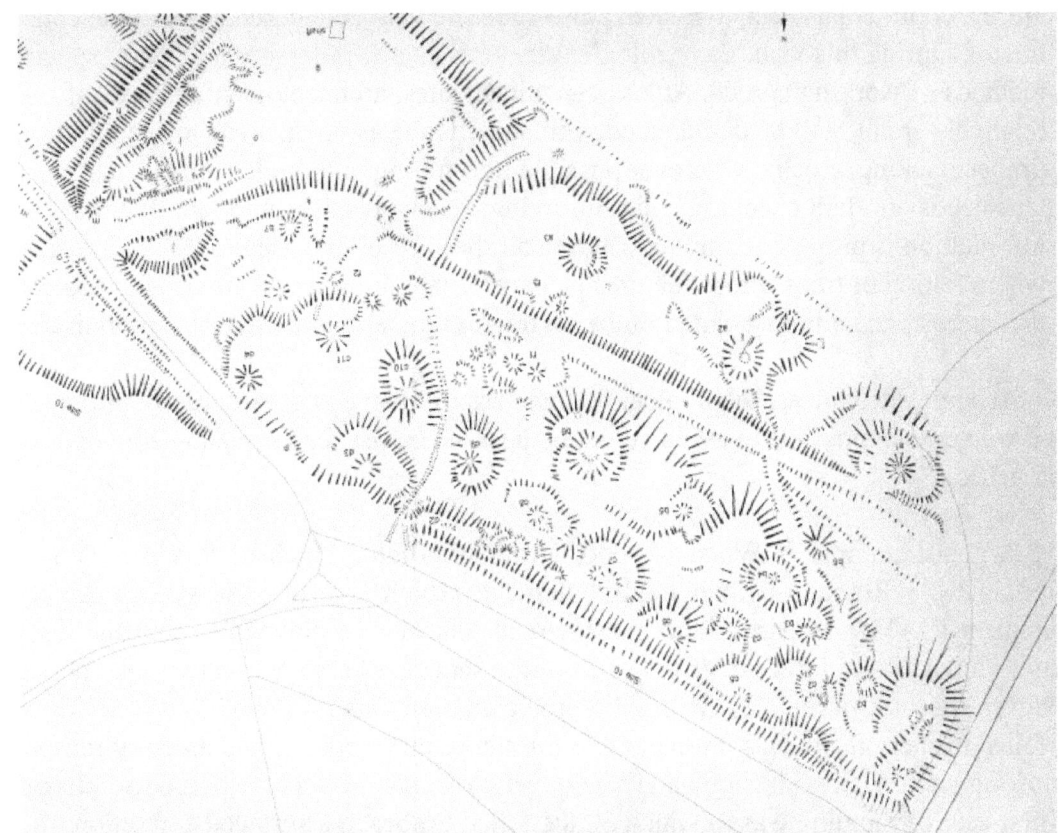

with introduced species (planted ancient woodlands). It is normal practice to remove the majority of felled timber, usually by machines such as small tractor skidders (where the timber is dragged out) or tractor forwarders (where the timber is carried out). Obviously this is potentially very destructive to features of archaeological interest. To minimise any problems the following practices are followed, building on the Forestry Commission's Forestry and Archaeology Guidelines (1995):

- In certain cases, a site visit is arranged with the South Yorkshire Archaeology Service at the planning stage. In all cases, SYAS are made aware of proposed work. The SYAS are consulted on all management plans at a draft stage and comments incorporated.
- All tenders sent out to forestry companies include maps and basic descriptions of the archaeological features in the wood to be worked. Contract documents include clauses related to prevention of damage to features by the contractor, and the need to avoid damage is mentioned in the site specification. This makes those tendering for the work aware at the start that features are present, that protection measures will be needed, and that implicitly, the time to undertake the operations and hence

the cost may be affected.
- Once a contract has been awarded, a pre-start site visit is undertaken with the contractor. During this visit, archaeological features can be pointed out and any special methods of working agreed. At less vandalized sites, archaeological features, if relatively small, will be demarcated with hazard tape as no go areas for vehicles, timber stacking, etc and wherever possible tree-felling, although even at such sites, tape needs constant checking and reinforcing. As always, its important that this information is properly communicated to all the staff on the ground. Sometimes, where felling of trees across features is unavoidable, brash mats are used to protect the interest, and any associated timber extraction undertaken only in dry conditions.

At some sites the archaeological features are extensive and particularly important, and it would be impossible to avoid vehicular passage across features using conventional approaches.

A good example is Wheata Wood, North Sheffield. Much of this woodland is underlain by a Romano-British field settlement, which is also a Scheduled Ancient Monument (SAM). As part of the management plan it was planned to thin the dense thirty to forty year old trees overlying part of the scheduled area over a two-year period. However, the use of vehicles within the protected area was prohibited, and leaving all the felled timber on site was unacceptable for nature conservation and amenity reasons. Following a site visit with English Heritage, who oversee SAMs, the agreed solution in the first year of thinning was to winch all the felled timber to a surfaced extraction track with a tractor, avoiding the need for vehicles to go across archaeological features.

In the second year, this was impractical because the area to be thinned was not crossed by an access track. The solution this time was to use heavy horses to draw the timber to rideside by a mixture of snigging and horse-drawn forwarder, combined with a conventional tractor helping to move the partly extracted timber to a collection point for haulage once it was placed next to a surfaced route. In both cases, wet weather conditions were avoided.

Both years the approaches taken proved a great success. At the same time, thinning of the woodland reduced the number of trees growing on archaeological features, and ultimately will reduce the risk of windthrow damage by allowing the retained trees to develop large, healthy crowns. As a general comment silvicultural operations within the woodlands in the Project can be used to deal not only with tree-related health and safety issues, but also reduce the risk of windthrow damage to archaeological features by careful felling or reduction of high-risk trees.

Some of the trees growing in the woods can be classed as living archaeological features in themselves – for example old coppice stools. Recent work in the Gleadless Valley, South Sheffield for example, where eight ancient woodlands are present, has identified a number of old coppice stools, potential veteran trees and stored coppice stools now grown to mature trees. Again, this information is used to inform management decisions by firstly recognising the value of these living artifacts; informing management prescriptions; excluding them from felling operations; and where appropriate, thinning around them to give them more light where they are suffering from too much shade and hence promoting their longevity

Recreation and access
In a few cases, the survey has highlighted that some monuments are suffering from inappropriate or unco-ordinated recreational use, related to paths, unauthorised vehicles like motorbikes, and fly-tipping

Perhaps the best example of this is Wincobank Iron Age Hill fort, a Scheduled Ancient Monument forming part of Wincobank Wood, North-central Sheffield (Figure 4). Situated on a hilltop overlooking the M1 corridor and with panoramic views of the surrounding area, this is a large structure approximately 125 metres long and eighty-five metres wide. The centre of the hill fort is generally covered in grass or heath vegetation, with extensive bare areas, as well as scrubby oak growing on some of the hill fort flanks, raising some concerns about tree root damage to the monument.

The hill fort is crossed through the middle by an unsurfaced public footpath along which serious erosion has taken place into the bedrock through what is a very shallow soil layer. More importantly the monument has long suffered abuse from motorbike scrambling, quad bikes and burning of stolen cars. This has led to rutting of the flanks of the fort in places, and extensive loss of vegetation and subsequent soil erosion (NAA, 2001b).

During 2003 it is hoped to secure the main vehicular access points into the woodland to prevent vehicular access, and reduce motorbikes access. At the same time, concerns over the potential for tree root damage (and less importantly, windthrow) have to be balanced against the protection the trees give to the monument from motorbikes, etc. For now the approach will be to selectively coppice dense areas of developing trees, allowing them to re-grow, but preventing them from reaching a size which would be more liable to windthrow. The footpath crossing the monument would be difficult to legally re-align and the route would continue to be used anyway. As such, the way forward will probably be to formalize the path surface, perhaps through laying a raised revetted surface, having first undertaken an archaeological survey of the route. In effect, the archaeology along the route of the path would be sealed and further damage prevented. Other paths around the monument will also be formalized or discouraged. Clearly these proposals are subject to approval by English Heritage and the SYAS.

Antiquity of the woodlands
In a few instances, the archaeological survey confirmed suspicions that some of the woodlands are not strictly speaking, ancient.

At both Chapeltown Park Wood and Thorncliffe Wood in north-east Sheffield, it is clear that woodland has been planted and/or naturally regenerated on what was industrial scale iron workings exploited during the eighteenth and nineteenth centuries. At Thorncliffe Wood these include bell-pits, suggested tramways, a railway embankment, and shaft mounds (Figure 5).

Whilst Thorncliffe Wood has the appearance of mature woodland, and is recorded as early as 1657 as part of a charcoal making contract (Jones, 2003), it is now clear that the part of the woodland owned by Sheffield City Council is secondary and relatively recent in origin. It seems clear that the presence of ancient woodland indicators such as Yellow Archangel and Wood Melick, which can both be locally frequent, is the result of the colonization from either small parts of the site not affected by the previous iron workings, or from adjoining parts of the greater Thorncliffe Wood less affected by mining, etc.

Whilst Chapeltown Wood and the Sheffield City Council part of Thorncliffe Wood may not be ancient, except in a few areas, they do have a ground flora generally characteristic of local ancient woodlands, and, with considerable areas of less disturbed ancient woodland adjoining or close by, have the potential to gradually acquire the ecological characteristics of more semi-natural ancient woodland. In general, the implication is that best practice will be followed to manage them as though they are ancient woodlands, although the control of introduced tree species such as Sycamore, which is now prevalent at both sites, is considered less of a priority than other more semi-natural woodlands like Wheata Wood.

Education and Interpretation
The work programmes for each woodland in the Project includes education and interpretation work. For some sites, leaflets and interpretative boards are appropriate and the archaeological survey work can contribute to this. Other uses of the archaeological knowledge of the woods have included input in education packs for each site, historical walks, demonstrations of traditional woodland management crafts like hurdle-making and greenwood turning, and schools work, as well as events with the Young Archaeolo-

gists Club. There is also a related website for the Project – www.heritagewoodsonline.co.uk - which includes historical and archaeological information.

Further work

The archaeological survey work undertaken will also be used to promote new scheduling and help in the reviewing and potential enhancement of existing scheduling, led by English Heritage. It has also identified areas where further research would be beneficial.

End piece

The archaeological survey and associated reports of twenty-three ancient woodlands in Sheffield in 2000-01 has greatly contributed to the archaeological knowledge of the city's woodland heritage, and strengthened the already well-recognised links between the woodlands of Sheffield and its industrial growth. On the ground the survey has helped to shape woodland management plans by identifying priority areas, fed into pro-active strategies on the ground to protect features, helped avoid damage during necessary management activities, and provided a wealth of information of value for educational and interpretative activities.

References

Coutts, C. (1996) *Sheffield's Heritage Woodlands An archaeological and archival study* Unpublished report

Forestry Commission (1995) *Forests and Archaeology Guidelines.* London: HMSO

Jones, M (1986) *Sheffield's Ancient Woodlands, Past and Present*. Sheffield City Polytechnic. Unpublished Report for Sheffield City Council

Jones, M (2003) *Sheffield's Woodland Heritage* (third edition). Green Tree Publications

Keen, L and Carreck, A (1987) *Historic Landscape of the Weld Estate, Dorset.*

Northern Archaeological Associates (2001a) *Sheffield Archaeological Surveys Volume 1: Level 2 Survey Woodlands* Unpublished report.

Northern Archaeological Associates (2001b) *Sheffield Archaeological Surveys Volume 2: Level 2 and 3 Survey Woodlands* Unpublished report.

South Yorkshire Forest Partnership (1997) *Fuelling a Revolution - the woods that founded the Steel Country.* Application to the Heritage Lottery Fund.

Embracing spaces: wood pastures, open pastures and historical geography
Brian K. Roberts

It is natural that we see the emergent historical geography of this country in terms of the material remains and survivals of obvious human activity, of villages, hamlets and farms, their fields, of towns, castles and monasteries, halls, parks and meadows, mills, forges and the like. These have long provided a focus for scholarly attention. Between these, however, once lay essentially unoccupied spaces, the woods, the commons and the wastes (Rackham, 1986; Winchester, 2000). This chapter is a pointer towards these 'embracing spaces', the far from neutral tracts of pastures and woodlands, areas of land that for a great deal of their history have been used as common grazing or as wood pastures. The objective of this study is to define a methodology exemplified by a descriptive examination of three pieces of evidence, a national map of woodland, the reconstructed medieval landscapes of County Durham and the topography of a single small territory in Durham, the 'small shire' of Heighingtonshire. The first of these is based upon work done with the support of English Heritage, and comprises a series of national maps. This was undertaken in collaboration with Stuart Wrathmell (Roberts and Wrathmell, 2002). The second presents one version of a map of medieval Durham based upon the mid-nineteenth century Ordnance Survey Old Series 1:10,560 maps, and is the product of collaboration between the author, Richard Britnell, Simon Harris and Helen Dunsford. The third map is an extract from this broader picture to view and analyse local detail, and is drawn from work in progress by the present author. Thus, within the argument a triple helix of scale is involved, national, county and local, with each level supporting, informing and interrogating the other two.

Underlying the argument, but not presented here, is a national map of English rural settlement, both nucleated and dispersed, which revealed distinctive spatial variations (Roberts and Wrathmell, 2002, Figure 1.14). A 'central province', extending from the North Sea lowlands, sweeping across the inner Midlands and extending into Somerset and Dorset, contains a large rather distorted diamond of countryside once almost wholly dominated by nucleation. On each side of this are varied landscapes, some containing vast concentrations of dispersed settlement, others with settlement either wholly absent. However, even in such zones, nucleated settlements are rarely absent: they are merely more scattered and often smaller, so that a market town of the uplands may be no larger than a large village in the favoured lowlands. These South-eastern and Northern and Western Provinces embrace and almost surround the Central Province, which only reaches the sea along the north-eastern coast, the Severn Estuary and the English Channel. Point by point mapping of all villages and hamlets, giving a pure, specific and generalised distribution

Working and Walking in the Footsteps of Ghosts: Volume 1 the Wooded Landscape

at a national scale, has allowed a close definition of boundaries, the *bêtes noire* of all regional divisions, and these have then been tested against distributions derived from other separate and diverse sources. Much remains to be explored and refined, but the map retains practical value and was the driving force leading to the construction of the national map of woodland (Roberts and Wrathmell, 2002).

Figure 1   **A national map of woodland between about 730 and 1086**

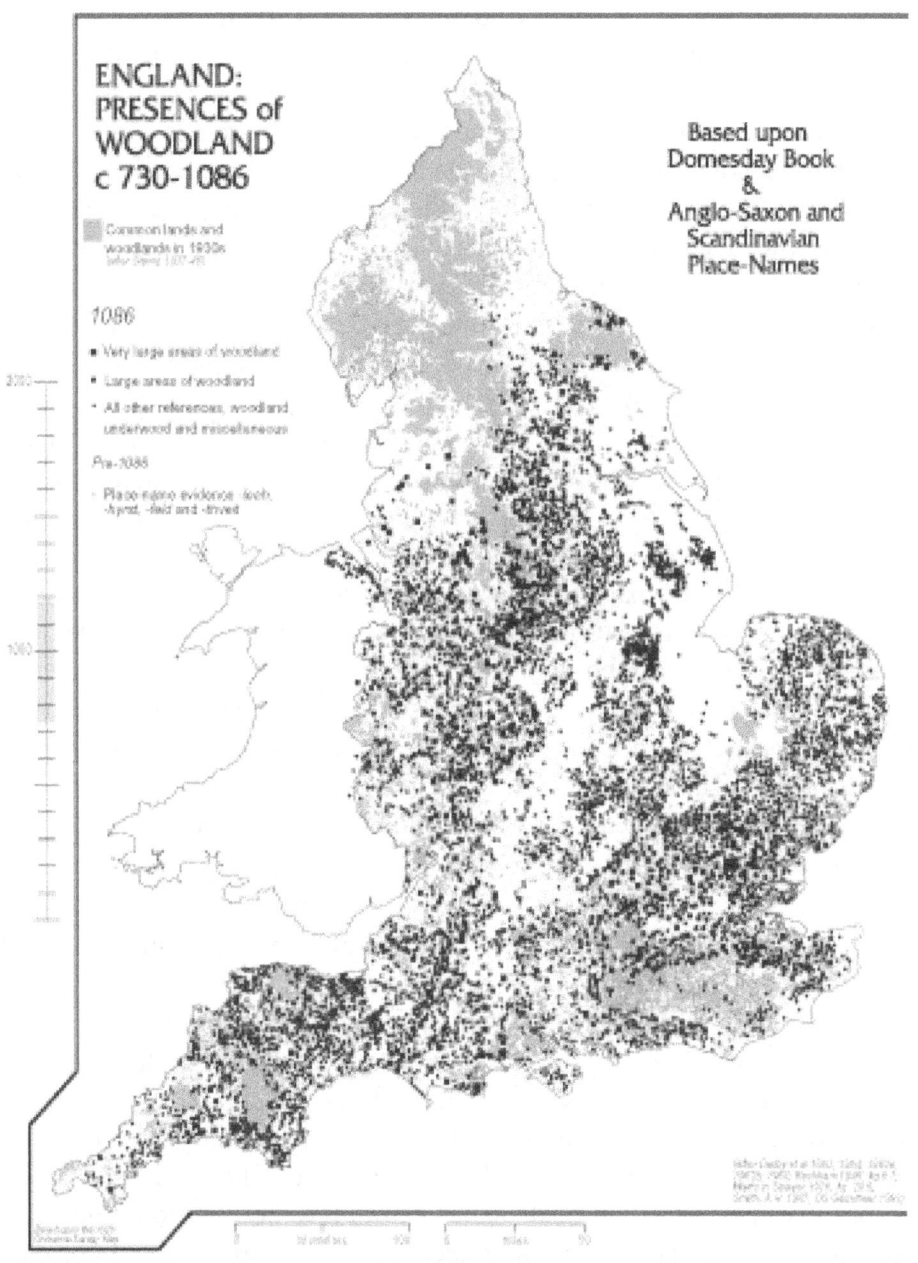

The first map of this present series, Figure 26, a national map of woodland between about 730 and 1086, is based upon the complementary evidence of Domesday Book and place-names. Although substantively reworked, this map owes vast debts to Sir Clifford Darby and his many co-workers, to Oliver Rackham and to Joan Thirsk (Darby 1952-1977, Rackham, 1986; Thirsk, 1984; 1987). In addition the great land use survey initiated and brought to completion by Sir Dudley Stamp was used (Stamp, 1937-44; 1962), while the little known Hilda Wilcox, who reconstructed the essentials of an accurate national distribution of medieval woodland in the late 1920s should not be forgotten (Roberts 2001). No map of such a remote period and integrating in a rather coarse manner the work of so many scholars can be perfect and indeed in its interpretation numerous caveats and qualifications are required. Nevertheless, the convergence of many types of evidence suggests we have indeed a broad picture of the national regional differences between cleared lands and open and wooded pasture landscapes. The map's accuracy is sufficient for the distribution of symbols within a ten by ten kilometre square to be locally meaningful. It is in fact three maps in one. First, there are open pastures, necessarily drawn from Stamp's distribution map of the 1930s. The author is currently working on an eighteenth century version of this map, which should provide a sounder basis for reconstruction. This land has long been dominated by extensive usages, primarily as grazing lands, but also as turbaries and sources of mineral wealth, and has always been subject to the greatest number of natural limitations, of altitude, climate and soil quality. Second, the woods and wood-pastures, also used as grazing, but, by 1086 indeed by 730, already being subjected to the sustained attrition caused by felling and fuel and wood cutting, grazing and fire and, above all, the inexorable advance of improvement and farming. This is not the place to discuss these, but a third distribution is germane: by mapping the open-pastures and wood-pastures the improved lands are also mapped, by a process of abstraction. The map of 'woodland' and open pastures, mapped 'positively', also reveals, as a 'negative', cleared, managed and cultivated tracts of varied character and dimensions.

There is no doubt that this is a very generalised picture, even within the limitations of the nature of the evidence and the manner in which it has been assembled. It is, as was once said, 'capable of improvement', for while this version was produced in Freehand, a graphics package designed to create publishable and attractive maps, the case of County Durham will show that computer systems can be used for both sustained and durable archiving and pursing active research. Nevertheless, at the national scale this synthesised picture supplies a setting within which all local studies can be pursued. However, the interaction need not be one way. Local studies can in turn be used to refine and correct the national picture. Each is of equal importance. Further, the real geographical contexts in which the Anglo-Saxon kingdoms crystallised can be defined, while the patterns of Roman occupation and exploitation, even the detail of their military advance, can be seen. There are clear links between the coppice woodlands developed to sustain pottery industries of the Roman period and woodland in 1086 (Wrathmell and Roberts, 2002; Wrathmell and Roberts in Hooke, 2000). In this map there are even important questions in respect of our view of prehistory and the fundamental nature of archaeological distributions, for settlement continuity in the cleared zones implies both early clearance and the presence of sustained attrition of all antecedent landscapes. Above all there is a real need for quantitative and qualitative assessments of the vast areas of temperate savanna implied by Figure 26. A revised county by county version of this map, reassembled to provide a historical national picture would be a worthy research goal; it would provide an unparalleled tool to which local studies could be keyed.

Figure 2. The Medieval Landscape Elements of County Durham

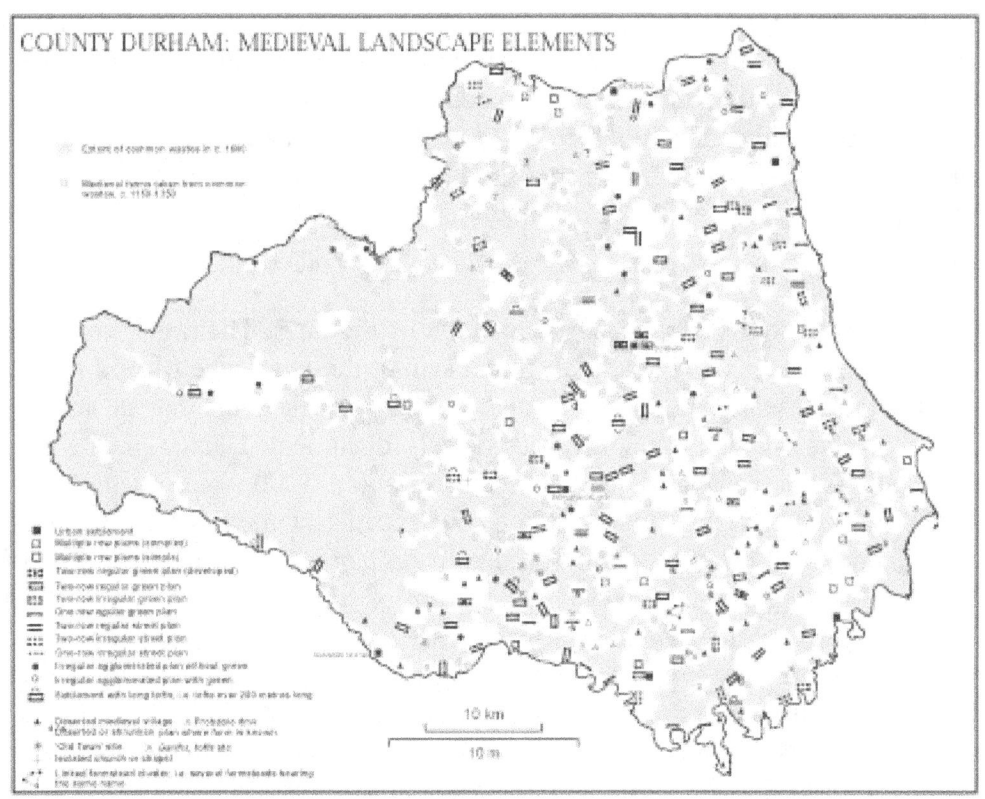

A second map, Figure 2, of County Durham, is based upon a reconstruction of common pastures in about 1600, by Helen Dunsford, but incorporating all of the known farmsteads developed in the waste between about 1150 and 1350, the work of Simon Harris. These were both substantial undertakings, and made possible by a grant from the Arts and Humanities Research Board to the author and Richard Britnell (Dunsford and Harris, 2003). This map is built around a framework of Ordnance Survey maps of the middle decades of the nineteenth century using ArcGIS. Durham County Council kindly provided digitised versions of these important historic maps. The software allows the development of research layers over base maps and the development of a tabulated inter-related data-matrix. Both maps and data-base can be used, and indeed constantly corrected and updated as new information becomes available. Furthermore, within this system it is perfectly possible to zoom from the detail of a single field to the whole county and the information included in Figure 2 is only a small proportion of that recorded. Within this structured framework it is feasible to reconsider the implications of place-names, the contexts of settlement forms and patterns, and above all, for this has also been mapped, the role of landownership and tenurial variations as forces in moulding individual elements of the landscape. The ability to create a synthesis is again a powerful research tool, and the author has no doubt that this is a precursor of what should be done for each county, standardising essential procedures and data-base fields, for eventual integration within a national synthesis. This is both feasible and necessary, and nothing illustrates the need better than the indispensable and imaginative leap made at the end of the eighteenth century from individual county maps to the standardised uniformity of the Ordnance Survey.

Some explanation is needed for the content of Figure 2. The rather complex key records the varied types of village plan found within the landscape of mid-nineteenth century Durham, a research interest of the author. There is little doubt that the antecedents of these same plans, which are sometimes closely documented, have medieval roots, indeed are all likely to have all been present by about 1200. These settlements are physical evidence of the way in which medieval farmers tamed and took possession of the land. Each comprised a small community, a hamlet or village, each of which cultivated surrounding lands, organised into a form of communal field system. Slightly emphasised in this map are a number of grey dots. These record the locations of farms taken from the waste between about 1150 and 1350. It is possible that some of these have been omitted because of defects in the documentary record, but the distribution is complete enough to be meaningful. They can be seen to concentrate to the north and west of a line drawn from Barnard Castle to Gateshead via Bishop Auckland and Durham. In contrast the villages and hamlets are concentrated in the south and east, and their Anglo-

Saxon, and occasionally Anglo-Scandinavian place-names, are indicative of the antiquity of permanent settlement within this zone. To the north and west lie countrysides where active colonisation was taking place-after 1150.

The embracing spaces of the common wastes provide a setting for these arguments. Reconstructed from evidence that takes them back to about 1600, not least the clear noting of former commons found on the Old Series Ordnance Survey six inch maps, these wastes, of varying physical character and normally subject to rights of common, define and frame the two other distributions. The negative, 'unmapped' areas define, in large, the communal fields of the villages and hamlets and the intaken lands of the medieval farms. To begin by reconstructing these positively would have been a monumental if not impossible task. However, by pursuing the objective of mapping the common wastes as *positive* space - and we believe that at least 80% accuracy has been achieved - we have defined the improved lands of the villages and the farms as *negative* space. The terms 'positive' and 'negative' are relative to each other, and do not correlate to the relative importance of either aspect. This would depend upon the research objective to which the map is applied. The map series, because that is what is really involved, gives a glimpse of the situation as it must have been in Durham on the eve the major economic changes of the fourteenth century - providing that we then see the deserted settlements as still populated centres at that early date. Further, by viewing the medieval farms not as steadings and lands, but as the 'waste' from which they were carved - hence the nature of the symbol adopted - then the map gives an impression of the landscapes of 1150. This is in spite of the varied chronologies of the materials from which has been assembled. This process of cartographic assembly, correction, addition and subtraction can be pursued indefinitely, using the map as an active research tool.

The emptiness of the vast wedge of open and wood pastures sprawling across northern and western Durham to merge with the wolf-haunted uplands of the Pennines is remarkable. This provides new nourishment for the imagination and reconsideration of such practical issues as the journeys of St. Cuthbert, the location of Monkwearmouth and Jarrow and the early acquisitions by the Cuthbertine community when based at Chester le Street. Pollen diagrams suggest the presence of vast open tracts by the end of the Iron Age and the early Roman period, with the pollen rains from trees being commensurate with those seen today, although lacking the recent resurgence of pine pollen, from recent plantations. Reaching forward in time, the location of mines, wagon-ways and railways and the settlements associated with them become part of the story, while the map is a pragmatic tool for contemporary landscape management. Its authors have no doubt that this is a foundation study at both a county and a national scale. We have yet to integrate it within studies of ancient woodlands, of the distributions of archaeological materials - contingent upon the duration of cultivation - and place-names, but these are 'in the system'. Revisiting Figure 1 it is clear that the contrast in countrysides revealed by the detailed Durham material is manifest within the generalised distribution of Old English 'woodland' names, in Durham, Northumberland, Cumberland and Westmorland used as a surrogate for the absent Domesday evidence (Watts 2002, xiv, xvi). Figure 1 captures one critical stage in the national transition from a wholly wooded landscape to that of the

Figure 3. The Small Shire of Heighingtonshire, County Durham

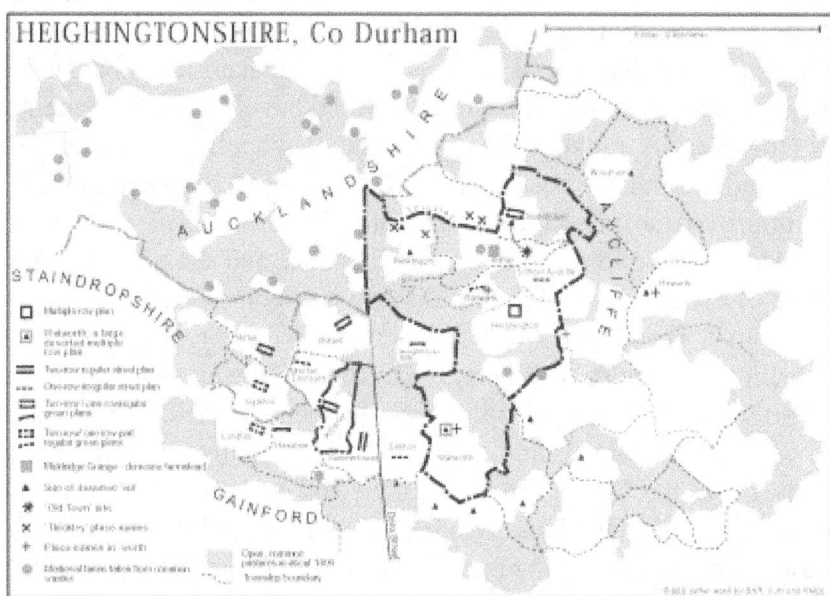

present, and the mapping is as precise as is currently possible. Figure 2 captures some of the detail for a single county, and given the storage of data within a standardised and widely available system, ArcGIS, corrections and additions can be made, driven by both the demands of scholarship and the pragmatic needs of countryside management.

Finally, the small shire, or multiple estate, of Heighingtonshire, County Durham, seen in Figure 3 provides insights into the power of the zoom effect, i.e. the ability to zoom in, and then cut out from the county map to focus upon particular small areas. In fact, we know little about local settlement sequences in any English county. In Durham the close definition of single-farmstead waste colonisation, together with a township by township identification of common wastes, permits a real understanding of the obscure processes of land development both after and before the Norman take-over. In this there can be an attempt to marry the intractable evidence of settlement morphology, seen in the complex key to Figure 2, to the equally intractable opacities of documentary sources such as the Boldon Book of 1183. Thus, Figure 3 is a complicated and specialist map. Outlined strongly is what became a parish, but which was recorded in 1183 as a 'shire', a unit of territory whose parts were integrated in such a way as to provide support for its lord (Barrow, 1973,1-68; Roberts and Wrathmell, 2002, Figure 1.7). Grain production, stock production, labour services, renders in kind and in cash were focussed upon and controlled from the hall at Heighington, and by 1183 this was in the ownership of the Bishops of Durham. The settlement detail is projected onto the background of the commons of about 1600, derived directly from the countywide map, and in this case it was clearly the policy of the estate not to grant large numbers of freehold farms within the 'shire'. Their relative absence may be compared with their abundance in Aucklandshire to the north-west. Three points are, however, applicable to the main theme of this paper. First, in the north-west of Heighingtonshire active twelfth century colonisation was taking place in the great woodland of Thickley, an Old English place-name implying 'a clearing made in thick woodland'. By the mid-twelfth century attempts were being made to plant new villages, as at Newbiggin - 'the new buildings' - but this was not successful and the foundation hamlets became farmsteads, part of a dispersed pattern. Nevertheless, the expansion of the Bishop's great home farm at Middridge led to the establishment of a new village on former commons to the north leaving behind an 'old town' site to appear on nineteenth century maps. Second, to the south-east, around Killerby, a Scandinavian place-name, a cluster of rather regular village plans tell of active colonisation, probably in the tenth and the eleventh century. Headlam, implies 'clearing with heather', Morton, a 'settlement by the moor', and Bolam, a settlement associated with the 'boles or tree trunks', while the name Summerhouse indicates that settlement arose at a place where summer grazing of stock took place amid once more extensive heaths, moors and commons (Watts 2002). Interpolating the distribution of common wastes provides a imaginary glimpse of a former large area of waste – perhaps even a reasonably accurate reconstruction - and a context for an otherwise inexplicable group of regular settlement plans set on the margins of four ancient shires. They are part of a process of communal colonisation and the date of this is assuredly before the Norman Conquest. The important point for this paper is that these details can be isolated and made meaningful within the broader context of the county. Once done, the ArcGIS county map obviates the need for countless local studies that begin from scratch and becomes an established survey beacon to which reference must constantly be made.

Third, and finally, this analysis emphasises both the vast extent of the commons before the Norman conquest of the north and their role as embracing spaces from which, and within which, medieval and post-medieval landscapes were carved. In this paper the *method* is at least as important as the content. Once the 'positive spaces' of the commons were mapped and an understanding of the tegulation, i.e. tiling, of the whole landscape of County Durham emerged, then the 'negative spaces' which remained could be gradually resolved. They are given substance with the documented enclosed farmsteads and the more shadowy townfields that once supported each of the nucleated villages, although there are, in addition, parklands and enclosed woods, coppice and timber. Ironically, it was mid-nineteenth century maps of the landownership patterns on the important North East coalfield, created in connection with valuable royalties and way-leaves, which gave essential clues to the medieval antecedent arrangements. Nevertheless, there is no intrinsic reason why this Durham study cannot be used as an exemplar for a national system. Figure 1, generated before the advent of easily accessible ArcGIS, represents an attempt to undertake this type of study on a national scale. The procedure differs fundamentally from the foundations on which it is built, namely 'maps of …', 'Domesday woodland', 'Royal Forests', 'place-names in *–leah*' and the like, because of potential, within a computer, for sustained usage and archiving. At all three scales the maps are more than mere representations of 'facts': they become interactive research tools capable of being used by all disciplines concerned with the countryside. The power and potential of the computer, now that it has come to maturity, can lift the map beyond mere illustration to become what it once was, a powerful and flexible tool of research. In this we have a glimpse of the historical geography studies of the future.

References:

This paper is not heavily referenced. The publications appearing below all have full bibliographic support.

Barrow, G.W.S. (1973) *The Kingdom of the Scots*. Edward Arnold, London

Darby, H.C. *et al.* (ed.) (1952-77) *The Domesday Geography of England* (7 volumes) : Eastern England (1952); Midland England (1954); South-East England (1962a); Northern England (1962b); South-West England (1967); Gazetter (1975) University Press, Cambridge.

Darby, H.C (1973) *A New Historical Geography of England*. University Press, Cambridge.

Darby, H.C. (1977) *Domesday England*. University Press, Cambridge.

Dunsford, H. and Harris, S. (2003) On the Distribution of Common Waste and Medieval Farms in County Durham. *Economic History Review,* LVI, no. 1, 34-56.

Hooke, D. (2000) *Landscape: the richest historical record.* (Society for Landscape Studies, Supplemental Series 1)

Rackham, O. (1986) *The History of the Countryside*. J.M. Dent & Sons Ltd., London.

Roberts, B. K. (2001) Woodlands in England. *Geographical Journal*, **167** (2), 163-73

Roberts B. K. and Wrathmell, S. (2002) *Region and Place – a Study of English Rural Settlement*. English Heritage, HMSO London

Stamp, L.D. (ed.) (1937-44) *The Land of Britain, County Fascicles*. Royal Geographical Society and Geographical Publications Ltd., London.

Stamp. L.D. (1962) *The Land of Britain: its Use and Misuse*. Longman's Green and Co. Ltd with Geographical Publications Ltd., London.

Thirsk, J. (ed.) (1984, 1985) *The Agrarian History of England and Wales 1640-1750*. vol 5, University Press, Cambridge.

Thirsk, J. (1987) *England's Agricultural Regions and Agrarian History, 1500-1750*. Macmillan Education, London.

Watts, V. (2002) *A Dictionary of County Durham Place-Names*. English Place-Name Socity, Popular Series, vol. 3.

Winchester, A.J.L. (2000) *The Harvest of the Hills*. University Press, Edinburgh.

Decaying Wood - Recycling in Arboreal Ecosystems
Andrew Cowan
Arborecology

Why decaying wood?

Decaying wood, which we have spent years removing, cutting off, and scraping out of cavities, because we have considered it to be dead and therefore of no use, is perhaps more important to the arboreal ecosystems than the living trees. The woody tissues of the tree may no longer be alive as far as the tree is concerned, but they are being decayed by a multitude of different organisms, while providing shelter for many more.

It is the process of decay which is the focus here, the progression of use by different organisms. Some like their wood served up fresh with the sap still ebbing from it's vessels, while there are those that prefer it when others have had their fill and all that is left is a mass of soft cellulose or brittle lignin. The diverse array of organisms that are involved in the breakdown of dead woody tissues is truly amazing. So much so that decaying wood can be considered a specialist habitat in it's own right.

The figures are quite astounding, just considering the invertebrates that exist and depend on the decaying wood habitat, there are includes 1700 species in Britain, six percent of total British Fauna, but the worrying fact is that forty percent are either British Red Data Book Species or labelled nationally scarce. In an effort to reduce potential losses, the Joint Nature Conservancy Council (JNCC) and the Royal Society for the Protection of Birds (RSPB) produced a practical handbook called '*Habitat Management for Invertebrates*', which was republished in 2001.

For those of you with a background in woodland management, Forest Enterprise produced a publication last year, called '*Life in the Deadwood – A guide to managing deadwood in the Forestry Commission forests*'. The cynical among you may think that this is a booklet on early retirement for foresters, as the Forestry Commission (FC) undergoes another change of identity, and yes, the FC is making changes in it's management strategies, but they are about new objectives that are evolutionary rather than revolutionary.

The current emphasis on biodiversity and protected species, which has come from European and international agreements and directives, has forced a change in management strategies and a shift in long term objectives. However, there is revolution afoot, with more and more people, and organisations, recognising the need to focus on a broader picture. In conservation the world over, the time and money has been invested in 'fire fighting', to protect and preserve endangered populations of particular species.

The solution is one that manages the system, rather than concentrating on its component parts, if we can maintain healthy ecosystems the biodiversity should take care of itself. However, we cannot and should not try to force long-term change, if we are to be successful in sustainable conservation, our role needs to be one of encouragement and persuasion.

Historically, woodland managers have removed dead wood on the basis of hygiene, to protect the timber resource from what have traditionally been perceived as pests, like insects and fungi. This is also true of many, parkland and garden sites managed by arborists, where dead wood in trees is seen as a liability, and is removed for fear it may fall and injure someone. The result is that there is simply not enough decaying wood habitat to sustain populations of many key species of conservation importance.

Dead and dying trees play a vital role in the functioning and productivity of arboreal ecosystems through effects on biodiversity, carbon storage, soil nutrients cycling, energy flows, hydrological processes and natural regeneration of trees (Humphrey *et al.*, 2002). This is a point now generally recognised by most of us, but this has not always been the case. The generations of managers that have religiously felled and removed dead and dying trees, has left us with a huge shortage, which is likely to take decades to replace.

The generation gap is aptly demonstrated when we look at the rare species, which are associated with our ancient and veteran trees. Many of these are only found on sites where there has been a continuity of decaying wood habitat for hundreds of years. However, ancient trees may appear plentiful today, but for how much longer? Next time you visit a site containing ancient trees, look around at the rest of the wood or parkland, and consider where the next generation will come from.

The organisms that rely on decaying wood habitat are becoming increasingly isolated, in time and place. This is made worse by their lack of mobility, which means that the creation of an intermediary 'bridge habitat' is essential if these species are to survive. This is a fundamental part of our involvement in the sustainability of arboreal ecosystems and the maintenance of biodiversity.

There are two distinct types of decaying wood habitat, the first is associated with standing dead trunks, limbs or branches left around the outside of the tree, while the second is found within the trunks and branches themselves, where the decay forms cavities. It is important to be aware of this distinction because the habitats that are created are quite different and require specific techniques to recreate them.

Standing dead wood, whether as whole trunks or branches within the crown of otherwise healthy trees, is relatively easy to replace by the resurrection methods described by Mark Robinson (see below). This type of decaying wood habitat breaks down from the outside in, providing a large surface area for occupation by invertebrates, fungi, lichens and mosses.

However, when it comes to the creation of the decaying wood habitat found within the trunks and branches of trees, the techniques involved are not quite so simple. The decaying wood inside living trees decomposes from the inside out, creates cavities, rot holes and hollow trunks, which are created by invertebrates and fungi, but go on to provide shelter for a diversity of birds, small mammals and reptiles.

Creating the habitat

Training as a practical arborist has progressed over the years, from the days of old when tree surgery work involved carting a hand axe and cross cut saw around the tree, through the era of flush cutting and cavity excavation, to the enlightenment of target pruning and an understanding of CODIT (Compartmentalisation Of Decay In Trees). However, modern pruning techniques may prolong the safe useful life of the trees in our parks and gardens, but they are threatening the sustainability of arboreal ecosystems, and potentially the life expectancy of the tree themselves.

There is a tendency to use pruning techniques, like reduction or thinning, to maintain trees in a particular form or shape. Our use of terminology is prone to describing a particular state, like dead wood for instance, rather than considering the process of decay, hence decaying wood. When we look at managing a process, the emphasis shifts, because this involves an understanding of how things change as they adapt within a natural system.

To create the bridge habitat so desperately needed by some of our rarest flora and fauna, we are going to have to adopt destructive pruning techniques, which will contradict much of our formal training. However, our knowledge of tree biology is going to be essential, because if these methods are going to succeed we need to mimic the natural processes of tree decline, which is a slow, progressional balance.

The term ***veteranisation*** is being used to describe destructive pruning methods, which accelerate the ageing process of trees, by inducing controlled stress. We do not have the knowledge or understanding to duplicate nature, because natural tree decline starts below ground, when the root system becomes exhausted and can no longer support a full crown of leaves. The transportation paths then start to break up and the tree progresses into a stage of retrenchment, like an army in retreat, resources are moved to a more central location.

The selective use of destructive pruning methods that involve natural fracture techniques and coronet cuts, encourages premature retrenchment, by reducing the crown area, while providing niche habitat for decaying wood organisms. his veteranisation of healthy trees is an essential part of the management of arboreal ecosystems, particularly in association with ancient decaying wood habitats where the generation gap is greatest. It can also be used instead of natural target pruning when managing hazardous trees, by reducing the potential for a lever arm to fail, while also retaining more structure within the trees crown.

Veteranisation

Taken from the English Nature publication '*Veteran Trees, A Guide to risk and Responsibility*' a question asked was, "*what is a veteran tree?*' – When a tree trunk is seen in cross section, a series of concentric rings are visible, which comprise of annual increments of new wood. Up to full maturity and under favourable conditions, the cross sectional area of individual rings tend to increase year by year; when this area begins to decrease consistently, the tree is at the veteran stage. This stage can be the longest period in the life of some tree species. A veteran tree is usually old having survived longer in relation to others of the same species.

During the ageing process and through the activity of wood digesting organisms, the tree progressively develops features such as hollowing, decaying wood and water pools. The tree is gradually transformed into a complex of habitats with often unique combinations of niches for many species, established sometimes over many centuries. The natural tendency to lose branches, to hollow and decay may initiate an adaptive growth process in the tree to compensate for potential weaknesses in the wood strength which may appear as a localised deformation i.e. a change in the shape of the trunk or branch.

To provide continuity of specialised saproxylic habitats found only in veteran trees, the concept 'Veteranisation' seeks to replicate over a relatively short period of time the morphological changes that occur during the often considerable life of a veteran tree.

Sustainable conservation

The creation of bridge habitats is a lengthy process, so consideration has to be given to the sustainability of the existing decaying wood, within our ancient arboreal habitats. As we are all aware the slow process of decay can significantly reduce the integral strength of trees, compromising their structural stability, ultimately leading to partial then total collapse. This is a natural progression and would not normally be a problem, but our obsession with the removal of, what has been perceived as, dead wood now means that for many organisms, there may be no where else to go.

Research into the sustainable management of ancient trees has been the focus of the Ancient Tree Forum for over ten years now. A pruning method known as restoration pruning became a recognised system of trying to reinstate lapsed pollards, which had become unstable. This involved the selective reduction work necessary to restore a more uniform and sustainable crown form.

There are some, who would express reservations about the use of the term restoration pruning. This is because it is in principle, a descriptive term for, a method of restoring, reinstating and imposing a physical state on the tree, which we perceive to be desirable with consideration to the management objectives of tree longevity and safety. However, ideas are evolving and a new term has been suggested by Paul Muir, of Treework Environmental Consultancy, that of 'retrenchment pruning', where the idea is to mimic the natural processes, encouraging a progression to a more sustainable structural form which considers the tree's physiological systems.

Summary

The recognition that decaying wood habitat is a dynamic system of processes, which are a constantly evolving part of the arboreal ecosystem, is an important step towards its successful and sustainable management. It is also a demonstration of how the terms we use can influence our perception of the management objectives. Our role as arboricultural managers is one of careful guidance, to encourage and support natural processes, not to impose a physical form or state to fit our ideas of what is right.

We must strengthen our recognition for the fact that trees live within a different time frame to us mere humans. Their living processes are almost the ultimate in sustainability, to a point where, in the right circumstances, they have the capability to attain immortality. A paper was recently published in the Arboricultural Journal '*Environmental arboriculture, tree ecology and veteran tree management*' by Neville Fay, which stresses the management impacts of tree life spans measured in hundreds of years, and in some cases millennia. The implications of this are that the component parts of arboreal ecosystems can undergo cyclic fluctuations, which are measured in centuries.

The knowledge we use to develop tree management strategies, must have a depth of understanding that considers the tree's interrelationship with its environment and other organisms, included within a broad arboreal ecosystem. It is also essential to have an appreciation of the ageing process of trees and be aware that different management methods are needed, which are sustainable in the context of tree longevity.

Conclusion

If sustainable conservation is to work we need to move away from management strategies that concentrate on individual species, and embrace an ecosystem based approach. This is needed, not least, because it would help define some common objectives for the various wildlife conservation organisations. As we are now, each group has it's own goals and it is common knowledge that these conflict and are in many cases counterproductive, often cancelling one another out.

These are not new ideas, and there is an evolution towards ecosystem-based management, with the concepts of ecosystem health and sustainability becoming strategic goals. However, it has taken us decades to get to this stage.

In conclusion it is clear that we need to think more carefully about the far-reaching effects and repercussions of our management decisions. This is hardly a new concept. Aldo Leopold proposed the following metaphor in an essay he wrote in 1949, called 'The Land-Health Concept and Conservation', which was published for the first time in a book called 'For the Health of the Land' in 1999.

The biotic clock may continue ticking if we:
    1 - Cease throwing away the parts.
    2 - Handle it gently.
    3 - Recognise that its importance transcends economics.
    4 - Don't let too many people tinker with it.

References

Alexander, K. (1999) The invertebrates of Britain's wood pastures. *British Wildlife*, **11**, 108-117

Anon, *Veteran Trees, A Guide to risk and Responsibility* English Nature, Peterborough.

Butler, J., Currie, F. and Kirby, K. (2002) There's life in that dead wood – so leave some in your woodland. *Quarterly Journal of Forestry*, **96(2)**, 131-137)

Fay, N. (2002) Environmental arboriculture, tree ecology and veteran tree management. *Arboricultural Journal*, **26(3)**, 213-238.

Humphrey, *et al.* (2002) *Life in the Deadwood – A guide to managing deadwood in the Forestry Commission forests.* Forest Enterprise.

Kirby, P. (2001) *Habitat Management for Invertebrates.* JNCC and RSPB, Sandy, Beds.

Leopold, A. (1949) The Land-Health Concept and Conservation, In (1999) *For the Health of the Land.*

Appendix 1:

Nectar Sources

A large proportion of the decay process is performed by juvenile invertebrates, which survive in the shelter of the decomposing wood, which provides them with all the nutrients they need to develop. However, when they leave the decaying wood as adults, they need a source of nectar to provide them with sufficient energy to fly, mate and disperse the population to the next available decaying wood habitat.

The information below has been taken from a paper, which was published in British Wildlife in December 1999, called *'The invertebrates of Britain's wood pastures'* written by Keith Alexander. In this paper Keith highlights the importance of decaying wood habitat to a diverse range of rare invertebrates, and the need to conserve their ancient habitat.

Nectar provides an energy-rich food, which can rapidly be assimilated and used to fuel flight, and pollen is a protein-rich food, which aids egg production. Flowering trees and shrubs are by far the most important sources, although other plants can also be very popular, notably Hogweed (*Heracleum sphondylium*) and Wild Angelica (*Angelica sylvestris*). Hawthorn (*Crataegus monogyna*) provides the classic insect blossom, partly because it flowers in late spring when so many wood-decay insects are in the adult stage.

Nectar sources are important throughout the year, and the presence of the following species can be particularly beneficial.

Common Name	Scientific Name
Holly	*Ilex aquifolium*
Wild Privet	*Ligustrum vulgare*
Crab Apple	*Mallus sylvestris*
Wild Pear	*Pyrus pyraster*
Rowan	*Sorbus aucuparia*
Bramble	*Rubus fruticosus*
Guelder-rose	*Viburnum opulus*

These are just some of the more obvious species, but even Elder (*Sambucus nigra*), with its poor reputation amongst entomologists, can be important for a select few species. For instance Elder is particularly favoured by the nationally scarce beetle *Aderus oculatus*, which develops in the decaying heart wood of oaks.

Appendix 2:

How much decaying wood and where?

An alliterative phrase adopted and promoted by Ted Green, is 'sustainable, successional, structural, supply of decaying wood', which sums it up neatly, but the implications may not be immediately obvious. However, it is clear that, an arboreal ecosystem needs just that, if it is to support a diversity of organisms, and maintain ecological integrity. It is a description of the level that needs to be achieved if our creation, management and maintenance of decaying wood habitat is going to be anywhere near natural.

It is, however, difficult to accomplish something even near a natural state, when we have no real idea what that might be like, since it infers the absence of human manipulation. We therefore face a challenge where the ultimate goal is unobtainable, so it is important that our aims are based on viable benchmarks. This is exactly what Jill Butler, Fred Currie and Keith Kirby have attempted to do with a paper called *'There's life in that dead wood – so leave some in your woodland'* published in the Quarterly Journal of Forestry, April 2002.

The arboreal ecosystem relies on a sustainable supply of decaying wood, because the process provides a range of habitat types, which are utilised by a large number of different organisms, which are in turn responsible for a particular stage of decomposition. It is therefore an absolute necessity that there is enough decaying wood around to provide the range of conditions needed to support these organisms.

To achieve a sustainable supply of decaying wood, with out the necessity to keep importing new material to a site, we have to encourage a successional ecosystem. It is fundamental part of managing decaying wood habitat, that there is the diversity of niches, available at any one time, to support the full range of organisms associated with decaying wood.

Finally, we have to appreciate that arboreal ecosystems have multiple levels, and the creation, management or maintenance of this habitat needs to work in a structural way. It is not sufficient to have a sustainable, successional, supply of decaying wood on the ground, in piles of logs or brash wood. There needs to be decaying wood in all of the following places:
- dead limbs on living trees;
- decay columns in trunks and main branches;
- rot holes in standing trees;
- sap runs from decaying cavities or recent wounds;

- dead bark on standing trees;
- standing dead trees;
- fallen trunks and large branches;
- fallen small branches and twigs;
- dead tree stumps and old coppice stools;
- exposed root plates of wind blown trees;
- decaying wood in water courses.

It is important to have all of the above in a diversity of locations, and conditions, in full sun, dense shade and various stages in between. Therefore our management goal is a Sustainable, Successional, Structural, Supply of Decaying Wood.

'*To stand in them is to feel the past*': Pinewoods and Birchwoods in the Scottish Uplands.
Chris Smout

"To stand in them is to feel the past."

These words in the introduction of Steven and Carlisle's milestone book of 1959 expressed the emotion that people have felt for generations about the great woods of Caledonian pine. Some 16,000 hectares remain, located in fewer than one hundred woods across the Scottish Highlands. This is sometimes said to represent one percent of the former extent, but such figures are meaningless, as they relate to woodland cover 5,000 years ago in totally different climatic conditions. We have little idea how much remained 400 years ago, before the Highlands were opened up in the modern sense, but it is very unlikely to have been even more than twice as much as we have at present. Within historic time a small number of Scottish pinewoods believed once to have been extensive have either vanished or been reduced to insignificant remnants – probably fewer than fifteen, and in some of those no human exploitation was ever recorded. A number of others have much declined in scale. Most of those that have disappeared are on the west coast or, if on the east coast, at high altitude, and it appears likely that their decline was due as much to climatic problems in the Little Ice Age as it was to economic exploitation. Felling episodes, which in the drier east would have been of little long-term significance, in the west were apparently often not followed by successful regeneration.

Twentieth-century foresters were kinder to pine than to other native trees, though all these things are relative. Steven and Carlisle's book was probably the first serious attempt to describe the ecological conservation value of any native forest-type in the UK, and to call for its protection. At about the same time, he was complaining that the work of clearing what he called 'birch scrub' was only half completed in Scotland: the Highlands were to lose about forty percent of their natural birchwoods in the next thirty years, largely to forestry. Similarly, sessile oak was regarded as a useless scrub even in locations like Loch Lomond and the Trossachs. The Scottish head of the Forestry Commission in 1944 complained that if a Nature Conservancy was created, it would 'sterilise' thousands of acres currently under oak.

But to a certain extent, Scots pine has always been regarded in a special light. The Forestry Commission itself established, at Glen Loy in the 1930s, what it called a forest reserve, though it soon forgot about it. Today, just about every fragment of Caledonian pinewood of any extent has been declared a Special Area of Conservation. Although in the 1960s, 1970s and 1980s, the Forestry Commission engaged busily in planting up some of the very finest of the ancient Scots pinewoods, as at Glen Affric, Glen More and Glengarry, with Sitka spruce. When policy changed in the 1990s, they became amongst the very first PAWS (Planted Ancient Woodland Site) to be restored, often at some expense, always with great energy, and apparently, so far, with some success. Private foresters were sometimes more protective still – as at Rothiemurchus – sometimes much less so. It was a proposal by Fountain Forestry largely to replace Abernethy with Sitka spruce and Lodgepole that led to the purchase of the wood by the RSPB, grant-aided by the NCC who gave the charity so much money that it had to be approved in cabinet.

In their original state – or at least as they were when they first became described in the eighteenth century – they were very much mixed woods of birch and pine, often mixed also with a certain amount of oak, hazel and aspen. As one eighteenth-century commentator explained, we call them pine woods or oak woods, bur what we really mean are woods predominantly of one or the other, because in reality the trees grow mixed together. Of the surviving woods, in some ways Glen Affric is the most natural, with a high percentage of birch, and birch and oak can be found freely growing with the pine in adjacent Glen Strathfarrar. Over time, some have tended towards less birch because of generations of foresters who have weeded it out – this was the policy at Abernethy. Alternatively, where heavy felling of pine was not followed by regeneration, birch sometimes took over almost completely, as at Glen Einig off Strath Oykell.

The Caledonian pinewoods are, in contrast to most Continental forests of *Pinus silvestris*, often open in structure with their distinctive, spreading granny pines, which give them great visual appeal. The trees can grow to be 3-500 years old, and the greatest of them had vernacular names: 'The Queen of the Forest', 'Lady Macdonald's tree', and so on. Nevertheless, Scots pine in Scotland can also grow as straight and trim and close as anywhere, even by natural regeneration, as was often noted on Speyside in the nineteenth century. The ground flora and fauna is highly distinctive, and includes a plethora of red data species. Some of them do very badly, plants like *Linnea borealis* which find it hard to set seed or to spread, and birds like the Capercaillie, which became extinct once in the 1770s and was the object of the first-ever reintroduction scheme in the 1830s, and now seems to be on the way out again despite the expenditure of a great deal of care and cash on its preservation. Species on the edge of their range are likely to be vulnerable.

"Our Highland woods shift their stances" was one eighteenth-century way of expressing the fact that neither pine nor birch regenerate easily in their own shade, nor do they coppice well – pine not at all, and birch not readily. They could not therefore be protected by simply putting a fence or a wall around them; maintained in the same spot like an English or a Scottish Lowland oakwood. Ideally they needed space at their margins on which to set seed, and they were threatened by fields being created up to their edges, or by heavy grazing on the moor next to them. Despite this, they were used as wood pasture on a seasonal basis certainly until the nineteenth century, usually for over-wintering cattle, horses and sheep though some held summer stock as well. When the main animal was Highland cattle, there was a certain benefit from breaking the mossy crust and pressing the seed into the ground, analogous to what one often sees in a modern pinewood where the best regeneration (sometimes the only regeneration) is by a path disturbed by machinery. In the nineteenth and twentieth centuries sheep and deer replaced cattle and horses, though a still nastier beast, the goat, which had once been common, was now excluded. Sheep, even if just confined to the moor, eat everything close to the ground and certainly prevent a wood from shifting its stance. Deer were sometimes enclosed *within* the wood, and this stopped regeneration in its tracks. Both sheep and deer are very much more numerous than they used to be historically. Red deer have multiplied about three times since the start of the twentieth century and perhaps by six times since the start of the nineteenth. The observation that "Our Highland woods shift their stances" is therefore not as true as it used to be, and historically it seems to be the case that the great pine forests like Abernethy or Rothiemurchus sit within much the same bounds as ever they did. Within those bounds, woods get cleared at one period, or a fire occurs or there is windblow, and an open space appears which, if grazing is not too heavy, fills up with new seed in time. With birch, however, it does seem to be the case that where trees were marked on Roy's map of the 1750s they are often on a slightly different spot today, having moved down the brae or to another location on the moor. This has some implications for the restoration of PAWS on old birchwood sites – it may be as useful to enclose an area of moor next to a Sitka plantation as to cut out the Sitka plantation itself. On Deeside it has been shown that there is a 'natural' alternation between forestry conifers and birch, which springs up immediately the conifers are felled and persists until they are shaded out by replanting.

The earliest records for the management of the Caledonian pine woods come from the seventeenth century, and suggest a relatively laissez-faire attitude, sometimes with modest regulation of grazing and prohibitions on the cutting of 'greenwood' but not much else. The owners of the pinewoods did, however, live in mortal danger of fire, and came down like a ton of bricks on any who caused it. At Abernethy in the 1690s, several children aged eleven or under who accidentally allowed muirburn to get out of control so that it spread to the forest, were charged before the Barony Court and sentenced to have their ears nailed to the gallows.

Fire, though, like grazing, can be good or bad. Some parts of Speyside have still not recovered from dreadful deep-burning fires of the post-Second World War period, and fifty years later present aspects of blackened heath by the A9. One part of Rothiemurchus is just showing recovery now from a similar event. On the other hand, at Glentanar fires are deliberately being set and carefully controlled to help grow a better ground flora for Capercaillie, and historically there are many instances of fire, like clearfell, being followed by dense pine regeneration. But I suppose if you were the Earl of Seafield and relying on a nice crop of 150-year old pines to help with the next rebuilding of Castle Grant, the sight of them going up in smoke due to the incompetence of kids would incline you to rage.

Exploitation of the Caledonian pinewoods was age-old, and left significant archaeological traces at its later stages in the form of embankments, weirs, sites of sawmills and floating canals. At Abernethy there are also traces of an iron-works, probably utilising the birch rather than the pine. The woods were always populous places, with clearings and small farms – in Rothiemurchus there are also prehistoric hut circles, and traces of prehistoric fields at Loch Garten, certainly not the dense and pristine wilderness of some popular fancy. The degree of exploitation and its intensity varied over time, but until the eighteenth century it was almost exclusively for local markets within, say, a radius of twenty-five miles. In the seventeenth century the inhabitants of a Speyside parish were said to "live by the wood, which keeps them all poor", presumably meaning they peddled wood produce round the countryside instead of being respectable farmers. There was a trade on ponyback from Glentanar into the Lowlands, and from Strathcarron into the Dingwall area, and from the Spey to Inverness, in deals, poles, battens, oars and so-on. 'Candle-fir' was a speciality of the Caledonian pinewoods, being splints rich in resin that burnt with a bright light to illuminate cottage homes. Peasants from the Black Wood of Rannoch were said to supply half of Perthshire with it. It damaged the timber to cut out the candle-fir from living trees, of course, and was a common occasion for prosecution before the Baron Courts.

The local market usually remained the main market, for the simple reason that most Scottish pinewoods were relatively inaccessible to the outside world, and for most Scottish consumers it was altogether cheaper and more practicable to bring building softwoods from Scandinavia. Norway was in practice as close as the Moray Firth, two days in sailing time from the Firth of Forth, and Scottish ships could tie up 'at the woods' in the Stavanger area and be assured of an excellent and efficiently delivered supply of first-rate pine: all the little burghs of the Lowlands were built using Norway pine or spruce, and when the great rebuilding of Edinburgh took place in the eighteenth century much of the wood came from the Baltic.

There were, however, certain exceptions to this rule. From time to time the Royal Navy had fantasies that it could supply itself from His Majesty's Dominions in Scotland instead of having to rely on untrustworthy foreigners, most determinedly so in the seventeenth century when the woods of Strathcarron were utilised by Pepys' navy at

Deptford – or would have been, had the timber not proved of such bad quality as to be hardly worth extracting. Pepys thought he might buy a cargo speculatively to sell for the rebuilding of London in the aftermath of the Great Fire, but nothing came of it, though the owner of Strathcarron did sell some for the reconstruction of Holyrood Palace. Another potential market for the west coast woods was in Ireland, where a good deal of pine was sold for building timber and masts from the now vanished woods of Glencoe, and from Glen Orchy and Loch Lhinnie where only vestigial woods remain. In Glen Orchy the Irishmen agreed to fell no trees under twenty-four inches at breast height, but when the work was completed it was found that they had felled every tree in some woods, because there had been none of the smaller size. Here, although the Irish were roundly blamed for the ensuing devastation, it is easy to see that a failure to regenerate, either through climate change or overgrazing, lay at the root of the problem.

War otherwise provided outsiders and, indeed, insiders, with their greatest opportunity to make money by cutting down the Caledonian pinewoods, as it either cut off Scandinavian supplies completely or made them inordinately expensive. Several times in the eighteenth century, English speculators were attracted to the woods in the expectation of making a quick buck, but they were normally foiled by a combination of the difficult terrain and the return of peace. One venture that did succeed was the felling of Glen More by a Hull-based shipbuilding enterprise that floated the wood down the Spey to its yards at Speymouth: even a Royal Navy frigate, named the *Glen More*, was built from this timber at the close of the eighteenth century.

It was the Napoleonic Wars, beginning in 1793, and their aftermath, which saw heavy duties placed on Scandinavian timber, lasting until around 1840, which also witnessed by far the heaviest phase of exploitation. The local lairds themselves, rather than outside entrepreneurs, now led the way, allegedly making in some cases up to £20,000 a year in timber sales – a truly vast sum for its period. By the 1830s, Glen More, Rothiemurchus and all the big woods on Deeside were virtually flattened and floated down to the sea, and the Red Squirrel and the Great Spotted Woodpecker became practically extinct. The Red Squirrel was reintroduced and became a major woodland pest in the twentieth century before becoming an object of conservation concern and the woodpecker made its own way back. One would think this was disaster, but clearfell only mimics a refreshing fire, grazing pressure was kept within acceptable limits, and the woods all recovered naturally at Rothiemurchus, only to be clearfelled a second time before Victoria's reign was half done, and then to recover fully a second time. So these great woods are still with us, outwardly as pristine as ever.

The moral, I think, was clear: even heavy exploitation of the pinewoods did not damage them in any basic way, providing the ecological processes necessary for their regeneration could function. Their true enemy was not a mad axeman but, in the west, climate change that made (and makes) it hard for seedlings to push up through the peat and moss, and, everywhere, the teeth of sheep and deer that nip off the seedlings before they have time to spring. Their third enemy, modern forestry that preferred the material returns from a Sitka spruce to the largely immaterial ones of old Caledonian pine, is no longer a direct threat, as the conservation tide has turned to protect them.

Finally, I have just to comment that although the ecological and aesthetic characteristics and value of the old woods are well understood, I do not think this is anything like as true of their archaeological characteristics and their social history. We have much further to go in seeing them not only as the remnants of a splendid wilderness, but also as containing the reminders of a busy workplace.

Just to take Speyside, there is an engrossing story to be told of the 'floaters', the men who took the wood down the river, initially attending it from wickerwork, skin-covered coracles, then in rafts of logs bound together, the latter functioning as little boats transporting butter, oak bark, skins and other upland produce for the Lowland market. There was irreconcilable conflict with the Duke of Gordon's salmon cruives (fishing traps), which in the eighteenth century led to expensive lawsuits and finally a compromise between the different interests on the river, so that floating was delayed in the year until the salmon had run – but this added such costs to an already shaky trade that the exploitation of Rothiemurchus (at least) was halted for a generation. There is a story to be told of the attempts to make water pipes for the London market by constructing boring mills at Rothiemurchus and Abernethy to hollow out the logs: they were floated down to Speymouth, too, but failed in the long term to compete with English elm. There were heroic efforts to blast away obstructions on the rivers, sometimes successful, as on the Spey, despite the protests and harassment by local people near the worst rock, who had previously made a small income from helping to get the logs around it. Sometimes they were not successful, as at Rhidderoch in Wester Ross, where the huge boulder of granite planned to be blown up in 1720 still churns the river there into an inferno of white water. Because of this, the wood turned out to be practically valueless and became a sheep pasture, while the valuable woods of Rothiemurchus and Abernethy were survivors despite their cutting. Finally, there is a story to be told about the revolution in organising how the woods were felled and processed in Speyside and Deeside. Originally the small tenants basically did their own thing, selecting trees in the forest and taking them locally to those who would mill them, and either float the logs or take the lighter wood produce by horseback to market. It became, *ca.*1810, a much more centralised system, where the laird of Rothiemurchus, for instance, organised the labour almost on an industrial scale, and replaced the many small mills with one bigger one, applying new technology, such as a circular saw to cut what had been valueless birch wood into useful staves for herring barrels. The family also planned to divide the wood into rotational sections (or 'haggs') and cut them in turn. These were good, sensible, sustainable decisions, but greed, impatience and shortage of ready cash to pay their many creditors scuppered the good intentions, and the family fled one night to India without even paying their miserable workers the back-pay owed to them. The result was an economic catastrophe for the district, and when one of the daughters of the family returned twenty years later she said the local people were much worse off than those on her husband's Irish estate. Woods do have economic and social histories as well as ecological ones, and when there is a good archive there are often remarkable opportunities for local historians and archaeologists to uncover this human aspect of their past.

References
Steven, H.M. and Carlisle, A. (1959) *The Native Pinewoods of Scotland*. Oliver & Boyd, Edinburgh.

Woodland Transport: the evidence for Derbyshire and the West Riding of Yorkshire

David Hey
University of Sheffield

Introduction

The evidence for transport within the woods of this district, both on the ground and in documents, relates mainly to the activities of the men who made charcoal for the ironmasters, white coal for the lead smelters and pit props for the coal miners. Few of the local woods are intersected by highways, for most of them lie on steeply-sloping ground at the edges of parishes and manors or are medieval deer parks that were converted to springwoods at the end of the middle ages.

Holloways

It is common to find short stretches of holloways leading to, or within, a wood, but the other visual evidence of the improvements to the transport system in the seventeenth and eighteenth centuries - guide stoops, packhorse bridges, causeys - are absent. Unlike the holloways on the moors, which were dug out to facilitate the movement of millstones, the woodland holloways appear to have been created by wear and tear. The depth of the holloways suggests that wheeled vehicles rather than packhorses were responsible.

Figure 1. Ancient Holloway in North Derbyshire

Figure 2. Burdett's Map of Derbyshire (detail) 1791

Methods of Transport

Documentary evidence shows that packhorses were used to transport charcoal from the woods to the furnaces and to move lead ore from the mines to the smelting mills near the woods. The platforms of the charcoal burners and the pits where white coal was produced for the lead smelters are often still evident. There is a great deal of documentary evidence to show that wheeled vehicles were used, both in the middle ages and in the early modern period, to move smelted lead to the inland ports and pig iron from the furnaces. These vehicles were often small, two-wheeled wains, though the sturdier cart was also used. The medieval bridges across the local rivers demonstrate the widespread use of wheeled vehicles, drawn by oxen or horses.

Development of Local Industry

The evidence for the transport system in and to the woods - and indeed the whole history of the management of the local woods - needs to be considered in the context of the development of local industries. From the 1570s the Derbyshire lead industry recovered

Figure 3. Thomas Jeffrey's Map of Yorkshire (detail) 1772

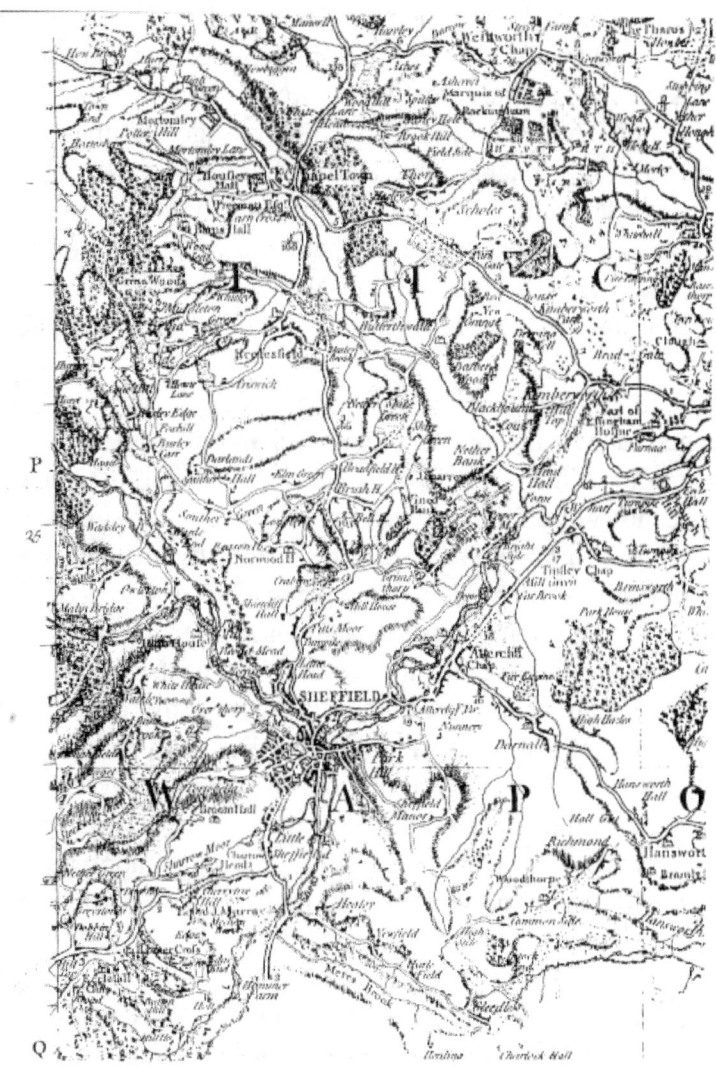

from a long period of stagnation to become the European leader. In 1614 it was claimed that twenty times as many miners were working within the county than fifty years previously. Improved smelting technology and expensive schemes to drain the mines yielded rich dividends. The new water-powered smelting furnaces were fired by white coal, that is small chopped wood that had been dried in a pit or kiln to a lower temperature than that required for the making of charcoal. The new smelting mills were sited in the wooded river valleys to the east of the river Derwent and west of a line drawn from Sheffield to Chesterfield. All the deciduous woods in this area contain small, Q-shaped pits where the white coal was prepared. This method was used for about 200 years until it was replaced by the coke-fired cupola or reverberatory furnace.

Surviving leases for some of these woods can be linked to the evidence of the whitecoal pits. Early leases do not mention them and make only brief references to transport. A lease of Linacre woods in 1513, for example, speaks only of free entry with 'all manner of cariage'. When the same woods were leased in 1596, however, the terms were specified in detail. The lessee was given free passage: 'to and from the said woode unto the over lead milne at Linacre ... withe horse Carte and other Cariages to leade drye beare and carie awaye the said woode, withe franke and free libertie to digg delve and make pittes and kylnes for white Coale and Charcoale withe sufficyant turffe braken and hillinge ... for the necessarie Coalinge of the said woode'. The lease gives details of the route to the lead mill and an alternative passage 'when Barnabie lane is fowle and not made sufficyent'.

The same period was the hey-day of the charcoal iron industry. Charcoal blast furnaces were introduced into the district in the 1570s and 1580s, and until the middle of the eighteenth century the industry was organised through a complicated system of gentry partnerships. The furnaces were sited alongside streams and woods within a mile or so of the ironstone pits. They produced on average 300-400 tons of pig iron per annum and required 1,000 to 1,2000 horse loads of charcoal a year. Two-thirds of this fuel came from within a five-mile radius, but for the rest the ironmasters had to go up to 15 miles away, even on to the magnesian limestone belt beyond the coal-measure sandstones. Between 1699 and 1705 Rockley furnace was supplied with charcoal from 43 different places, mainly from a north-easterly direction. Wheeled vehicles were also used. In 1595, for instance, the Earl of Shrewsbury's steward wrote of the need for more oxen to carry ironstone and charcoal, and in 1683 eight men paid a landowner for passes for the: 'carying of Charckcole ... with our waines & Carts from Cawthorne Parke' to the furnace at Rockley.

Many of the local woods contain evidence of former coal mining and holloways leading to small pits and the minor place-names recorded in leases can often be identified. Some woods were not felled for over 30 years to allow the trees to grow to sufficient thickness for use as pit props or 'punch wood'. Thus, in 1637: 'a Spring wood called Cooke wood wherein they get Punch wood for the use of the Coale pits', was divided into sections: 'some parts thereof is above 32 yeares growth and some part newly Cut downe and every yeare Cut as occasion serveth'.

Most carriage was undertaken in summer months, when the going was relatively firm. In 1534 Master Fitzherbert (a Derbyshire man) wrote in The Book of Husbandry: 'And in May, whan thou hast falowed thy grounde, and set oute thy shepefoulde, and caryed oute thy dounge or mucke, if thou have any wodde, cole, or tymbre to cary, or suche other busynes, that must nedes be doone, with thy charte or wayne, than is it tyme

Figure 4. Map showing industrial and processing sites across the region

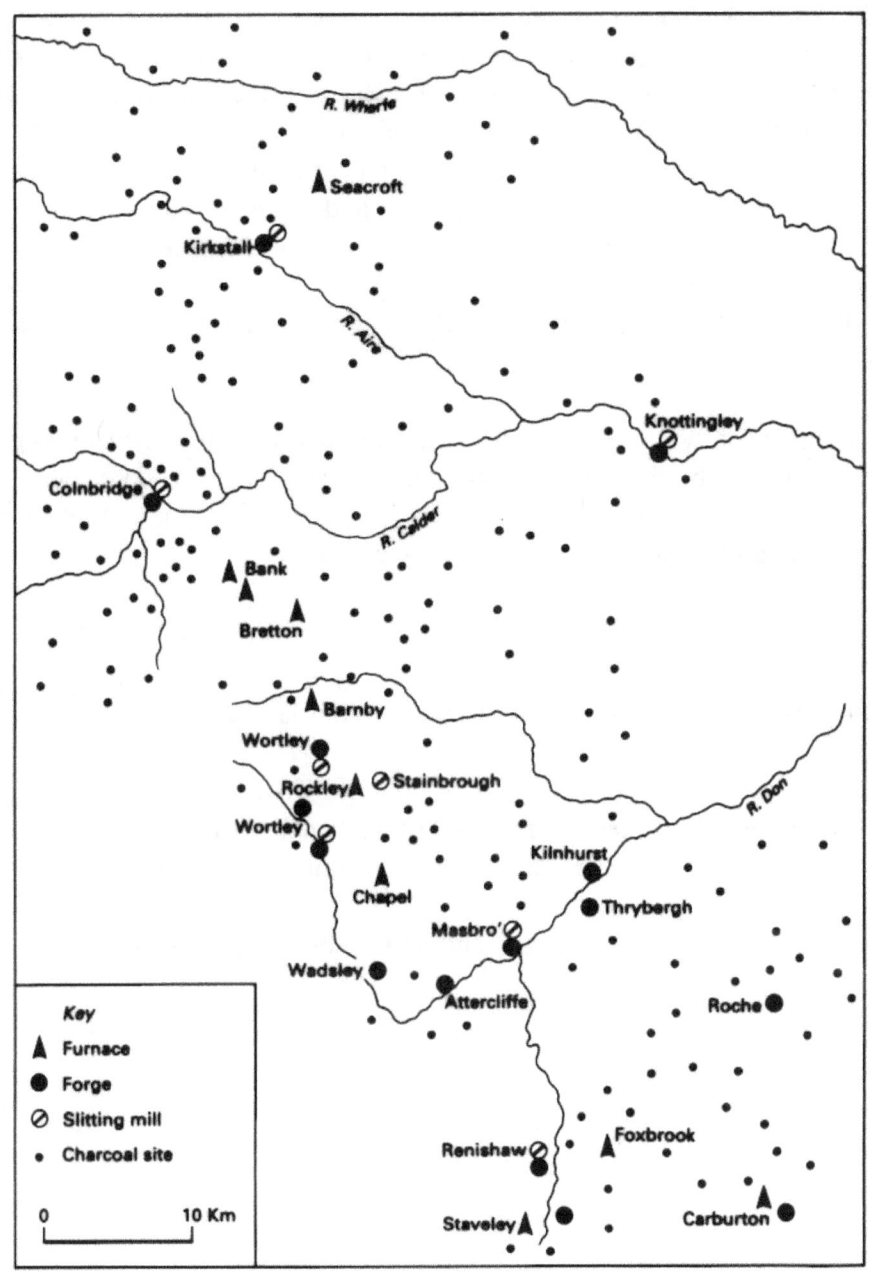

to do it. For than the waye is lyke to be fayre and drye, and the days longe, and that tyme the husbande hath leste to doo in husbandry.'

Local farmers were free between the hay and corn harvests to carry loads, using their draught animals and equipment, but other men obtained regular employment as carriers. In 1586, for example, the lessee of the Barlow smelting mill was given free passage through the woods for his: 'servants workmen cariers and jaggers with horses oxen waynes carts and cariedges ... for bringing and carieing of lead ore'. Another lease of Linacre woods in 1683 granted free passage 'in and on the usuall wayes to and from the said woodland ground commonly in the time of cutting and felling thereof to and for them their servants, workmen, Agents, Draughts, Oxen, Horses, Waines carts and carriages to fell cut cole and carry away all the said wood, Whitecole, Charcole, Barke and rammell'.

The documentary evidence provides the context for an understanding of the holloways and pits in the local woods, but we are rarely able to date these features precisely. The deepest holloways are not necessarily the oldest; they might have been formed during a relatively short period of intense activity.

References

Hey, D.G. (1979) *The Making of South Yorkshire*. Moorland Publishing Company Ltd. Ashbourne.

Hey, D.G. (2001) *Packmen, Carriers and Packhorse Roads: Trade and Communications in North Derbyshire and South Yorkshire*. Landmark Publishing. Ashbourne.

Hey, D.G. (2002) *Historic Hallamshire*. Landmark Publishing. Ashbourne.

Oak, the footmark of ghosts
Frans Vera

It is a generally accepted theory that in the natural state, that is if there had been no human intervention, the lowlands of Central and Western Europe, with their temperate climate, would have been covered with a closed canopy forest in places where trees can grow.

This theory is at first based on the observation that after people withdrew from arable fields, pastures and wood-pastures, these changed spontaneously into a closed canopy forest. The forest that developed without cattle and horse was considered to be the natural vegetation, because cattle and horse were considered as alien species introduced by humans. The effects of fencing parts of forests grazed by livestock where there is prolific regeneration of trees is said to prove the threat of large ungulates to the regeneration of trees and therefore of forests.

Secondly, this theory is based on the interpretation of historical sources. These concern the regulations from the beginning of the Middle Ages onwards for cattle grazing in the last forest wildernesses in the lowlands of Europe. These regulations are supposed to aim to protect the regeneration of the trees in the forest. They are therefore interpreted as proof of how people in the Middle Ages took measures to preserve the originally present forests. The fact that these regulations concerned forest is based on the observation that abandoned fields and pastures where livestock are removed develop spontaneously towards closed canopy forests.

Pollen studies are said to confirm that the natural vegetation was a closed canopy forest, because up to 90% of the pollen originates from forest trees and shrubs. According to the pollen the forest consisted of species like oak *Quercus robur* and *Q. petraea*, small-leaved lime *Tilia cordata* and broad-leaved lime *T. platyphyllos*, elm *Ulmus spp.*, ash *Fraxinus excelsior*, beech *Fagus sylvatica* and hornbeam *Carpinus betulus* with a shrub layer which included hazel *Coryluas avellana*. From forestry the palaeoecologists were familiar with the potential threat of ungulates for the regeneration of trees in forests as mentioned. Therefore, they concluded that the original fauna of large herbivores must have lived in very low densities in the primeval forest. Otherwise, the natural vegetation could not have been a closed canopy forest.

Forest reserves in the lowlands of Central and Western Europe are supposed to develop as modern analogues of this vegetation. Oak and hazel are also very well represented in pollen diagrams dating from the period in the Holocene (Flandrian) when the vegetation was supposedly undisturbed by man. However, light-demanding pedunculate oak and sessile oak hardly regenerate successfully or do not do so at all in these reserves. Shade tolerant species like beech *Fagus sylvaticus*, broad-leaved lime *Tilia platyphyllos* and small-leaved lime *Tilia cordata*, elm species *Ulmus* spp. and hornbeam *Carpinus betulus* replace them.

Many of these forest reserves are former wood-pastures; park-like landscapes grazed by the true grazers among livestock, namely horse, cattle and sheep. They consisted of a mosaic of grassland, scrub and thickets, solitary trees and trees grouped together (groves). Grazing livestock made forests increasingly open and changed (degraded) them into a park-like landscape, so-called wood-pastures. Finally, these park-like landscapes were supposed to change into grassland and heathland because of retrogressive succession. Therefore, wood-pastures are considered human artefacts. When the reserves were established, cattle, horse and sheep were removed, because they were considered as alien species, introduced by people.

In wood pastures however, both species of oak regenerate successfully in the presence of the shade tolerant species that push them aside in forest reserves. All tree species regenerate in open grassland grazed by true grazers like cattle and horse when they are within or near to thorny or spiny shrub species like sloe *Prunus spinosa*, hawthorn *Crateagus monogyna*, juniper *Juniperus communis* and bramble *Rubus* spp. Like oak, these shrub species are light demanding. The thorny scrub acts as barbed wire protecting the young trees against the browsing and trampling of the large ungulates.

In this landscape the oak is very well represented because of the activity of the jay *Garrullus glandarius*. Jays collect acorns of pedunculate and sessile oaks and bury them at some distance from the tree where they collect the acorns. This distance varies from a few metres to several kilometres. The jay has a preference for a transitional area of short to long grass or brushwood (the periphery of fields), the outer edge of hedges and the fringes of thorny scrub of blackthorn, or at the base of the stem of a thorny shrub like hawthorn, and thorny mantle vegetation of forests. These structures develop when there is grazing by bulk grazers like cattle and horse in wood pastures. The large number of pedunculate and sessile oak seedlings which grow in open grasslands, abandoned fields, roadside verges, the periphery of hedges and fringes of scrub and forest mantle at a great distance from the old fertile oaks show how oak benefits from the jay.

Clonal growth of shrub species in wood-pastures, such as that of blackthorn, results in an ever-spreading group of trees, forming a grove, commonly called woodland or forest. Species that lack vegetative reproduction like hawthorn will mostly protect a single tree. Because of the activities of the jay this is often an oak. A single hawthorn can therefore result in an open grown solitary oak tree and many hawthorns in a savannah-like landscape. Within the grove trampling and browsing of the animals prevent the regeneration of all tree species. Therefore, shade-tolerant tree species cannot regenerate under the canopy of oak and out compete it. Because the large herbivores prevent the regeneration of all trees within the grove, the grove becomes eventually more open and changes ultimately into open grassland by the so-called retrogressive succession. "Catastrophes" such as drought, and storms can accelerate this change. In the open grassland eventually thorny or spiny species establish themselves in which trees grow up successfully.

Summarised, in wood–pastures the vegetation follows a cyclical process of grassland → scrub → grove (or single tree or savannah) → grassland. This is a non-linear succession steered by large grazing ungulates. This process results in a dynamic park-like landscape consisting of various biotopes that are permanently present but all the time at different places. Contrary to the common beliefs on wood-pastures, trees regenerate very well in the presence of large ungulates, especially oak. The trees regenerate outside the grove (forest) in open grassland grazed by bulk grazers like cattle and horse. Considering this, it is concluded that oak in wood-pastures tell us something about processes in the past. The question then raised is whether the wood-pasture is a modern analogue of a bygone landscape?

The wood-pasture can be traced back in history by means of regulations of the use of the uncultivated wilderness. These regulations are known from the seventh century onwards. Merovingian and Frankish kings declared the uncultivated wilderness as "*forestis nostra*" (our "*forestis*"). "*Forestis*" was a legal concept that described or confirmed the royal rights concerning the ownership and the right to use. Over many centuries the word "*forestis*" evolved in German to "*Forst*", in French to "*forêt*", in English to "*Forest*" and in Dutch to "*foreest*", "*forest*", "*voorts*" and "*vorst*". The "*forestis*" (the uncultivated wilderness) was called in common language in German "*Wald*", "*wold*" and "*weld*", in Dutch "*wold*", "*wald*" and "*woud*" and in Anglo-Saxon "*weald*". The king passed the administration and management of the "*forestis*" to officials he appointed, so-called "*forestarii*". They regulated use like cutting firewood, grubbing up timber, pasturing cattle and pannaging pigs. They dealt with this use as well as with the infringements of the regulations in a legal forum, a court, in accordance with the "*ius forestis*", "*iura forestarorium*" or the "*ius nemoris*" (literal translated: forest law; not to be confused with the Forest Law issued in England in 1066 by William the Conqueror). Analysis of the meaning in the context of the regulations show that the terms "*Forst*", "*foreest*", "*forêt*", "*wold*", "*woud*", "*weld*" "*Wald*" and "*weald*" did not imply a solid cover of trees. They implied the uncultivated "outside", the wilderness that consisted of a park-like landscape like the wood-pasture.

If the wood-pasture is a proxy wilderness then livestock in wood pastures can be proxies of the indigenous bulk grazers, namely aurochs *Bos primigenius* and tarpan *Equus przewalski gmelini*. Cattle and horse are domesticated forms of these indigenous species. They have the same feeding strategy and can therefore be considered as modern analogues of their wild ancestors. These wild ancestors lived in the Holocene up to the Middle Ages in the European uncultivated "outside", the wilderness. They did so with other wild ungulate species of the indigenous fauna, namely European bison *Bison bonasus*, red deer *Cervus elaphus*, elk *Alces alces*, roe deer *Capreolus capreolus*, and wild boar *Sus scrofa*.

In former wood pastures livestock like cattle lived more or less like wild fauna; that is roaming freely. According to the old regulations the density of the domestic animals in wood pastures was not beyond the carrying capacity of the parts of the wilderness they grazed. Therefore, the food supply regulated the number of livestock likewise it did with the number of wild ungulates. At the highest level the number of animals was at saturation density. The regeneration of oak both in the wood-pasture and primeval vegetation implies that the densities of the wild large bulk grazers must have been analogues to that of their domestic descendants in wood-pastures.

If the primeval vegetation was a park-like landscape, it must be responsible for the low percentage of ten percent of Non Arboreal Pollen (NAP) in the pollen-diagrams originating from this vegetation. This low percentage can be explained as follows. Firstly, the mantle vegetation in wood-pasture prevented the horizontal movement of pollen from grasses and herbs by wind to raised bogs further on, where pollen samples have been taken. Secondly, large herbivores that graze the grass in park-like landscapes, at least partially prevent the grass from flowering and therefore from producing pollen. This means an inverse relationship between the densities of large grazing ungulates and the percentage NAP. At third, trees reach high into the air and flower abundantly, producing much pollen. These can be picked up by air currents and transported over tens of kilometres to raised bogs from which pollen diagrams are derived. The result is a bias in sampling places towards tree pollen. The accumulated effect of all these factors can explain the very low percentage of pollen of grasses and herbs. Added to this, modern pollen analyses of wood-pastures show that the percentage of non-arboreal pollen (NAP) is an unreliable measure for the openness of the landscape. Very open areas give pollens-spectra that are commonly interpreted as being descended from closed canopy forests.

Summarised: oak and other tree species in wood pastures protected by shrubs and thickets armed with thorns and spines against browsing by large herbivores tell us about processes and landscapes in the past. Closed canopy forest reserves without grazing cattle and horse are not modern analogues of the primeval vegetation. They are recent anachronisms.

Oak is also very well represented in pollen diagrams from interglacials from before the Holocene like the Eemian (Ipswichian) and Holstein (Hoxnian). These pollen diagrams are also commonly interpreted as originating from a closed canopy forest as well. These interglacials are characterised by a fauna not only consisting of the species present in the Holocene. The fauna also consisted of elephant *Palaeoloxodon antiquus*, rhinoceros *Dicerorhinus kirchbergensis*, hippopotamus *Hippopotamus aniquus* and giant deer *Megaloceros gigantheus*. Therefore, oak may be the foodmark of a menagerie of ungulate ghosts whose heritage is a diversity of trees, shrubs, grasses and herbs that we nowadays try to preserve.

References
Vera, F.W.M. (2000) *Grazing Ecology and Forest History.* CAB International. Wallingford.

Bringing the Ghost to Life: woodland ecology and landscape history
John Rodwell

The National Vegetation Classification (Rodwell, 1991) provides a sound scientific methodology for describing the woodland vegetation of the UK and understanding how the composition and distribution of different woodland types and their replacement plant communities relate to variations in climatic, terrain and biotic factors. The NVC is now widely accepted as a standard by all UK wildlife, forestry and agriculture agencies, local government, corporate industry, utilities, wildlife NGOs and environmental consultancies, providing a common language for describing, mapping and assessing the extent, quality and value of existing woodland resources. Further extensive woodland sampling since the NVC, much of it in conjunction with Ancient Woodland Inventories, has provided a detailed national overview of the survival of this country's semi-natural woodlands (Kirby & Hall, 1998) and many individual sites have been surveyed and described in compatible style.

In fact, though climatic conditions varied even in historical time and the patterns of earlier woodland management were often very different to those familiar today, it is possible to use the NVC in a predictive fashion to develop past scenarios that can greatly inform landscape history and our understanding of the roles that woodlands played in local and regional economies in former times. In the lower Dearne Valley in South Yorkshire, for example, we can sketch the patterns and processes of past woodlands and their semi-natural replacement communities on the Coal Measure grits and shales and flood-plain alluvium that form the basis of the landscape there. Such knowledge can then be used as a backdrop to appreciate the dynamics and limitations of the agricultural use of the waste, ploughland and meadow, as well as woodland remnants, in the pre-enclosure period (Harvey, 1974; Rodwell, unpublished).

Even without such extensive modelling, it is possible to incorporate historical resonances into woodland surveys so as to give depth to an understanding of their existing heritage of biodiversity and landscapes. Such an ecological historical perspective can also inform projections for future landscapes and develop a richly-embedded sense of community ownership in restoration programmes. For example, the Outwood Project *'Bringing the Ghost to Life'* in Wakefield MDC (Rodwell, Wildsmith & Cartwright,1999), is using the local Manor Court Rolls, place-names and landscape history to help local schools and community groups understand the past and present woodland scene and the diverse medieval economies that were based upon the timber, mineral and agricultural resources of the local landscape. Theatre, photography and arts projects, reminiscence therapy and an electronic forest – the Virtual Outwood – are among the project ideas being developed in this suburban part of West Yorkshire.

Such approaches can be applied on a variety of scales. Modelling potential vegetation cover across the whole of West Yorkshire, for example, and in more detail across the Wakefield Metropolitan District Council area, is helping develop a woodland strategy for the REACT programme of post-coalfield restoration in the area that is sensitive to the historical heritage (Handley, 2003; Rodwell, 2003). This project also provides an example of the way in which a county-wide plant species computer database (Lavin & Wilmore, 1994) can be used to model the coincidental survival of woodland trees, shrubs and herbs often widely dispersed in landscapes that are now often devoid of any kind of woodland. This can help scope the prospects for recruitment from remnant seed-parents in surviving woodland fragments and hedgerows into new spontaneously-developing or planted woods.

For Groundwork's *Changing Places* programme, such a dynamic perspective on woodland development was developed at Darwen Parkway in Blackburn to illustrate successions of plant communities that might be expected to occur in particular habitats of a post-industrial setting (Rodwell & Dring, 1999). Combined with sensitivity to recent industrial history, this ecological understanding can help nurture the kind of local distinctiveness that is very hard to find in technology-driven brownfield restorations where landscape design has only repetitive off-the-peg solutions to offer to local communities that have been all too often been left bereft of landscape signifiers. Groundwork's EU *Life* project (www.ecoregen.com) incorporates such an approach in a toolkit for ecologically-informed, community-led restoration projects, which is of Europe-wide application.

In the county of Cheshire, this kind of predictive apporoach has been used in a more thoroughgoing fashion to describe and map ecoscapes as a framework for linking historic woodland remnants in ecological networks for the EU *Life* ECOnet project (Rodwell & Skelcher, 2003). Nine such ecoscapes have been defined as envelopes of unique vegetation patterns and processes related to distinctive landscape-scale terrain and climatic conditions and with particular cultural resonances. Different woodland types are the climax vegetation in most of these ecoscapes but equally important to having such plant communities as targets is to see such indicative mapping units as linking surviving woodlands in networks of dynamic landscape processes rather than static patterns. This kind of approach can then be incorporated into multifunctional landscapes that might provide a more sustainable option for post-industrial situations (Handley, Ling & Rodwell, 2000).

Across Europe as a whole, the European Vegetation Map (Bohn, Gollub & Hettwer, 2000) provides a spatial model resolved at a scale of 1:2.5m and an integrated legend that enables landscape patterns and their woodland remnants to be understood on an international scale. The river valley floodplain mapping unit around the North Sea basin shows how these landscapes possess shared cultural resonances that are often reflected in such things as architectural styles and artistic perceptions of scenic quality – as in the paintings of Constable and Rubens in East Anglia and the Low Countries.

Creating New Native Woodlands (Rodwell & Patterson, 1994) pioneered the notion of using an ecological approach like the NVC in a practical predictive fashion to provide planting guidelines for establishing new woodlands using sustainable mixtures of native species of trees and shrubs ecologically suited to the environmental conditions of particular sites. Combined with the Ecological Site Classification (Pyatt, 2003), such plantings could incorporate productivity as one of a series of multiple objectives. There is no reason why such new and commercially-viable woodlands should not be part of networks which also sustain valuable fragments of previous wooded landscapes that are cherished for historic and biodiversity value. After all, such a varied dynamic was the basis of much previous land use.

References

Bohn, U., Gollub, G. and Hettwer, C. (2000) *General Map of the Natural Vegetation of Europe. Scale 1: 10 million*. Bonn, Germany, Federal Agency for Nature Conservation.

Ling, C., Handley, J. and Rodwell, J. (2000) *Multifunctionality and Scale in post-industrial land regeneration* Conference on Multi-functional landscapes, Centre for Landscape Research, University of Roskilde, Denmark.

Hall, J.E. and Kirby, K.J. (1998) *The relationship between Biodiversity Action Plan Priority and Broad Woodland Habitat Types and other woodland classifications*. Joint Nature Conservation Committee (Report No 288), Peterborough.

Harvey, J. (1974) Common Field and Enclosure in the Lower Dearne Valley, *Yorkshire Archaeology*, **46**.

Lavin, J.C. and Wilmore, G.T.D. (1994) *The West Yorkshire Plant Atlas*, City of Bradford MDC, Bradford.

Rodwell, J.S. (1991) (ed.) *National Vegetation Classification: British Plant Communities - Woodland and Scrub*. Cambridge University Press, Cambridge.

Rodwell, J. and Patterson, G. (1994) *Creating New Native Woodlands* Forestry Commission Research Bulletin, 112, Forestry Commission.

Rodwell, J. and Skelcher, G. (2003) *ECOnet & the National Vegetation Classification: The ecoscapes & plant communities of Cheshire*. Lancaster: Unit of Vegetation Science report to Cheshire County Council.

Rodwell, J.S., Wildsmith, C and Cartwright, R. (1999) *Outwood Future Landscapes*. Lancaster: Unit of Vegetation Science Report to WWF (UK).

Identifying and protecting archaeology in the woodland environment in Northern Scotland
Jonathan Wordsworth

There has been a considerable amount of archaeological survey work carried out in Scotland on behalf of forestry interests in recent years. Figures from 1999 -2001 show the areas being surveyed rising from 9,736 hectares in 1999/200 to 14,954 hectares in 2000/1. However the majority of the surveys being carried out were in advance of Woodland Grant Scheme applications and were carried out on previously unplanted ground. Few of these surveys were carried out in areas of existing woodland, though some work has been done in existing conifer plantations in advance of felling and restocking or as part of long term management plans. Archaeological survey in conifer plantations, especially of unbrashed sitka, can be an extremely unpleasant experience and often not very rewarding in terms of archaeological sites identified.

Archaeologists have tended not to have the skills to recognise historical significance in the woodland itself and do not regularly record human adaptation of existing woodland. Few archaeologists would be able to distinguish pollarded trees from mature coppice or maidens and as a result such features are rarely listed in the archaeological record. This even extends to features related to the working of the woods like pitsteads and sawpits. The national archaeological database, CANMORE, covering the whole of Scotland has only three sawpits recorded as surviving and twelve records for coppice (and two of those are mis-transcriptions for copse!). Plantation Banks are slightly better represented by being covered by 112 entries and this does include some banks protecting ancient woodland. Traditionally the archaeological record has been best at recording point-based features rather than linear boundaries or areas but the shift to GIS systems of recording is dramatically changing how information is stored.

However the archaeological survey work that is being carried out is supplying important information as to how our woods evolved and were managed in the past. Such work can only be done in conjunction with documentary work and the pioneering work of the Centre for Environmental History in Stirling and St Andrews and the Woodland History Discussion Group have gone a long way to understanding how woods have been managed.

While not proposing to venture into the documentary background of Scottish Forests, it is worth remembering that the majority of the oak and other native woodlands that are identified as ancient woodland, with associated biodiversity interest, survive in most cases precisely because they had an economic or social value to the human population. It is only in gorge refugia or the remoter regions of the highlands that any extensive undisturbed woodland now survives.

The primary sources for the Scottish Ancient Woodland Inventory such as the Roy Military Survey, a sketch of Scotland drawn *c*1750, give an approximate but very imperfect picture of woodland cover in Scotland (*cf* Whittington's example of Glenmore Forest comparing variations between estate maps and the Roy map).

This is reflected in sites such as Rassal Ashwoods, the most northerly substantial ashwood in the UK and significant enough to be designated as an SSSI. Archaeological examination shows just outside the SSSI is a prehistoric roundhouse 2,000 -3,000 years old pointing to a long history of human settlement in this area. This may also be connected to a significant outcrop of copper which was described by Williams, a mineralologist writing in 1810, as '*the best copper ore he had ever seen*'. The mine was worked from 1775 but closed fairly shortly afterwards. Tree ring dating of ten trees in 1960 revealed trees dating from 1730 to 1820 with a 'cluster' of five dating from 1790-1820. Stone dykes, level terraces and pollarding of trees show that the ashwood survives in a managed landscape. A more detailed archaeological survey linked to further dendrochronology would go a long way to understanding how this woodland was formed and managed. This is not to deny its biodiversity value of this woodland but it does stress the human element in biodiversity, a feature often under recognised in Scotland.

On the eastern side of the highlands the great pine woods edging the Cairngorm plateau are a significant natural heritage asset but their present structure cannot be understood without reference to their archaeology and history. The Forest of Mar, for example, on the east and now owned by the National Trust for Scotland, has had a detailed archaeological survey done by officers of the RCAHMS. This has identified a number of shieling and farming settlements that were established in the eighteenth and early nineteenth century in this former hunting reserve and which were themselves abandoned when it was converted back into a deer forest in the mid nineteenth century. The discovery of these settlements and their relation to surviving stands of pine led to a re-examination of the nature of the woodland and an adaptation of the proposed woodland expansion.

Further west the great forests of Abernethy and Rothiemurchus cannot be understood without reference to the long history of exploitation in the eighteenth and nineteenth centuries. Archaeological work has been less extensive in these areas, though some survey work has been done in the Forestry Commission woodlands in Glenmore and a one kilometre square was examined in Abernethy. This revealed at least three neolithic chambered cairns in an area where no prehistoric settlement had previously been recorded. This emphasises the extent of human settlement in this area from earliest times - information belying the traditional picture of virgin forests and emphasising the dynamics of woodland expansion and retreat.

The extent of human penetration by c2,000 BC is emphasised by the work of palynologists in Loch Clair and Glen Affric and in some areas by the surviving remains on the ground. At Morvich in East Sutherland, for example, there is a fine oak woodland now used as wood pasture. The mature oak trees could be an escape from the well-preserved woodlands within the gorges, but equally the age structure and solely oak specimens visible may point to this being a planted woodland. Certainly the evidence higher up the slope point to intensive human settlement on this sheltered and fertile slope for at least 3,000 years. Few traces of such settlement are now visible within the mature woodland. But traces of cairns suggest that when this was converted from a series of traditional joint stock farms into a commercial farming unit in the early nineteenth century (by the notorious Patrick Sellars) that originally the area of woodland was cultivated. This may be significant in understanding the present biodiversity interest of this woodland.

The most significant archaeological survey in the highlands was carried out by the Sunart Oakwood Research Group (SORG) around Loch Sunart in an area of great natural beauty as well as significant botanical and mycological interest. Of the 266 fungi taxa recorded two are found nowhere else in the UK. A detailed documentary and archaeological survey was carried out over 12.7 square kilometres funded by the Millennium Forest and involving 1,900 hours of survey. A total of 1,799 sites were recorded including 233 buildings and 499 platforms and stances. The majority of the latter were probably used to produce charcoal for the iron furnaces while some may have been used for buildings. The documentary survey showed a continuous history of woodland exploitation and protection from the early eighteenth century until the present day. This was associated with the lead mining industry at Strontian which by 1851 was employing 115 miners. At the same census three woodland workers and twenty-eight workers with wood were also recorded. At this time estate records show the standard methods of planting were at the rate of 800 oaks per acre with 1,200 scotch firs and 400 larch as nurse trees. Pit planting was the norm with four to five year old saplings used. Pruning and weeding were carried out. By this time the trees were grown primarily for their bark for the tanning industry as the iron furnaces were closed and the former industry was itself shortly going to shift to aniline dyes, ending the commercial value of these woodlands.

This survey is significant not just because of the detail of work carried out but also because it included the humanly altered trees, a total of forty-seven pollarded oaks being recorded with their positions being marked by GPS. Fifteen core samples were taken with the oldest clear sample being a 168 year old Scots pine , though incomplete samples suggested other surviving trees might be as much 200 years old. Many of the oaks are known to have been felled when this was converted to a forestry plantation (though this is now being reversed) and so a fuller understanding as to how the woodland was managed is difficult. A look at a neighbouring woodland at Rahoy which had a more rapid archaeological survey shows some of the problems in detailing the woodland history during survey.

In conclusion some progress has been made in using and integrating archaeological information in woodland history in northern Scotland. It is a useful tool but limited to the classes of information that survive. Much of the archaeological record is either difficult to spot or is no longer visible above ground and archaeological excavation is intrusive and expensive. Archaeologists also need to develop better skills in recognising significance in the features of woodland both in the shape and modifications of trees as well as using species type and size as indicators of past human activity. We also need to be better at recognising colonisation patterns and associated vegetation with different tree species and finally we need guidance on what features are significant in terms of biodiversity, both intrinsically and as overall indicators. In return practitioners working in the natural environment must be better equipped not only to recognise and protect archaeological features but also to use these features as sources of information for understanding the dynamics of the woodland being studied.

The Use of Woodlands by Mammals - Past and Present

Derek W. Yalden
University of Manchester

The present interactions between mammals and forestry need to be considered in the light of historical information on how they came about; this is particularly true given the current emphasis on creating something more like a "natural" broadleaved woodland cover in lowland Britain. Just what was that "natural" cover, what mammals inhabited it, and how have six millennia of human interference changed it?

The maximum of the Devensian (last) Glaciation about 20,000 years ago saw a high arctic fauna in Britain of lemmings, reindeer and musk ox. Neither trees nor any of the forest mammals could have lived here. The record of the pollen rain shows first birch scrub, then hazel and pine, followed by oak, elm and alder returning over about 2,000 years from 10,000 to 8,000 years ago, by which time the English Channel and the North Sea had probably been flooded and rendered them the British Isles. From about 8,000 to 5,500 years ago (when Neolithic farmers and their livestock appeared, and started to interfere seriously with the landscape), high forest of species such as oak (especially in the west and north), lime and elm (in lowland England), ash (on chalk and limestone), and alder and willow (in the river valleys), blanketed most of Britain. In Highland Scotland, and as altitudinal bands around higher mountains further south, Scots pine would have persisted, with birch scrub even higher uphill and further north (Bennett, 1988). Only on very high northern mountains would open ground, perhaps analogous to moorland, have been evident.

If most of Britain was blanketed by high forest, what exactly would it have looked like? We know from the archaeological record of such sites as Star Carr in Yorkshire and Thatcham in Berkshire that mesolithic hunters were pursuing a large mammal fauna that included roe and red deer, elk, aurochs, wild boar and beaver. Though archaeological remains of elk are few, those of aurochsen are quite numerous, as are red deer (Yalden 1999). High tree foliage could not have supported these: there must have been river valley grasslands, glades where soil conditions or accidents of windthrow or lightning provided grazing, and considerable amounts of low-level scrub and young growth to support browsers. Indeed, the mammals themselves must have played a role in creating (beavers) or maintaining (large ungulates) such conditions, and the pollen analysts point out that the pollen rain, which creates the illusion of almost complete forest cover, is itself deceptive. Because most trees are wind pollinated, they produce copious amounts of pollen that therefore dominates the pollen rain. A fairer assessment of the actual vegetation associated with any particular pollen flora has to be derived by adjusting the figures; dividing birch, alder, pine and hazel by four, multiplying lime by four, grasses by 3.33, heather by five and sedges by two (Maroo & Yalden, 2000). On this basis, the high forest seems to have included rather more grassland, and could have supported the mammal fauna. Deciduous woodland is likely to have covered 43.2 percent of the landscape (cf. 3.7 percent now), but there might have been about 19.3 percent grassland.

Many of the larger mammals here then are now extinct, perhaps hunted out, but perhaps because their habitat has gone. Red deer and roe deer survive, and in sufficient numbers to cause problems for foresters, though they too were nearly exterminated in the seventteenth century. That red deer prefer a forest habitat is indicated by their greater densities and better reproductive rate in woodlands (Clutton-Brock & Albon, 1989: Figure 7.2). We may regard roe deer as marauders of farmland, using woodland to provide shelter, but they take territories that neatly divide the woodland between themselves, so they certainly regard it as their prime habitat. Other surviving forest mammals include the red squirrel, now reduced to a remnant of its former range and population size, but then much more widespread, and responding not only to the density of pine cones, in its favoured conifer habitat, but also to the hazel crop (but not the acorn crop) in deciduous woodlands (Kenward *et al.*, 1998). Hazel dormice too are now reduced to a remnant of their former range and abundance, perhaps out-competed for hazel nuts by introduced grey squirrels, but dependant on a range of flowers, fruits and berries, and making much greater use of tree holes for nesting than we formerly suspected (Bright & Morris, 1992, 1993). Tree holes are also critical to a number of woodland bats, among them some of our rarest species - Bechstein's bat, Barbastelle and Leisler's bat - while foraging conditions inside woodland are also the preferred hunting grounds for several of them, including lesser horseshoe and Bechstein's bats. Others, including Leisler's bat, prefer to forage outside or around, rather than within, woodland.

If we take some guidance from the nearest analogue to our mesolithic countryside, the Bialowieza Forest in eastern Poland, together with what we know from the archaeological record, we can hypothesise about the mesolithic mammal fauna and the extent of the changes since then. We do not know enough about the densities of bats, then or now, to estimate their population changes, though we know that Bechstein's bat used to be more widespread, and relatively much more numerous, in earlier times (Yalden, 1999). For the other mammals, we estimate that numerically, small rodents and insectivores dominated the fauna then, just as now, though bank voles and common shrews would have been the most numerous, rather than field voles. However, the greatest ecological impact would have come from the large biomass of large ungulates already mentioned (Maroo & Yalden, 2000). There would perhaps have been 1.2 million red deer, rather than 0.36 million, 0.8 rather than 0.5 million roe, and in addition 0.9

million wild boar, eighty thousand aurochs and sixty thousand elk. There might have been 11.8 million red squirrels, rather than 0.16, and 25.8 million dormice rather than only 0.5 million. Numerically, the mammals might have then totalled 535, rather than 281 million (fifty-three percent), but their biomass has reduced rather more, by loss of the larger species, from 304 kt to 129 kt (forty-two percent). The modern figures include an introduced mammal biomass (rabbits, fallow deer, brown hares, *etc.*) about equal to that of the surviving natives. However, this latter figure still overlooks the enormous biomass of humans and of our domestic species. The total biomass of mammals in the British countryside is now some 6,743 kt, 2,218 percent of what it then was. It is not surprising that our woodland mammals are squeezed into a rather small segment of the countryside, nor that, when they become too numerous within it, or extend outside it, we notice them and categorise them as pest species.

References

Bennett, K.D. (1988) A provisional map of forest types for the British Isles 5000 years ago. *Journal of Quaternary Science*, **4**, 141-144.

Bright, P.W. and Morris, P.A. (1992) Ranging and nesting behaviour of the dormouse *Muscardinus avellanarius,* in coppice-with-standards woodland. *J. Zool. Lond.*, **226**, 589-600.

Bright, P.W. and Morris, P.A. (1993) Foraging behaviour of dormice *Muscardinus avellanarius* in two contrasting habitats. *J. Zool. Lond.*, **230**, 69-85.

Clutton-Brock, T.H. and Albon, S.D. (1989) *Red Deer in the Highlands.* Blackwells, Oxford.

Kenward, R.E., Hodder, K.H., Rose, R.J., Walls, C.A., Parish, T., Holm, J.L., Morris, P.A., Walls, S.S. and Doyle, F.I. (1998) Comparative demography of red squirrels (*Sciurus vulgaris*) and grey squirrels (*Sciurus carolinensis*) in deciduous and conifer woodland. *J. Zool. Lond.*, **244**, 7-21.

Maroo, S. and Yalden, D.W. (2000) The Mesolithic mammal fauna of Britain. *Mammal Review*, **30**, 243-248.

Yalden, D. (1999) *The History of British Mammals.* T. & A.D. Poyser, London.

The work with old trees and saproxylic beetles in Östergötland, Sweden

Nicklas Jansson
County Administration Board of Östergötland, Sweden

Introduction

The county of Östergötland is situated in the southeast of Sweden at the same latitude as northern Scotland. The climate is warm despite being so far north. The forests in the northern and southern areas are dominated by coniferous trees, with birch and aspen; but in the middle and coastal areas the proportion of broadleaved deciduous trees is greater.

Inventory and survey

Since 1990, there have been a variety of activities in the county concerning old trees and their associated organisms. Different kinds of mapping and inventories have been carried out. The County Administration Board has been running a project since then, involving threatened species and their distribution. The organisms that so far have been sought on and around old trees are lichens, fungi, beetles, pseudoscorpions and bats. Early on, we realised that the health of the trees and the microclimate around and inside them and their younger successors was the key for long term successful preservation.

The trees

In 1998, we started a project aimed at mapping all the big and hollow trees in the county. We believe that they are of such a high conservation value that it is worth trying to identify and describe all of them at a landscape level. The information can then be used to select areas suitable for protection, for monitoring, for more detailed surveys and in early planning for exploitation. The criteria used for selection of trees is minimum girth size (greater than one metre for oak and greater than seventy centimetres for other trees, in diameter at breast height) or if the tree has a hollow in the trunk. The hollow trees are categorised into four stages. We think that this gives us a quite good picture of the age structure in an area. The work started with a survey of infrared aerial photographs to help us narrow down which areas to visit. Other information gathered during the field visits was the condition of the tree, particularly in terms of overgrowth and light conditions. With the help of thirty unemployed people during the winter seasons of 1999, 2000 and 2001, an area of 7,150 ha (fifty-five percent of the county area) was been inventoried. So far 60,000 trees have been registered, fifty-five percent of which are hollow.

The saproxylic beetles

The areas chosen for more in-depth studies of saproxylic beetles not only depend on the amount of old and hollow trees, but also where the area is situated in the county. We want to find the most valuable sites and get a picture of the species' distribution. So far the studies have targeted sites dominated by hollow, old oaks. Trees in old avenues, parks and pollards have also been studied, along with both oaks in forests and grazed pasture woodlands.

Since most of the beetles can fly, they are caught most easily by window traps (or flying interception traps). The traps were hung in branches of high stumps, dead, dying or hollow trees. This investigation resulted in thousands of new records for threatened species in this area and we have learnt a lot about their demands for light, moisture, substrates, and also about their distribution patterns.

In one study carried out together with Dr Thomas Ranius (Swedish University of Agricultural Sciences) we compared three methods – window trapping, pitfall trapping and wood mould sampling - to survey saproxylic beetles in hollow oaks in a smaller area with a radius of 700 metres (Ranius & Jansson, 2002). We used these methods at the same sites and to a large extent in the same trees. The same ninety oaks were surveyed with the traps and wood mould was sampled from fifty-three trees. Useful information was obtained from all methods, but partially targeted different assemblages of species. A total of 125 saproxylic species were identified, including fifty-one on the Swedish redlist (Gärdenfors, 2000). Window trapping collected the highest number of species. Pitfall trapping collected many beetles associated with tree hollows. Window traps rarely collect these species, and it is therefore useful to combine the two methods. As wood mould sampling is the cheapest method to use, indicator species should preferably be chosen among species that are efficiently collected by this method.

The next step in the study is creating "species pyramids" by making NSS-analyses (Nested species subsets) and find out if there are species that indicates many other species presence in a certain site. This could in this case be used in monitoring programmes.

References

Gärdenfors, U. (2000) Population Viability Analysis in the Classification of Threatened Species: Problems and Potentials. *Ecological Bulletins*, **48**, 181–190.

Ranius, T. and Jansson, N. (2002) A comparison of three methods to survey saproxylic beetles in hollow oaks. *Biodiversity and Conservation*, **11**, 1759–1771.

Traditional Woodland Management: the Implications of Cultural Severance and Knowledge Loss

Ian D. Rotherham
Sheffield Hallam University

Summary

English wooded landscapes result from millennia of human interaction with nature. Their early beginnings were as various forms of pasture woods, and originally an expansive patchwork landscape of forest, wetland, grassland and other naturally occurring 'habitats' with large grazing herbivores. The descendants of these original ecosystems and landscapes persist today as woods and other 'unimproved' landscape features, and as 'shadows' and 'ghosts'. Unlike many countries, most English woodlands are small making them vulnerable to clearance and neglect at times throughout their history.

This chapter focuses on 'woods' and on the cultural knowledge of their traditional management. In South Yorkshire, in the English North Midlands, there are around 350 known ancient woodland sites, only one over 200 hectares, and many undocumented fragments. Indeed, over 150 sites are smaller than five hectares. Successions of different woodland management regimes have influenced the ecologies of these woods over time - wood pasture, coppice-with-standards, high forest, amenity woodland, and abandonment. These variations reflect changes of function, ownership and importance, as perceived economically, culturally and socially. In recent centuries, urban influences have also been important and have caused significant disturbance, both directly and indirectly. With nearly eighty documented ancient woodland sites, and numerous fragments and 'ghosts', Sheffield in South Yorkshire, England makes an informative case study. For around 600 to 800 years, most of these sites were managed as traditional coppice-with-standards woods. The production from such working woods included constructional timber and small wood, plus underwood for fuel and especially for charcoal and whitecoal (kiln-dried wood), for metal smelting and working. Providing energy and materials, these woodlands fuelled the region's industrial revolution before this demand declined from around 1850 to perhaps 1910. They were then 'converted' to high forest plantations and ultimately local authority-owned, amenity woods.

In the region's woods we see a process, which I have described elsewhere as 'cultural severance'. Many of these sites are now 'locked' into the urban area or at least urban-based management, though some are islands in a sea of intensive agricultural landscapes.

The spatial isolation and the severance from traditional woodland management proceed at different speeds and in different times. Indeed, it can be argued that the first stage was the change in the intensity of management with industrialisation in the 1700s and 1800s and the 'enclosure' and 'improvement' of the wider landscape. With the growth of iron and steel industries in the region, a landscape of open pasture woods and smaller coppices, in a little less than 300 years, was transformed to a rigorously and intensively organised system of wood production. The marks, scars, and ecological impacts of this transformation remain visible in the woods today.

Figure 1. Charcoal Burner's Hut at Parkwood Springs, Sheffield, UK in the 1930s.

For many of these woods, their status and functions varied though the twentieth century depending on whether they were managed as 'amenity' or 'recreational' woods (and mostly abandoned), or as a productive estate. In the latter cases, they were generally converted to exotic conifers or completely new plantings of beech, sycamore or conifers. In all cases, the traditional woodland or forest management ceased during the late 1800s, apart from a few exceptions where coppice work lingered on farm-managed woods until the 1950s. All the local authority estates were more-or-less intensively drained, and the amenity woods had periods of rigorously clinical safety and tidiness management. Sometimes, there were significant periods of replacement plantings with exotic trees, and under-plantings of exotic shrubs, often without any real rationale other than the personal whim of the managers. During the same period, but increasingly towards the latter end of the twentieth century, the woods were being actively invaded by alien plants and cultivars from gardens; either deliberately introduced, or by accident. At the same time, rare or showy native flowers such as Wild Daffodils and Primroses were being stripped from the woods for planting in gardens or to sell in Sheffield Market.

Key Words: woodlands, shadow woods, ghost woods, cultural severance, traditional use, and cultural knowledge

Introduction

Forest and woodland landscapes reflect and influence community cultural history. These are multi-layered palimpsests of archaeology bearing testimony to human exploitation. Some uses were sustainable but others were not. Evidence for this cultural past relates to both woodland and non-woodland uses of the landscape (Muir, 2005). In order to understand better the processes at work and the legacies that they have produced, over a period of nearly thirty years, we have undertaken detailed studies of wooded landscapes and their ecology, history and archaeology. These intensive studies in the UK show the depth of evidence and the diversity of interactions between people and their woods. A major output from the research was the *Woodland Heritage Manual* (Rotherham *et al.*, 2008). Furthermore, our understanding of the nature of these landscapes and of the drivers that shape them has changed radically over the last twenty years. New concepts have emerged and developed to change our perceptions of these landscapes. These are of traditional knowledge (Agnoletti (ed.), 2006, 2007; Parrotta & Trosper (eds.), 2012; Rotherham, 2007), of cultural severance (Rotherham, 2008), and of woodland shadows and ghosts (Rotherham, 2012). During the 1980s, interest in ancient woodlands in Britain grew with the research and writing of woodland and forest enthusiasts such as Oliver Rackham (1980, 1986), George Peterken (1981, 1996), Charles Watkins (e.g. Kirby & Watkins, 1998), Richard Muir (2005) and Melvyn Jones (2009). This re-kindled an interest in the unique histories and values of forested or wooded landscapes. The ideas and enthusiasms have influenced site management. In the last twenty years, there have been moves to reinstate native broadleaved tree species and to encourage demonstrations or targeted conservation programmes of 'traditional' management. This has developed in parallel with an increased recognition of the benefits that woods and forest landscapes bring through public health benefits (Crowe, 2001), ecosystem functions, and local economic values such as house prices and a desire to live in an area (O'Brien & Claridge, 2002). However, despite the increased interest in woods, and awareness of wooded landscapes, it is clear that there has been a steady loss of understanding and knowledge of their traditional management and cultural origins. At the same time there has been increased interest in attempts to broaden the 'value-base' for forest and woodland management (e.g.

Helliwell, 1992), and in the influence of perceptions of trees and woods in determining management priorities (e.g. Hare, 1988). Alongside the passion for woods has been an emerging enthusiasm for trees themselves with the dramatic and influential growth of the Ancient Tree Forum, and a realisation of the importance of ancient parks and wood pastures. These landscapes are now recognised as holding some of our most iconic and precious wildlife resources yet for decades were the 'Cinderellas' of conservation.

The management of woods and forests across Europe has changed dramatically over the centuries. The balance between grazing of wood-pasture and of coppice woods or other uses has varied hugely and given rise to local and regional character and distinction. The spatial extent, the balances and interactions, and the drivers of change are still a matter of much debate but a degree of consensus is emerging. Undoubtedly, over a period of millennia, a primeval landscape was converted to one of human-driven utilisation, with compartments, large and small, with long-term, often traditional management. Sometimes the rights and ownership were vested in an individual or an estate (large or small), and sometimes they were held in common (De Moor et al., 2002). The exact mechanisms were complex and varied over time and from place to place. By the medieval period, wooded landscapes occurred in a number of clearly recognisable forms; broadly divided into wood-pastures and woods or coppice; with perhaps limited or at least localised areas of natural, closed-canopy woodland.

Ever since Rackham's seminal works, *Ancient Woodland* (1980) and *The History of the Countryside* (1986), it has been clear that wood-pasture was once the most widespread and common wooded landscape in north-western Europe. Essentially wood-pasture is a landscape or system of land management where trees are grown, but grazing by large herbivores (domesticated, semi-domesticated, wild, or a combination) is also permitted (Rotherham, 2007a, b). Wood-pasture in England is well documented for over a thousand years, and the Domesday Book (1086) records a landscape in which this is a dominant feature. Vera (2000) stressed the importance of large grazing and browsing mammals in determining the landscape and ecological successions in European primeval environments and their persistent influences into historic times. Indeed, it has been suggested that managed wood-pasture evolved from grazed forest or a savannah as an ancient system of management in a multi-functional landscape where woodland was plentiful. In this context, there was little need for formal coppice since this is a more intensive and rigorous system which ensures vital supplies of wood and timber in a resource-limited landscape (Fowler, 2002; Hayman, 2003; Perlin, 1989). Pasture-woodland is an older and more 'natural' system. Significantly, most livestock, wild or domesticated, will take leaf-fodder or browse if available rather than grazing (Vera, 2000; Rotherham, 2012).

Today's landscapes of woods, parks and forests derive from a suite of medieval landscape types that mixed trees and grazing or browsing mammals. These included wood-pasture, wooded commons, heaths, moors, fens, bogs, and forests, as the relicts of what was probably in prehistory a great wooded savannah with extensive wetlands, across much of north-western Europe. Along with the main historic 'woods', and often embedded within them, were coppices, holts, hags, heys, and hollins managed in controlled and specialist ways to produce particular woodland materials (Jones, 2003). Both of the main types of wooded landscape would have been characterised by 'working trees' that included pollards and stubs, and in the protected 'woods' coppice stools and evidence persists today as 'ancient trees' in the landscape. Interestingly, in the various inventories of ancient trees compiled in recent years, most coppices are omitted. In the 1700s and 1800s, two major drivers affected many of these woodland areas. Firstly, there was the imposition of formal estates and grand landscape parks for the aristocracy, reflecting status and offering opportunities for recreation such as hunting. Secondly, there was the emergence of industrialised plantation forestry. In regions such as South Yorkshire in England, these were to fuel the emerging industrial revolution (Perlin, 1999). They produced massive amounts of wood for charcoal to smelt iron and other metals, and then later pit props for coalmines. Some aspects of this are discussed by Rotherham & Jones, 2000) and presented in detail by Rotherham & Egan (2005).

These changes fragmented the earlier landscapes and weakened, changed or removed the social systems and common rights relating to environmental resources. They helped generate the wooded landscapes we see today. Then, as the industrial demands were replaced by other technologies, and rural traditions lapsed too, the forest or wood was often abandoned. The other scenario was that management intensified through twentieth century agri-forestry (Fowler, 2002; Hayman, 2003; Rotherham, 2011). By the late twentieth century, in countries such as Great Britain, the economic driver for woods and forests was no longer related to the primary production of timber and wood, but to tourism and recreation (Rotherham & Jones, 2000). However, the economic benefits from such modern post-industrial landscapes are problematic in that they often do not relate to the actual management of the land and the forest. The cost of care and management bears no direct relationship to the benefits provided, and in the time of new 'austerity', this does not bode well. The wooded landscape is seen as a 'natural' backcloth that can be taken for granted and which will take care of itself; which is clearly not the case. In many cases, where traditional management died out between 100 and 150 years ago, almost all the local knowledge of forest-use systems that spanned maybe 1,000 to 1,500 years has gone too. A recent observation in the Roztoczański Park near Zamość in Poland supports this analysis. The forest here is full of archaeological evidence of former woodland crafts and management, with charcoal hearths, possibly potash pits, and numerous boundary features. Relict coppice stools and other working trees also occur. However, interviews with local forest rangers and other local experts revealed almost no knowledge of the archaeology or of the traditional management systems. Following persistent questioning it was revealed that charcoal had last been made around a hundred years ago. Rotherham & Ardron (2006) and Rotherham (2007) address the issues and consequences of the lack of awareness of woodland archaeology, and the implications for contemporary management.

In considering the Sheffield case-study area, but with a European context, it must be recognised that England is one of the least wooded countries in Europe (Rackham, 1986; Rotherham & Jones, 2000). Not only this, but its surviving semi-natural woodlands are small; with woods over fifty hectares uncommon and those over 100 hectares generally rare. South Yorkshire with its 333 ancient woodland sites has around 4,451 hectares or just 2.8 per cent of the land surface recognised as wooded (Eccles, 1986). Of these woods, only one woodland exceeds 200 hectares, four are in the range 100-200 hectares, five are 50-100 hectares, and 157 (47%) are less than 5 hectares in size. There are many smaller fragments, which remain unaccounted and large areas of young, semi-natural woods now establishing on former heaths (Rotherham, 2009a, b, c). The ecologies of these South Yorkshire woodlands, like those in the rest of Britain has active and passive management regimes, which have transformed sites, species, and soils (Rotherham & Doram, 1992; Rotherham, 2007). These reflect changes of function, ownership, economic, cultural, and social importance with significant urban and industrial impacts. Rotherham & Jones (2000) considered the social, political and economic drivers of change in these wooded landscapes; and Rotherham &Ardron (2006), and Rotherham (2007), presented specific issues of knowledge loss. This chapter develops the themes further and addresses the serious impacts of the loss of local cultural knowledge, and of cultural severance.

Figure 2. Charcoal Burner's Hut, New Forest, F.G.O. Stuart, 1910s or early 1920s.

Methodological approaches

In essence, the work has been a multi-methods study which combines scientific applications of detailed field survey (ecology, archaeology, soils), with social sciences, historical and ethnology work. Long-term action research of sites and of the social structures and stakeholders across the study region has been hugely informative. The research approach combined long-term field surveys (of archaeology and ecology) at a number of study sites (see Figure 3), social case studies, detailed searches of archival materials and published literature on woodland and forest management, and the gathering of oral histories. At several core sites, very detailed surveys were undertaken to over-lay and compare woodland ecology, woodland landscape archaeology, soils and hydrology, and known management drivers. Where appropriate, GIS (Geographic Information Systems) and GPS (Global Positioning Systems) technologies were applied in the mapping of finds, features, vegetation etc; and subsequent analysis involved interrogation of the GIS maps. The final studies are currently being completed. Ethnological studies obtained oral histories from local woodworkers and foresters. The findings from the different approaches were then triangulated and placed in a context of social, economic, and political changes and drivers over the period considered, based on the initial analysis of Rotherham & Jones (2000). The results of the detailed case study at Ecclesall Woods in Sheffield are presented in Table 1, and based on the regional study, the drivers of change and their impacts, are presented in Table 2.

Figure 3. South Yorkshire Survey Map.

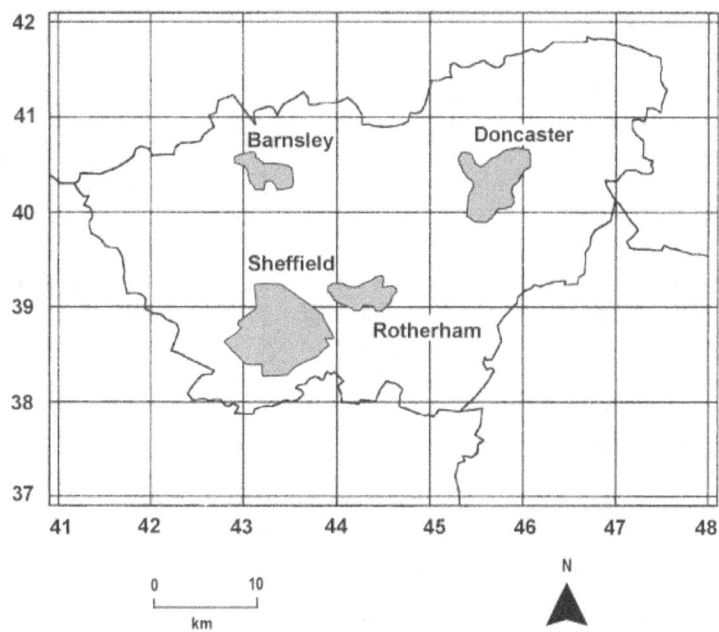

Table 1. Ecclesall Woods, Sheffield since Domesday: a selective timeline from the last millennium.

Dates	Landscape condition	Consequences
c. 4,000 BP onwards The early landscape and its evidence	Open landscape with farming, grazing, habitation, and woodland in wet areas and along streamsides.	Dominance of non-woodland plants and spoils over most of the study site.
Pre-1300 AD	Farmed agricultural landscape close to open heathy commons and riverside meadows.	Wet and streamside woods.
1317 AD	Robert de Ecclesall – granted licence to impark the area. Hunting of deer and other game including a rabbit warren.	Enclosure and grazing – pollards?? Laund for grazing; tracks and routeways through the landscape. Probable survival of veteran tress and dead wood.
1500s–1600s	Industrial coppice-with-standards for underwood – whitecoal and charcoal; and for timber. Whitecoal and charcoal needed for lead smelting and other metal-working.	Probable introduction of rare shrub, Alder Buckthorn, associated with coppice. Massive drainage and de-turfing to cover the charcoal clamps. Associated loss of woodland flora to woodland edges and wet areas. Loss of deer species.
1700s-1800s	Changing technology in lead smelting; loss of need for whitecoal manufacture, continuing industrial charcoal production. Surface mining of mineral coal.	Introduction of some Sweet Chestnut?? Heathland vegetation and fauna widespread.
Mid-1800s –1900s	Extraction of ganister for furnaces and smelting industries. Creation of wooden-tracked railways. Continuing drainage and decline of coppicing with replacement by Victorian High Forestry. Introduction of Beech (*Fagus sylvatica*), Sweet Chestnut (*Castanea sativa*), European Larch (*Larix decidua*), Scot's Pine (*Pinus sylvestris*). Theft of Wild Daffodils (*Narcissus pseudonarcissus*), Snowdrops (*Galanthes nivalis*), Primroses (*Primula vulgaris*) for sale and gardens.	Progressive closure of canopy, and so decline of open forest and heath vegetation and beginnings of recovery of ancient coppice wood ground flora. Deliberate and accidental introduction of exotic trees, shrubs and herbs, including *Rhododendron ponticum* and *Prunus laurocerasus*. Significant heathland element remaining in flora and in bird fauna by early 1900s.

Table 1. Ecclesall Woods, Sheffield since Domesday: a selective timeline from the last millennium. (continued)

Dates	Landscape condition	Consequences
Early-Mid-1900s	Massive air pollution with fallout of around 3.35 tons of grit and grime deposited per square mile per week in 1920s. Consequent acidification of remaining soils. Urbanisation and severance by major roads. Establishment of Bird Sanctuary as the region's first nature reserve. Set aside for zero management and no access. Major threat of loss of most of site (perhaps 80% of the 100 hectares), for urban development.	Deliberate planting in woodland compartments of exotic Sycamore (*Acer pseudoplatanus*), and then later of Norway Maple (*Acer platanoides*) along roadsides. Continued recovery of woodland flora but also increasing occurrence of garden escapes and introductions: Himalayan Balsam (*Impatiens glandulifera*), Variegated Yellow Archangel (*Galeobdolon argentatum*), Narcissus var., Spanish Bluebells (*Hyacinthoides hispanica*).
Mid-1900s–late 1900s	Continuing urbanisation and threats of felling and 'parkification' (1970s). Proposed felling and re-planting with exoticsfor 'amenity'. Many more visitors and dog-walking. Increased atmospheric fall-out from road traffic but declining smoke pollution from industry and housing. Assumed increase in nitrogen levels in soils. Increased in micro-disturbance and fly-tipping of litter, plus encroachments into woods by adjacent domestic gardens. Closure of local authority-owned Sawmill.	Spread of exotics, and recovery of ancient woodland ground flora. Increase in high forest birds and loss of open forest or heath species. Spread of Sycamore and then later of Norway Maple. Loss of dead wood as a tidiness measure.

continued ...

Table 1. Ecclesall Woods, Sheffield since Domesday: a selective timeline from the last millennium. (continued)

Dates	Landscape condition	Consequences
Late 1900s–early 2000s	Establishment of local community 'Friends Group'. Experimental conservation management.	Continued spread of exotics, and recovery of ancient woodland ground flora. Loss of Elm (*Ulmus* sp.) to Dutch Elm Disease.
	Glades plus non-intervention areas, and then experimental coppice.	Further spread of Sycamore, Norway Maple, *Sorbus* sp., and Highclere Holly (*Ilex*).
	Footpath, access and interpretation work.	Decline of some exotic plants in some areas due to selective controls.
	'Weed' control.	
	Still getting drier!!	
	Recognition of historic landscape and its importance.	
	First funded research programmes and development of management plans. Abandonment of experimental coppice after less than 10 years.	
Early 2000s	Opening of visitor and woodland craft centre and continuing footpath improvement works.	
Major threats averted – here but not elsewhere		

The regional work was placed in a national context by the Woodland Heritage Research Project, which produced the Woodland Heritage Manual (Rotherham *et al.*, 2008). This provided for the first time a coherent and integrated approach to the assessment and evaluation of wooded landscapes. There is an on-going programme of research to analyse trends at a UK national level, whichhas been supported by the Woodland Trust, the Forestry Commission, Natural England, English Heritage, and the British Ecological Society. Internal context has been provided by members of the European Cultural Forest Network, by IUFRO (International Union of Forest Research Organisations), andespecially by conferences organised by, and contributions from colleagues across Europe.

Table 2. A thousand years of Social, Economic and Political Drivers of the Wooded Landscapes of South Yorkshire, England

EVENT, ACTION, AND DATE	Economic Driver	Political Driver	Social Driver	CONSEQUENCES
1086 AD According to the Domesday Book around 15% of the area was wooded. Over 95% of the woodland was wood-pasture. Land had been cleared for arable, meadow and grazing.	✓	✓	✓	Woods grazed by deer, cattle, sheep, and horses; many ranging over unenclosed commons, waste, moor and chase.
From 1250-1325 AD there were 44 grants of free warren; and between 1200 and 1441 AD there were 70 more	✓	✓	✓	Woods as canopy high forest and then coppice-with-standards preserved within demesne lands; and old trees such as pollards protected in enclosed deer parks and chase (such as Rivelin Chase and Wharncliffe Chase).
1421 AD first records of coppice-with-standards management.	✓	✓	✓	
1550-1800 AD The 'golden age' of coppice-with-standards management.	✓			Surviving woods protected by banks and ditches, and walls and hedges or fences. Gazing animals only allowed into woods in middle or later stages of the coppice cycle. Particular tree species favoured by the woodwards, especially oak, hazel, holly, and alder. Coppice management results in regular opening of the canopy and light input every 15-20 years depending on the cycle. This along with the micro-scale disturbance of management allows the development of the characteristic ancient woodland ground flora.

Table 2. A thousand years of Social, Economic and Political Drivers of the Wooded Landscapes of South Yorkshire, England

EVENT, ACTION, AND DATE	Economic Driver	Political Driver	Social Driver	CONSEQUENCES
This was associated with the production of charcoal for iron and lead smelting and working (both furnaces and forges); white coal for lead smelters, bark for tanning leather, oak and other timber for building, and poles for many other uses. Widespread and long-lasting lead pollution of soils across the region. Woodland soils stripped for covering charcoal burns and typical ancient woodland vegetation much reduced.	√	√	√	Ground flora and soils extensively disturbed as coppice, charcoal and whitecoal industries become increasingly industrial scale, and woodlands are 'de-turfed'.
From around 1600 AD, there was rapid disparking of deer parks (with some incorporated into grand landscape parks), and gradual extinction of chases through agricultural intensification (e.g. Rivelin Chase) or drainage and then agriculture (e.g. Hatfield Chase).	√	√		Deer probably generally extinct in the wider landscape and lost from deer parks and chases, and maintained in ornamental deer parks in landscaped areas around country houses. The exception is Wharncliffe where the ancient herd survives until the mid-twentieth century and to form the nucleus of a feral population of Red Deer.
From 1775 AD, lead was produced in coal-fired cupola furnaces and iron in coke-fired blast furnaces. The markets for whitecoal disappear and for charcoal are much reduced.	√			Coppice-with-standards begins a long decline as estates increasingly convert to high forest plantations and there is more use of exotic tree species as nurse crops and as the main harvest.

Table 2. A thousand years of Social, Economic and Political Drivers of the Wooded Landscapes of South Yorkshire, England

EVENT, ACTION, AND DATE	Economic Driver	Political Driver	Social Driver	CONSEQUENCES
From 1750-1830 AD, Parliamentary Acts of Enclosure remove almost all wooded common. Tiny fragments remain but today are often unrecognised for what they are.	√	√	√	
The last coppice in Ecclesall Woods is around 1850.	√			
By around 1900 AD almost all coppicing in the region has ceased. There are still charcoal burners and gamekeepers at Parkwood Springs in Sheffield, but within the next 10-15 years, the woodland and all of its workers are removed. Two tiny areas of coppice remain today.	√			
Some small woods in the Gleadless Valley were still coppiced into the 1950s by the local farmer / landowner, but this ceased with the compulsory purchase of the area for urban expansion of Sheffield, and the farm and hall were demolished.	√	√	√	
Late 1700s – early 1900s saw massive conversion of traditional coppice-with-standards woods to high forest.	√			Coppice declines steadily after 1800, and increasingly after 1825. Gradual conversion to high forest utilising natural regeneration, selection thinning and re-planting. Coppice stools neglected, physically removed, or 'singled' to form a canopy tree.

Table 2. A thousand years of Social, Economic and Political Drivers of the Wooded Landscapes of South Yorkshire, England

EVENT, ACTION, AND DATE	Economic Driver	Political Driver	Social Driver	CONSEQUENCES
Late 1700s – early 1900s saw massive conversion of traditional coppice-with-standards woods to high forest.	√			Exotic conifer and broadleaved trees widely planted and many naturalise; in both ancient woodland sites and in new plantations. The first major post-industrial restoration plantations established on former ironstone workings.
From 1900 AD onwards, many woods acquired by Local Authorities as recreational Woodlands. Either neglected or managed on a tidy care and maintenance basis.	√		√	Here begins a long period of often very minimal management in woods both in public and in private ownership. This lasts at least until the 1980s and beyond for many sites. The woods become even-aged and under-planted with beech, sycamore and sweet chestnut the ground floras become very impoverished and there is massive erosion and loss of topsoil.
From the 1920s, some held in productive forestry estates and new plantations were established in both existing woods and on former farmland.	√			
From 1850-1970 AD woods in the region and especially those in the urban catchments were increasingly affected by chronic air pollution.	√			Sensitive species including some trees, ferns and especially lichens were lost and soils affected.
Many woods encroached upon, reduced in size, increasingly fragmented and isolated.	√	√	√	Birds typical of open and coppice woods decline - replaced by birds of high forest.
1850s-1900s Victorian 'Wild Garden' and 'Gardenesque' movements.			√	Woodland flowers such as primroses, wild daffodils and snowdrops taken from woods into gardens. Exotic rhododendrons, laurels, Japanese knotweed, Himalayan balsam and others introduced into local woods.

Table 2. A thousand years of Social, Economic and Political Drivers of the Wooded Landscapes of South Yorkshire, England

EVENT, ACTION, AND DATE	Economic Driver	Political Driver	Social Driver	CONSEQUENCES
By the 1970s, public pressure was building for conservation of old woodlands and for both non-intervention areas for conservation, and for active 'traditional' management. There was also increased pressure for free recreational access to all areas of open land.		✓	✓	Dramatic impacts of Dutch elm Disease and loss of mature trees in many areas.
		✓	✓	Zoning of access and non-intervention areas.
			✓	Pioneering experimental management of ancient urban woods led by the late Dr Oliver Gilbert. This is the first time such woods have been managed in this way for over 100 years. Conservation glades created and prove popular with the public and with wildlife!
1980s woodland conservation projects established and a diversity of 'Friends Groups' and 'Trusts' set up to promote, conserve and manage local woodlands.		✓	✓	Recovery begins of lichens moving back into the area. Ferns recovering too probably re-establishing form spores escaping from garden collections.
			✓	Garden plants increasingly introduced into or escaping into the woods.
At the same time, the last local sawmills close down, and local government funding cuts force the massive reduction in the public woodland and forestry management services.	✓			Populations of red deer and roe deer recovering and moving back into local woods. Alien muntjac deer also arrives.
1990s Initiatives such as *South Yorkshire Forest* established followed by projects such as *Fuelling the Revolution*.	✓	✓	✓	Increase in positive management work in woods, much footpath and access improvement, new educational and interpretation initiatives.

Table 2. A thousand years of Social, Economic and Political Drivers of the Wooded Landscapes of South Yorkshire, England

EVENT, ACTION, AND DATE	Economic Driver	Political Driver	Social Driver	CONSEQUENCES
		✓		Renewed enthusiasm for native species broadleaved planting; some unfortunately was damaging to local wildlife habitats such as heath and unimproved grassland.
Only limited re-establishment of economic and social function and relationship with ownership and management. Most management is dependent on short-term charitable funding.	✓	✓	✓	Lack of long-term economically based, landscape-scale, recovery or plans.
Continuing process of 'parkification' with much work driven by funding for access and education but not conservation.		✓		Nature conservation management and strategies or commitments, as agreed in 1980s and 1990s, often ignored or forgotten.
New woodlands still being created as plantations on high quality unimproved grasslands and even on heaths and moors – but under the guise of 'conservation'.		✓		Continuing loss of and damage to ancient habitats of high nature conservation and heritage value.
Recognition of importance of heritage and archaeology of wooded landscapes.		✓	✓	Little practical implementation.
Many active local groups, friends groups etc but now threatened by cuts associated with the new austerity and loss of countryside management services and a general de-skilling in local authorities and agencies.	✓	✓		

Table 2. A thousand years of Social, Economic and Political Drivers of the Wooded Landscapes of South Yorkshire, England

EVENT, ACTION, AND DATE	Economic Driver	Political Driver	Social Driver	CONSEQUENCES
Move to extract industrial biofuel and energy crops from ancient woodlands.	√	√		Serious damage to woodland heritage landscapes including scheduled archaeology, and loss of veteran trees.
Recognition of wider resources of wood pasture and shadow woods – hitherto overlooked.		√	√	But threatened by inappropriate management including tree planting.

Expanded from Rotherham and Jones, 2000 and Rotherham, 2007.

Wood Anemone (left) and Bluebell (right); two local ancient woodland indicators.

The Sheffield Area case study: change, severance and loss of cultural knowledge

In the Sheffield area, the loss of traditional and industrial coppice woodlands was quite rapid. From the mid-1800s, there was piecemeal conversion to plantation high forest by owners of large estates, and the loss or abandonment of sites to either urban spread or farming. This continued until the 1920s and 1930s, as many woods fell victim to urban development, were abandoned, or passed to local authorities for recreation and amenity. From the 1920s to 1980, local authorities purchased many ancient woods for community benefit. Until the 1990s, a substantial workforce managed these sites, which was in part for commercial exploitation. Many woods were converted to coniferous plantations, and extensive new conifer forests were established. Remarkably, by the 1970s there was almost no local memory of the earlier traditional uses, functions, or origins. With oral traditions lost, some technologies and processes that were unrecorded have remained undocumented and enigmatic. This process in the case-study region largely mirrors the trends described earlier, but is sharply focused due to the intensity of regional industrial and urbanisation processes. Remarkably, with over eighty 'ancient' woodland sites in the city, Sheffield itself remains one of the most richly wooded cities in north-western Europe due largely to the need for industrialists and landowners to protect woodlands for vital coppice production (Jones, 2003; Perlin, 1989). However, many contemporary managers and conservationists still fail to realise that these woods were transformed by intensive use as industrial coppice, particularly by widespread soil-stripping (Rotherham, 2007, Rotherham & Doram, 1992; Rotherham & Jones, 2000; Rotherham & Ardron, 2006). Soil and turf were cut from the woodland surface to cover charcoal and perhaps whitecoal burns, available nutrient levels in woodland soils were depleted by this turf cutting, and by the massive, regular removal of biomass as coppice. Furthermore, atmospheric fallout from gross air pollution (around 3.35 tons of grit and grime deposited per square mile per week in 1920s), acidified and leached the soils during the nineteenth and twentieth centuries. The soils, which remained after several centuries of charcoal and whitecoal manufacture, were often just layers of charcoal dust and a sub-soil.

By the late twentieth century, local cultural memories were of the now commercial, plantation, high forests not of the traditional coppice woodlands. Despite photographic evidence of traditional charcoal burners working the woods in the early 1900s, local people had lost all knowledge after fifty years or less. It was the same with associated local woodland crafts and workers; making baskets, clog making, besom making, basket making, hurdle making, and others such as tanning. It was almost as if these practices had never happened. The harvesting of winter Holly from managed 'hollins' and 'haggs' for winter fodder is another long-term cultural use that declined and was lost from memory (Jones, 2003). Yet the abandoned Holly woods with their dense cover of remain, along with place-names and road-names. The imprint remains in place-names and familynames but not in the community itself. In the late 1970s, in Sheffield, local people including foresters and other woodland managers believed that no woods in the district were 'ancient'; all were believed to have been planted over the last 200 years. The period of planting in the 1700s was seen and recognised but with an absence of obvious older trees, it was assumed that this was planting into non-woodland landscapes.

One reason that local people did not recognise the antiquity of their woods was the absence of big trees. In their minds, they associated 'ancient woods' with large veterans and as a consequence of centuries of industrial coppice, most of these have gone. For the public, ancient trees are big and impressive, since in Sheffield there are very few obviously old trees, these woods cannot be ancient. Yet palimpsests of archaeological evidence bear testimony to centuries of woodland use, sometimes sustainable and at other times not. The impacts of cultural and later industrial uses are deeply embedded in the wooded landscapes, with dramatically altered ecology, hydrology, and pedology. This is now an archaeological and heritage resource of huge interest. Throughout the period 1960-1980, approaches to site management reflected this lack of awareness of either antiquity or history.

However, research and detailed site case studies have dramatically altered contemporary understanding of these cultural landscapes, with similar trends witnessed across the UK. Scoping work and information exchange across Europe and the USA, also suggest close parallels. There is interest in both conserving and in re-creating past uses, at least for demonstration purposes. In today's context, these wooded landscapes are recognised as of immense social and economic value, but recognition of their cultural historical significance is limited. This results in lack of protection for archaeology, and low awareness of changed soils and vegetation from the 'natural' forest. 'Working' and other culturally significant trees are frequently over-looked and mismanaged. Even with increased awareness of old pollards and open-grown trees in parklands, ancient coppices are still mostly ignored. These are cultural landscapes and the future vision of Europe's forests and wooded landscapes must recognise this (see Agnoletti (ed.), 2007; Parrotta & Trosper (eds.), 2012).

It is important to recognise, identify, and assess typical processes and landscape evidence, and factors of regional character and distinction are clearly of great interest and vulnerable to loss. Across Europe, there is excellent research, and findings need to be sharedto foster wider appreciation something that triggered the establishment of the *European Cultural Forest Network* and of the *Ancient Tree Forum*. On-going work has improved the recognition of the importance of forest and woodland archaeology and history, and has promoted cross-disciplinary collaborations. The approach taken by the *Woodland Heritage Manual* should inform visions of future, sustainable, forest landscapes.

There are key issues to be addressed such as the degree to which these woods are natural. It is increasingly obvious that they are not, but many people think they are. The public now think that 'ancient woods' somehow link to 'primeval forests'. There is even a legacy of misinformation, such as a loose quote from an early 1900s introduction to forestry: '...... *Our forests and woods today are pretty much as they would have been 15,000 years ago*'. Furthermore, ancient woodland plants, such as the Bluebell (*Hyacinthioides non-scriptus*), one of the UK's most iconic plants may tell a subtly different story from that usually assumed. Occurring in dense swarms across former coppice woods, it probably reflects succession to high forest, abandonment of medieval management, and replacement of a more diverse community (Vickers & Rotherham, 1999). I argue that the working, medieval coppice wood would be dominated by a diverse, mixed flora of 'ancient woodland' wildflowers. These plants have been displaced by the impacts of turf stripping, by drainage and desiccation, and finally by shading due to high forest management or successional canopy closure following abandonment and severance. Forested and wooded landscapes reflect the cultural, economic, and industrial histories of their communities.

Drivers of change and a shared history

In the 1980s, a new appreciation of woodlands and especially ancient woodlands emerged. However, what does this mean in terms of conservation and continuity of management? Understanding of the nature and drivers that shape these landscapes has emerged and changed radically over the last twenty years. This has answered some questions but also posed further paradigms for the landscape historian. Rotherham & Jones (2000) discussed some of these for South Yorkshire. Mills (1994) presented an overview of forest landscape history for the nearby West Yorkshire region, and related the trends to utilisation and traditional crafts. It is important to recognise these drivers and their impacts for future sustainable management of wooded landscapes. Similar trends and evidence are emerging across Europe and North America, but further detailed research is required. There are differences in detail, but common underlying principles. The impacts of management histories are massive and in many cases have more immediate influence on contemporary ecology and landscape than the original environmental character of the area. Yet there are still serious problems in terms of establishing wider recognition of the significance of cultural nature of forest and wooded landscapes. In many situations, forest and woodland management has both affected the ecology, and left a legacy of landscape features and artefacts. This is the archaeology 'of' the woods. Increasingly these features are considered to be an important component of the archaeological resource (Rotherham *et al.*, 2008), but general lack of recognition results in a lack of protection for archaeology. There is a low awareness of changed soils and vegetation from the 'natural' forest; and 'working' and other culturally significant trees, are frequently overlooked and mismanaged. There is still a widespread tendency for archaeological surveys in wooded landscapes to be supervised and implemented by professionals unable even to identify trees to species level. Trees and archaeology 'of' the woods are mostly overlooked, and what is recorded is the archaeology 'in' the woods. This resource is itself often important because being in a wooded landscape has often, though not always, limited the impacts of major disruption.

Ecological trends

The implications of woodland management were generally totally unseen by ecologists working in Britain in the mid- to late twentieth century. Indeed, this led to often a complete misunderstanding of the nature and quality of the woodland resource. In the 1980s, in Sheffield for example, Ladies Spring Wood was the only woodland Site of Special Scientific Interest (SSSI) in the city and designated because it was a good example of a 'semi-natural Pennine oak-birch woodland showing zonation of vegetation associated with the steep slope on which the woodland stands. However, most of the wood was re-planted in the 1700s and 1800s, and prior to that, it was intensively turf-stripped for charcoal burning. The slope has a major influence on soils and vegetation here, but the human exploitation is an equally important determinant.

There have been major changes in the ecological dynamics and balances of these sites, with shifts in key aspects of site character. In particular, there was the dramatic impact of drainage and turf stripping for industrial coppice and charcoal. Perhaps associated with this, but maybe beginning with an earlier coppice-with-standards phase, there was a massive decline in the impact of grazing herbivores on the region'swooded landscapes. However, despite a shift from early medieval wood pasture, it is suggested that some impacts remained throughout the bulk of the period as woodland industries were powered by draft animals and humans. By the mid twentieth century, even these localised impacts ended and with regional extinction of most wild deer, the woods were freed from herbivore impacts. This was not always so and in some situations, mostly in the western upland parts of the region, numbers of ancient woods now privately owned, had lost their economic value as productive wooded landscapes. In many cases, the consequence of this severance was the removal of fences, walls and other barriers, and the destructive use of these as stock shelters. The impact of this grazing on the woodland ground flora, and on the trees was devastating and clearly not sustainable. Soils and archaeologywere badly affected.

A further and more subtle change has occurred in these wooded landscapes consequent on their release from either traditional, rural coppice or industrial coppice management. The small-scale, micro-disturbance of soil and vegetation associated with woodland workers and their animals also stopped. Over the period since then, a very gradual but ultimately dramatic change has occurred as ecological succession has proceeded (Vickers & Rotherham, 2000). We suggest that relatively species-rich ground flora has given way to domination by a few species such as Bluebell (*Hyacinthoides non-scripta*) and the typical woodland grasses such as *Holcus mollis*. With canopy closure and a move from open coppice to high forest, the species-poor acidic heathland vegetation of the industrial coppice woods has also declined and been replaced by shade-tolerant forest species. Some key trends are:

- Eutrophication from atmospheric nutrient fallout and decreased limited removal of biomass compared with a coppice wood;
- Successional change following canopy closure, competitive effects, lack of micro- disturbance from woodland workers and their animals, but often macro-disruption;
- Removal of topsoil and vegetation for charcoal manufacture;
- Decline in dead wood components and of associated species;
- Response to long-term trends of environmental change;
- Destructive but localised winter grazing of farm livestock;
- Inevitable urbanisation impacts;
- Socio-ecological influences with planted trees, theft of attractive herbs, and introduction of garden throw-outs and aliens, plus nutrient inputs.

Hydrological Trends

All the woodland areas reported on are suffering from desiccation and drought caused by various long-term factors. This is the case in both urban and rural locations and some of these are the consequences of deliberate actions, others are unplanned. The causes include:

- Extensive networks of internal drains that are often still active and still desiccating;
- Continuing drainage maintenance associated with recreational and amenity uses, and the perceptions of an urbanised population;
- Urbanisation and 'water theft' associated with road building and housing development; with woods often left as isolated islands of habitat;

- Services such as power-lines and water supplies embedded in underground channels filled with aggregate provided active site drainage and reduction of water reaching the woods;
- There is much talk of hydrological sustainability in both urban and rural areas, but this is little more than policy statements. Continued trends of development threaten wooded landscapes.
- New developments still occur without regard for sustainable drainage or their impacts on nearby wooded areas.

Drainage of woods and of commons began very early but perhaps reached a peak in the early to mid 1800s. Early accounts confirm that the landscape was once far wetter, and that owners and managers of woods in the 1700s and 1800s were obsessed with drainage. Owler Car Wood in the Moss Valley, and Ecclesall Woods in Sheffield are examples with extensive drainage networks, and both are now substantially desiccated. De-watering continued through the 1900s and the period of amenity woodland uses, with added and catastrophic impacts from urban development and intensive arable farming. Yet there are no attempts to remediate these impacts. Early forestry texts provide details of how to drain, and books and papers abound that advocate the need for drainage in terms of good husbandry. It is clear that foresters and woodland managers over the last century and a half have applied these guidelines to the full. These impacts have been maintained, and often enhanced by more recent management ever since. It is likely that in the long-term, particularly with expected climate change scenarios, this is one of the most serious threats to the sustainability of the wooded landscape resource in the study area.

Loss of dead wood habitat

A major cultural impact on forested landscapes has been the loss of dead wood habitat (Kirby & Drake, 1993). This is in all its forms: standing and fallen, on both living and dead trees. After decades as tidy woodlands, sites are depleted in dead wood compared with natural forests. Victorian foresters and then twentieth century amenity woodland managers, liked clean, tidy woods; so do many members of the public which is bad news for dead wood and the associated wildlife and history. However, it is worth considering how medieval woodland, the 'cultural forest', would compare with the present-day scenario. Contemporary (50-150 years) economic management of woods, generally leaves them impoverished in terms of dead and decaying wood, so the regional woods are depauperate in dead / decaying wood resources. These amounts are probably reduced to below 5% of that in *'natural woodland'* and less than 15% of that in traditionally managed woodland. More recent concepts about the nature of traditional forests and wooded landscapes may push these figures even lower (Parrotta & Trosper (eds.), 2012). The *Sheffield Nature*

Conservation Strategy (1991) noted the rarity of trees over 200 years old in Sheffield. Developing ideas in the *Sheffield Woodlands Policy* (1987), it stated that the Local Authority would continue to implement policies and proposals set out in this policy. In particular, the City Council (Bownes *et al.*, 1991), committed itself to active support for the EEC Committee of Ministers Recommendation No.R(88)10 '*On the Protection of Saproxylic Organisms and their Biotopes*'. This was a European priority target for conservation and to which Britain was a signatory. Since then however, there has been only limited action in support of this objective and it is likely that today neither members nor officers are actually aware of their obligations. There have been sporadic moves by some local authorities to maintain dead wood with both fallen and standing trees, and brash piles left after forestry of woodland management works. However, overall there is limited application of these approaches at a wider level. Conservation '*non-intervention zones*' were identified and agreed as promoted by local entomologists and ornithologists in the *Sheffield Woodlands Policy* (1987). Again, however, since then these seem to have fallen from favour and rather than being actively overturned, the commitment is ignored or overlooked. In amenity woodlands, there is also a significant public pressure for tidiness even at the expense of woodland sustainability. This can only be overcome by active and informed educational activities to explain why this management is taking place, and that it is not simply neglect. However, again, despite once being a national leader in community engagement and environment in woodland management, the City Council has relinquished its obligations, commitments and resources.

Stripping of soils, turf and vegetation

These changes have been compounded by massive removal of soil and vegetation for industrial coppice and charcoal manufacture. Rotherham & Doram (1990) and Hart (1993) described the impact on woodland vegetation of topsoil disturbance and turf stripping associated with charcoal production. Surveys of woodland ground flora in the Sheffield study area suggested a causal link between charcoal and whitecoal production, and the absence of mature soil profiles or typical ancient woodland vegetation. Researchers had previously overlooked the extent of this anthropogenic impact, and the consequences for woodland vegetation. Charcoal and whitecoal production in the woods of the study area and impacts on vegetation, were later described by Ardron & Rotherham (1999).

The combined or individual impacts of charcoal production and whitecoal on woodland soils and plants are potentially very significant. Woodland zones apparently unaffected by coaling have well developed soil 'A' horizons with a neutral or only slightly acid pH. They have typical ancient woodland plants such as *Mercurialis perennis* (Dog's Mercury), *Lamiastrum galeobdolon* (Yellow Archangel), *Anemone nemorosa* (Wood Anemone), *Allium ursinum* (Ramsons), *Galium odoratum* (Woodruff), *Sanicula europea* (Sanicle), *Stellaria holostea* (Greater Stitchwort), *Veronica montana* (Wood Speedwell), *Circaea lutetiana* (Enchanter's Nightshade), *Melica uniflora* (Wood Melick) and *Milium effusum* (Wood Millet). This vegetation occurs in either areas unaffected by coaling (such as Nether Spring Wood at the western end of Ladies Spring Wood), or as a fringing 'halo' around the external boundary of the wood. Other species-rich areas include wet flushes and streamsides. Areas influenced by intensive 'coaling' (often over several centuries and for industrial coppice), had thin 'A' horizons, and low pHs (*c*.3.5-4.5) often with raw charcoal dust directly over a clay 'B' horizon. Their typical plants were *Holcus mollis* (Creeping Soft-grass), *Rubus fruticosus* agg. (Bramble), *Lonicera periclymenum* (Honeysuckle), *Deschampsia flexuosa* (Wavy Hair-grass), *Pteridium aquilinum* (Bracken), with *Dryopteris dilatata* (Broad Buckler Fern), *Hyacinthoides non-scripta* (Bluebell), and sometimes *Luzula pilosa* (Hairy Woodrush). These differences are dramatic and significant.

However, at a national conference on ancient woodlands, held in Sheffield in 1992 (Beswick & Rotherham 1993), ecologists and archaeologists from all over the UK visited our core case study sites including Ecclesall Woods. This was before our observations had been more widely disseminated. The view of participants concurred with the published opinions of earlier writers on the woods of the district; that these sites are of inherently low botanical diversity and are 'naturally' relatively species-poor. Consequently, it was also considered that these were sites of low conservation interest. In fact, the species-poor vegetation, which whilst widespread is not uniform throughout the sites, is a direct consequence of air pollution and of turf stripping.

Many of the landscape archaeology features are easily overlooked or misunderstood. At the 1992 conference on the archaeology and ecology of ancient woods, experts were presented with evidence of a variety of features (since evaluated and reliably 'typed'). Senior archaeologists and ecologists gave interpretations of what they saw (or did not see) in the Ecclesall Woods case study site. This was an interesting exercise with some features recognised and correctly identified but most overlooked and / or misunderstood. The participants included foresters and woodland managers with knowledge of wooded landscapes across the region for several decades. The Q-pits (so-called because of their typical shape and mostly but not all associated with the manufacture of kiln-dried wood) are obvious and the 100 ha wood has over 100. However, charcoal platforms on level ground are more difficult to recognise and may be superficial. Prior to the conference an intensive field survey by an experienced archaeologist in preparation for the 1992 conference found only 60-70 'coal kilns' and 'charcoal hearth pits'. More recent, intensive surveys confirmed 3-400 charcoal hearths plus over 100 Q-pits (Rotherham & Ardron, 2001). The group on the conference field visit suggested that some of the larger pits were building sites, and that an early industrial tramway was a medieval hollow-way. They also overlooked a major Romano-British field system and a sizeable early Iron Age hilltop enclosure.

With training and practice, it is reasonably easy to find and confirm suspected charcoal hearths. In many cases, the typical form (a sub-circular and recessed levelled surface) on level or sloping sites is a first clue. Blackened earth, rich in charcoal dust and fragments provide confirmation; with deposits often exposed in bare ground due to dense shading or to animal activity. True charcoal can be separated from burnt firewood by its hardness, not readily crumbling to dust if squeezed. From these early observations, detailed audits have been carried out for many woodland sites around Sheffield. The findings have helped increase awareness of charcoal manufacturing features in woods. However, the implications of this for a thorough understanding of contemporary woodland ecology and pedology are still not always realised.

It is particularly interesting that all local and professional knowledge of these uses of and activities in the region's woods has been lost. This has occurred within a period of only 100-150 years since the last traditional charcoal burns in the region, and fifty years since their virtual demise nationally. Furthermore, the phenomenon should be considered in the context that these were the major industrial and management activities in these wooded landscapes for around 5-600 years.

Wider ecological impacts

The impacts of charcoal burners, coppice men and associated crafts run deep in the ecology of these wooded landscapes. Medforth & Rotherham (1997) described the changes in bird populations following cessation of coppice and return to high forest. However, other species are affected too. The Grass Snake (*Natrix natrix*) is an interesting species, local and uncommon in Sheffield, a Local Red Data Book Species (Bownes *et al.*, 1991). At Ecclesall Woods, it is at the extreme western edge of its regional distribution and survives because of the open, sunny nature of the former coppice woods, and associated warm piles of bark and woodchip. In this case, it is an 'indicator' of the medieval, working coppice wood, which survives opportunistically. However, although highlighted as important for action in the draft site management plan produced in the 1990s, with experimental and conservation coppice areas now abandoned its future looks bleak. This parallels the declines of open-wood bird species described by Medforth & Rotherham (1997). An exciting project to reinstate a cycle of coppice Hazel management (Rotherham & Vickers, 2001) was terminated after nearly ten years of implementation and monitoring when, without any consultation, the site was re-planted as high forest. The opportunity to re-create the open habitat of traditional coppice was lost. Monitoring showed dramatic increases in Bluebells and the open areas being used by hawker dragonflies, woodland butterflies, and birds.

Discussion

Cultural Landscapes

Where does this leave these cultural, semi-natural landscapes? It is important to recognise, identify, and assess typical processes and evidence in these landscapes. Factors of regional distinction are of particular interest. Excellent research is now being done across much of Europe, and it is essential that findings be shared to foster a wider appreciation of the resource. Modified for economic use the woods have been used and managed often continuously for decades and sometimes centuries. Some of the oldest trees are smaller species such as Holly clones or Rowan coppices; not what people expect to see. Relicts of former management, a 'singled' coppice or 'elephant's foot', are unique archives of woodland and landscape history, but easily removed and lost through uninformed management. Yet there are ancient trees but these are mostly relatively small or otherwise not obvious. Some modestly sized oak coppices in Sheffield woods, when incrementally felled and excavated because of a road-widening scheme, turned out to be at least 500 to 600 years old. Remarkably, when approached for support to protect such trees, a spokesman for the agency Natural England in the region stated that they were not of any particular interest.

The case study of Sheffield is now famous for its old woodlands (e.g. Jones, 2007), and consequently has received over a million pounds of National Lottery Funding for site management. However, it has few obviously veteran trees, and this still causes confusion; for in old woods, people expect old trees. The region's woods were mostly managed as industrial or rural coppice-with-standards that were worked, used, and extracted. Veteran trees might survive on boundaries such as trackways, and outside the woods, in parks and on commons. Remaining woods are often affected by conversion to Victorian high forest, with exotic species; and then neglect or planting with conifers. Many old trees were lost through management, and then 'Dutch Elm Disease'. In urban areas, vandalism, removed many others. What remains reflects these impacts through time. Today most of the traditional crafts and the industrial or subsistence uses of these wooded landscapes have stopped. In the 1990s there were still just a few traditional clog makers in West Yorkshire's Calder Valley Woods (Mills 1994), but for how long?

Contemporary management

There remain serious problems in relation to contemporary management of wooded or forest landscapes. When management is introduced to sites abandoned for decades, the impacts may be undesirable or unpredictable. Contemporary site works often fail to take account of the history of site management, or the consequences of often deep-seated ecological trends. The context of the woods is changed radically from times past; they may be urbanised and fragmented, or isolated within intensively farmed rural landscapes. The soils, archaeology, working trees, and vegetation are a precious resource; an ecological archive through pits and platforms, soil profiles and sediments, plant indicators, banks and ditches, trackways and roads. This tells a story of land-use and human activity, and can help guide future conservation.

In the case study region, there is a Working Woodlands Trust and there has been a major funded project to promote public awareness of woodland history, called *Fuelling the Revolution*. Public open-days and woodland craft exhibitions are becoming immensely popular, and there are local people once again making a living as woodland craft workers. All this should be, and is very good and very encouraging. However, it seems that deep-seated problems remain. The interactions of environment and people for thousands of years have driven and shaped these landscapes. For the last millennium or more, these relationships were forged through economic and political influences. It could be argued that the present phase is merely an extension of the process. However, there are significant and fundamental differences. The utilisation of the resource for fuel, for building materials, for food, for minerals etc has largely ceased; this is so in the UK but increasingly across the whole of Europe too (Rotherham, 2005). In some cases, the memory is preserved in museums and through demonstrations. Yet the context of the wooded landscape has also changed and as increasingly, we become an urban society. The daily link to and dependence on the natural world is severed.

Moreover, when woodland workers and demonstrators carry out their activities in the woods today they often do not work in the same ways as their forebears. They may utilise modern equipment and technologies quite reasonably to process and deliver their product. Their educational message may refer to the old ways, but it is unlikely that they will use them. Whilst this is understandable it may have subtle consequences that affect resource sustainability. Kirby & Woodell (1998) observed that experimental and conservation coppice in the UK often failed to achieve hoped for outcomes because the processes were not applied as they had been traditionally. After coppicing, there was no harvesting of bramble for fuel and fodder, and there was no grazing by pigs. Absence of these dramatically affects the ecological succession outcomes of management, as confirmed by Vickers & Rotherham (2000). How do we balance the old and the new? For example, is it reasonable that a modern-day metal charcoal kiln be placed on top of an early industrial or medieval site, potentially compromising the heritage? Is this a continuity of traditional use or inexcusable damage to the unique heritage of anciently worked woods? Similarly, having established that these woods were indeed ancient and medieval, and industrial wood-fuel production sites, it is now argued that modern, industrial biofuel extraction is reasonable and appropriate. Discussions with senior government advisors in both the Forestry Commission and Natural England were peppered with phrases like *'Well, these woods have to work for a living'* and *'.....you know, even ancient woods have to pay their way'*.

Difficult issues

The long-term impacts of management on hydrology, deadwood, and soils present huge problems for future conservation. Furthermore, on the back of urbanisation and eutrophication, invasion by non-native species raise issues and prove controversial. Widespread colonisers include Highclere Holly (*Ilex xaltaclerensis* or *aquifolium* x *I. perado*), Portuguese Laurel (*Prunus laurocerasus*), Sweet Chestnut (*Castanea sativa*), Swedish Whitebeam (*Sorbus intermedia*), and Variegated Yellow Archangel (*Lamium galeobdolon* var. *argentatum*). There are basic questions of what to do, why, when and who decides? Science and history inform but decisions are inherently subjective. They may be valid but are a choice that we make. How do we conserve the ecology and the imprint of human activity in the past, but maintain the dynamic stability of these cultural landscapes? This challenge is in the face of the fickle nature of human whim and fashion, and the vagaries of funding. It is increasingly clear that in many or even most situations neither decision-makers nor local people really understand how their wooded landscapes evolved and were managed. The long-term stakeholder observation research suggests that there are major issues, challenges and problems. Management of sites still shows little sign of any long-term continuity but varies with individual stakeholder whims and fashions, and with grant aid opportunities. In particular, what is most worrying is that commitments, policies, management plans, strategies and other agreements are frequently set aside. Often this is not that they are overturned by any discussion or debate, but they are simply overlooked, forgotten, or discarded without any due process.

Recognition of the heritage resource

For the case study sites, the continuation of archaeology and ecology surveys begun in the 1980s has led to a radical change in perceptions. Local archaeologists did not believe the initial findings, since the local Sites and Monuments Record had only 4-5 records for the whole of Ecclesall Woods, and the surveys indicated in excess of 1,000. Ardron & Rotherham (1999) identified a major resource in Ecclesall Woods, with features dating back over 3,500 years. This revolutionised the perception of these landscapes. Similarly work by Rotherham & Avison(1997) (Owler Car Wood), totally changed perceptions and subsequently the conservation management implemented by the Woodland Trust. Guidance on site evaluation and management has now been published (Rotherham & Avison, 1998; Rotherham *et al.*, 2008)

Recognition of the resource is hugely important, and becomes more urgent as time passes; memories are lost and management tends towards either abandonment or intensification. This raised awareness is needed in order to help evaluate the importance of forest archaeology and history, and to inform visions of a future more sustainable forest landscape. The *European Cultural Forest Network*, launched at the Florence 2006 conference supports this process of recognition, evaluation and assessment, promoted though the UKECONET website www.ukecoent.co.uk.

Shadow woods and ghosts in the landscape

Today, we see shadows and imprints of an ancient ecology in the modern landscape. Old meadows and pastures, ancient heaths, medieval coppice woods, and similar features bear testimony to this remarkable lineage. Ancient parks are the most visibly obvious remnants of formerly extensive grazed wooded landscapes. However, even where deer parks survive (and this is rare), they do so as unique landscapes separated in time and function from their origins. It may be that the greater medieval parks have shared common origins from the legacy of Vera's primeval savannah. However, other areas, upland moors and moorland fringe, and lowland heaths, commons and downs, probably reflect this same lineage; even today, many of these lands are grazed, and many have ancient albeit small, trees. These are the lands unenclosed in medieval times and linked, albeit tenuously, to Vera's open, fluid primeval landscape. For example, some of the species-rich grasslands such as the Derbyshire Dales limestone pastures are in effect, the remains of the open areas of Vera's landscape. Here are anciently complex, species-rich grasslands within landscapes of hazel and patches of ancient woodland (identified by Pigott in the 1960s). These and other wooded sites are now being recognised as 'shadow woods' or 'ghosts woods'; either relicts from once obviously ancient woodland sites, or perhaps more excitingly, ancient wooded landscapes until now overlooked.

Parks are the most obvious landscapes that mix trees and grazing animals. However, once one starts to examine the landscape more critically, it is apparent that many other systems have a similar approach. Heaths, commons, and unenclosed pastures (like Longshaw, North Derbyshire), mix ancient trees and open grazing lawns with long-term continuity of management to match that of the nearby Chatsworth Park. A major difference is that ancient trees in these landscapes are generally small and may be species such as hawthorns, which are often overlooked. Examining ecology and pedology in these wider landscapes reveals the imprint or '*shadow*' of former 'woodland' status; they are '*ancient wooded landscapes*'.

The origins or at least the recognition of, the components of these ancient landscapes are apparent in medieval legislation. In particular, the Statute of Merton (Act of Commons) (1235) provides a window into a watershed moment for these landscapes. The Act probably reflected what was happening and provided legal recognition setting down rights of land-use and function at manorial level; what was previously very fluid and extensive, became fixed and localised. A named 'wood' was now set in its landscape, bounded by fence, wall, hedge or ditch, and given a name. Similarly, common, heath, fen, field, and waste, were marked and recorded. This process transformed Vera's landscape to what we see today, including 'wooded' areas left outside the 'woods'. Greater, early medieval deer parks enclosed the landscape, as it existed before Merton, including woods and other wooded features and so these are good places to search for the ecological shadows of once extensive wooded landscapes. Our case study of Ecclesall Woods in Sheffield demonstrates very clearly the huge influence of changes from wood pasture to coppice and then high forest in a wooded landscape. However, a new and emerging challenge for our research concepts and paradigms is to step outside the boundary of the medieval 'woods' in search of the shadows, ghosts, and footprints of a wider wooded landscape.

Conclusions

Changing influences in the Ecclesall Woods case study: an ebb and flow of woodland and grazing

Ecclesall Woods in Sheffield is the region's premier conservation woodland today, but detailed studies of deadwood indicators of ancient woodlands, undertaken in the 1980s, identified it as an anomaly. Ecclesall Woods lacks key species of invertebrates that its assumed antiquity would suggest that it should have. Following in-depth studies of field archaeology and archival research however, the circumstances make eminent sense. Ecclesall Woods was open farmland with small areas of very wet carr woodland and riverside woodland. This was the case throughout a long period from Late Neolithic, and through the Bronze Age, Iron Age, and Romano-British periods even until the late Saxon. Following the Norman Conquest, the lands changed hands and the site has its origins as a medieval hunting park. In 1317, Robert de Ecclesall was granted a licence to impark, and this is reflected in modern place names such as Parkhead, Warren Wood, Park Field, and Old Park (Hart, 1993). Rotherham & Ardron (2006) present an overview of the issues of interpretation of the landscape here. As noted by Hart (1993), there is further evidence of the use of the Woods for hunting from a set of depositions taken on October 2nd 1587. These were from George, Sixth Earl of Shrewsbury. He stated that he, his father and his grandfather:

'……..used sett and placed Crosbowes for to Kyll the Deare in Ecclesall Afforesaied and to hunte at all tymes when it so pleased them there.' Thomas Creswick noted that '………..ye said Erle George grandfather to ye said now Erle of Shrewsbury hath sett Netts & long bowes to kill deare in Ecclesall and hunted dyverstymes there and he thinketh that ye said Erleffrancis father to ye Erle that now is did the lyke.' Richard Roberts confirmed that '…..he hath sene the lord ffrancis hunting in Ecclesall byerlow and that said lords officers sett decoers there at such places as they thought convenyent.' (Hart, 1993).

In the early 1700s, there were also livestock pastured in the woods with horses, mares, foals, cows, heifers, calves, and sterks recorded. Gelly's map of 1725 shows a 'laund' in the centre of the Woods and this was planted up in 1752 (Jones & Walker, 1997). In the 1587 deposition (Hart, 1993), it is also clear that wood and underwood are also being taken, and it was this use that was to dominate the former deer park for the next few centuries. It seems perhaps that the hunting use was falling from fashion by the late 1500s, with references to deer hunts certainly from the late 1400s and early 1500s. Was this the reason for the deposition? Excitingly, in the late 1990s, Paul Ardron, working with the author, located the western boundary bank of the medieval park (Rotherham & Ardron, 2001). Here we have some insight into the evolution of a specific wooded landscape, for which the medieval imparkation was probably the critical moment in it becoming woodland today. However, this 'ancient' woodland is not all it seems, and its ecology and pedology reflect its unique history. From the 1500s onwards, the Woods were individually named and being exploited for intensive manufacture of charcoal and whitecoal. By the mid-1800s, the coppice exploitation ended. Gradually the woodland was converted to high forest with exotic tree species. It was then largely abandoned as 'amenity woodland'. This site is now locked within a sea of urbanisation and separated from its past by the process of 'cultural severance' (Rotherham, 2008, 2010). However, the key issue is that for long periods of time this site was mostly un-wooded and included large areas of arable land. For much of the rest of its history it was grazed parkland. Today, culturally severed from its working past and managed as an urban amenity space, it is rapidly becoming 'parkified' but aside from occasional deer and rabbits, there is no grazing. Importantly, the absence of the ancient dead wood invertebrates now makes eminent sense; the site lacks essential continuity.

A wider context

Many fundamental drivers in the wooded landscape have gone or changed. Woods and forests are now more highly valued for recreation and for tourism, not for subsistence and survival. Rackham (1986) noted the fact that woods were under threat when their economic importance waned. Today's forests and wooded landscapes risk severance from their direct, local economic functions. In place of this, they provide a backdrop to tourism and leisure, to the visitor's gaze and the community's recreation (Crowe, 2001). This has real value (O'Brien & Claridge, 2002) and along with the value of ecosystem functions such as carbon sequestration, provides a real economic reason for forest maintenance. The problem seems to be, that in the past the economic value, management cost, and control of the resource and its management were placed or held, at least by the same community, if not by the same person. This is no longer the case and today's 'value' and 'cost' are generally separated. Furthermore, it was the day-to-day community impacts of management over centuries, that made the forest and woods what they are; they are not merely 'natural'. They are complex palimpsests of culture and nature. It is clear that with the loss of cultural memory and knowledge these landscapes are misunderstood. The woods are seen as ancient, natural and primeval on the one hand, and young and secondary on the other. To let nature take its course as is so often advocated (see Skeggs, 1999 for example) will lead inevitably to major changes and these may not represent sustainability.

In the 'cultural forest', we can see the woodman through the trees such as relict coppices, ancient pollards, pits and platforms, and in soil, vegetation, and lack of water. The woodman has left an indelible imprint on the woods, along with loss of soil and loss of water. These are cultural landscapes and the future vision of Europe's forests and wooded landscapes must recognise this. Across much of Europe there is far more local fuelwood use, and often for local, domestic supply than is the case in Britain. Perhaps such local, cultural attachment might be encouraged to give local people a real functional link to the forest landscape. This would be community-led fuel lots rather than economically led industrial exploitation.

Our wooded landscapes have been affected dramatically by a number of specific human impacts, for example air pollution as described earlier. However, two major impacts were through the enclosure and naming of woods under the Act of Commons (1235), and then the widespread enclosure of commonlands and open spaces through Parliamentary enclosures during the 1700s and 1800s. The impacts of these two seismic events were in the first place to spatially fix and name the 'woods' and their boundaries, and then secondly to separate the woods from the commons. The first enclosure also affected the balance of pasture woods and coppices, with the removal of most grazing and browsing animals from the woodland environment. The second period of wider enclosures took the commons from the commoners and the local people from their woods. I suggest that this has broken the ancient connection of community and wood. Commoners became poachers and trespassers, and cultural severance began in earnest. Only recently have community groups begun once more to be actively involved in their woods, but the nature of the relationship is changed. Even groups, which began in the 1980s, as nature conservation campaigners, are now mostly delivering access and footpath works. Biomass removal and on-going, small-scale micro-disturbance through subsistence and early industrial uses maintained open areas and often-distinctive vegetation. Increased biomass, closed canopies, and pulses of macro-disturbance by machines now replace these former impacts. The predominant uses for the woods today are as recreational pleasure grounds where the users do not interact as managers but demand well-surfaced, metalled, drained footpaths and ever-wider access routes to all areas.

Cultural knowledge loss – yesterday and today

Finally, the speed with which local cultural knowledge of forest landscapes is lost is worrying. The loss has not been uniform, so in the UK for example, traditional charcoal manufacture with clamp kilns died out entirely by the 1950s with only one traditional charcoal man left. Fortunately, some record was made of this dying art. Around the Mediterranean countries and some parts of Eastern Europe, the practice continues to the present but is clearly on the wane and in many areas has stopped in the last twenty years. The history and knowledge of some woodland crafts, such as potash manufacture, and tar production, remain elusive in the UK but can be informed by reference to research elsewhere such as for example in Sweden (Lars Östlund pers. comm.). Other activities like whitecoal manufacture for sixteenth century lead smelting in the UK, had a profound and intensive impact on woodland ecology, but local knowledge was totally lost and there was almost no documentation. This is a precautionary note for regions that still have the remains of traditional crafts, in that they can so easily disappear.

Interesting but worrying too, is the fact that recent site and management memories also seem to be lost. This was a most unexpected finding, and it applies to site-based information, but also to policy and practice. During the 1970s, 1980s and 1990s, there emerged commitments to good nature conservation practice at local and regional levels but supported by national legislation and policy guidance too. Some of these have already been noted, but there were also agreements on basic matters such as management plans, consultation, and review, and on the staff skills and necessary professional training. Any significant site management was to be undertaken only following detailed site survey and appraisal, a formal management proposal or plan, and a full public consultation including expert stakeholders and the public. This process involved both indoor and outdoor meetings. The implementation teams were qualified foresters, arboriculturists, and countryside managers or rangers, and they operated within multi-disciplinary teams that had expertise and experience in management planning and site monitoring. Almost all this has been abandoned and most work in local woodlands is undertaken on an opportunistic and ad hoc basis with little or no consultation or review. Staff with minimal or no formal conservation training or qualifications, do much of the work. Site management and timing are dependent largely on available finance through grant aid. This is often for access improvement works and not for ecological management as such and so driven not by conservation need of policy but by opportunity. Furthermore, the nature of grant aid for site management (such as the Heritage Lottery Fund monies for '*Fuelling the Revolution*'), is generally available in relatively large 'dollops' but all at once. This leads to a 'boom and bust' approach to management with either all or nothing. The situation is very different from the long periods of cyclical management, which occurred for centuries to create today's woodlands.

Future vision

The issues and challenges raised in this chapter become even more acute in the context of environmental change (particularly climate change and eutrophication) and with the Frans Vera debate about forest origins and dynamics in Europe (Vera, 2000; Rotherham (ed.), 2012). For sustainability, our vision of wooded landscapes needs to be much more dynamic and much more fluid; and yet it must preserve its cultural attachment and its local values. This is a serious challenge. The answer may lie in part with individual 'champions' willing to lead on the conservation management of woods, and these may be within local authorities or government agencies, or in local conservation groups. 'Friends' groups are especially valuable in this respect, and our core case study site of Ecclesall Woods has a long-established voluntary group called the Friends of Ecclesall Woods. A result of work which I began with the group back in the 1990s, is that they now have a state-of-the-art visitor centre with working woodland craftsmen and women, artists, sculptors and more. This is a wonderful achievement and testimony to the Friends and the City Council officers who have driven this through to completion. However, such success is tinged slightly with a worry for the long-term future of the unique heritage and ecology of this and other wooded landscapes. Accumulated impacts of human activities over several thousand years make for a remarkable and rich palimpsest of landscape heritage. Cultural severance, urbanisation, and destruction management are now ever-present threats and it only takes one event to erase the heritage of centuries.

Acknowledgements

Research colleagues Paul Ardron, Christine Handley, Barry Wright, Adrian Vickers, Melvyn Jones, Colin Avison, and local woodland friends groups are all thanked for their help, advice and encouragement.

References

Anon. (1987) *Sheffield Woodland Policy*. Sheffield City Council, Sheffield.

Agnoletti, M. (ed.) (2006) *The Conservation of Cultural Landscapes*. CAB International, Wallingford, Oxon, UK.

Agnoletti, M. (ed.) (2007) *Guidelines for the Implementation of Social and Cultural Values in Sustainable Forest Management. A Scientific Contribution to the Implementation of MCPFE – Vienna Resolution 3*. IUFRO Occasional Paper No. 19 ISSN 1024-414X

Ardron, P.A. & Rotherham, I.D. (1999) Types of charcoal hearth and the impact of charcoal and whitecoal production on woodland vegetation. *Peak District Journal of Natural History and Archaeology*, **1**, 35-47.

Beswick, P. & Rotherham, I.D. (eds.) (1993) Ancient Woodlands – their archaeology and ecology - a coincidence of interest. *Landscape Archaeology and Ecology*, **1**.

Bownes, J.S., Riley, T.H., Rotherham, I.D. & Vincent, S.M. (1991) *Sheffield Nature Conservation Strategy*. Sheffield City Council, Sheffield.

Crowe, L. (2001) *Fresh Air .....Fitness and Fun.* Yorkshire Sports Board, Sheffield.

De Moor, M., Shaw-Taylor, L. & Warde, P. (2002) *The Management of Common Land in north west Europe, c. 1500-1850*. Brepols Publishers n.v., Turnhout, Belgium.

Eccles, C. (1986) *South Yorkshire: Inventory of Ancient Woodland*. Nature Conservancy Council, Peterborough.

Fowler, J. (2002) *Landscapes and Lives. The Scottish Forest through the ages*. Canongate Books, Edinburgh.

Griffiths, P., Simpson, F. & Rotherham, I.D. (1995) *A Hydrological Assessment of the Meers Brook Catchment.* Sheffield Centre for Ecology and Environmental Management, Sheffield

Griffiths, P. & Rotherham, I.D. (1996a) *Ecclesall Woods: A Preliminary Hydrological Assessment.* Sheffield Centre for Ecology and Environmental Management, Sheffield.

Griffiths, P. & Rotherham, I.D. (1996b) *Bowden Housteads Wood: A Preliminary Hydrological Assessment.* Sheffield Centre for Ecology and Environmental Management, Sheffield.

Griffiths, P., Simpson, F. & Rotherham, I.D. (1996) *Hydrology and water Quality in the Upper Don Catchment. Results of the research feasibility study and proposals for further research.* Sheffield Centre for Ecology and Environmental Management, Sheffield.

Hare, A.D.R. (1998) Woods Ancient and Modern. *Arboricultural Journal*, **12 (2)**, 177-180.

Hart, C.R. (1993) The Ancient Woodland of Ecclesall Woods, Sheffield. In: Proceedings of the National Conference on Ancient Woodlands: their archaeology and ecology - a coincidence of interest, Sheffield 1992. Beswick, P. & Rotherham, I.D. (eds.), *Landscape Archaeology and Ecology*, **1**, 49-66.

Hayman, R. (2003) *Trees.Woodlands and Western Civilization.* Hambledon and London, London.

Helliwell, D.R. (1992) Benefits of Multi-purpose Forestry: Who Assesses, Who Pays and How? *Arboricultural Journal*, **16 (1)**, 5-10.

Jones, M. (1997) *Woodland management on the Duke of Norfolk's Sheffield estate in the early eighteenth century.* In: M. Jones (ed.) *Aspects of Sheffield: Discovering Local History, Vol.1.* Wharncliffe Publishing Ltd, Barnsley, 48-69.

Jones, M. (1998) *The rise, decline and extinction of spring wood management in south-west Yorkshire.* In: Watkins, C. (ed.) *European Woods and Forests: Studies in Cultural History.* CAB International, Oxford, 55-72.

Jones, M. (2009) *Sheffield's Woodland Heritage.* 4thEdition (revised), Wildtrack Publishing, Sheffield.

Jones, M. & Walker, P. (1997) From coppice-with-standards to high forest: the management of Ecclesall Woods 1715-1901. *Peak District Journal of Natural History and Archaeology Special Publication*, **No. 1**, 11-20.

Kirby, K.J. & Drake, C.M. (eds.) (1993) *Dead wood matters: the ecology and conservation of saproxylic invertebrates in Britain*. English Nature Science, 7, English Nature, Peterborough.

Kirby, K.J. & Woodell, S.R.J. (1998) The distribution and growth of bramble (*Rubus fruticosus*) in British semi-natural woodland and their implications for nature conservation. *Journal of Practical Ecology and Conservation*, **2 (1)**, 31-41.

Medforth, P. & Rotherham, I.D. (1997) The Birds of Ecclesall Woods. *Peak District Journal of Natural History and Archaeology Special Publication*, **No.1**, 21-33.

Mills, E.J. (1994) Woodlands of the Upper Calder Valley, West Yorkshire. *Arboricultural Journal*, **18 (4)**, 365-380.

Muir, R. (2005) *Ancient Trees Living Landscapes*. Tempus Publishing Ltd, Stroud, Glos.

O'Brien, L. & Claridge, J. (2002) *Trees are Company. Social Science Research into Woodlands and the Natural Environment*. Forestry Commission, Edinburgh.

Perlin, J. (1989) *A Forest Journey*. Harvard University Press, Massachusetts.

Peterken, G.F. (1981) *Woodland Conservation and Management*. Chapman and Hall, London.

Peterken, G.F. (1996) *Natural Woodland – ecology and conservation in northern temperate regions*. Cambridge University Press, Cambridge.

Rackham, O. (1980) *Ancient Woodland: its history, vegetation and uses in England*. Edward Arnold, London.

Rackham, O. (1986) *The History of the Countryside*. Dent, London.

Rotherham, I.D. (1996) The sustainable management of urban-fringe woodlands for amenity and conservation objectives. *Aspects of Applied Biology*, **44**, 33-38.

Rotherham, I.D. (2005) Fuel and Landscape – Exploitation, Environment, Crisis and Continuum. *Landscape Archaeology and Ecology*, **5**, 65-81

Rotherham, I.D. (2006) *Historic Landscape Restoration: Case Studies of Site Recovery in Post-industrial South Yorkshire, England*. In: Agnoletti, M. (ed.) *The Conservation of Cultural Landscapes*. CABI International, Wallingford, Oxfordshire, 211-224.

Rotherham, I.D. (2007) The implications of perceptions and cultural knowledge loss for the management of wooded landscapes: a UK case-study. *Forest Ecology and Management*, **249**, 100-115.

Rotherham, I.D. (2006) *Working landscapes or recreational showcases – sustainable management and the implications of cultural knowledge loss.* In: Parrotta, J., Agnoletti, M. & Johann, E. (eds.) *Cultural Heritage and Sustainable Forest Management: The Role of Traditional Knowledge*. Proceedings of the Conference 8-11 June 2006, Florence, Italy, Volume 1, Published by the Ministerial Conference on the Protection of Forests in Europe, Warsaw.

Rotherham, I.D. *et al*. (2007) *Guidelines for the Implementation of Social and Cultural Values in Sustainable Forest Management. A Scientific Contribution to the Implementation of MCPFE – Vienna Resolution 3*. IUFRO Occasional Paper No. 19. ISSN 1024-414X.

Rotherham, I.D. (2008) *The Importance of Cultural Severance in Landscape Ecology Research*. In: Dupont, A. & Jacobs, H. (eds.) (2008) *Landscape Ecology Research Trends*. Nova Science Publishers Inc., New York, 71-87.

Rotherham, I.D. (2009a) *Hanging by a Thread - a brief overview of the heaths and commons of the north-east midlands of England*, in: Rotherham, I.D. & Bradley, J. (eds.) (2009) *Lowland Heaths: Ecology, History, Restoration and Management*, Wildtrack Publishing, Sheffield, 30-47.

Rotherham, I.D. (2009b) *Habitat Fragmentation and Isolation in Relict Urban Heaths - the ecological consequences and future potential*. In: Rotherham, I.D. & Bradley, J. (eds.) (2009) *Lowland Heaths: Ecology, History, Restoration and Management*. Wildtrack Publishing, Sheffield, 106-115.

Rotherham, I.D. (2009c) *Cultural Severance in Landscapes and the Causes and Consequences for Lowland Heaths*. In: Rotherham, I.D. & Bradley, J. (eds.) (2009) *Lowland Heaths: Ecology, History, Restoration and Management*. Wildtrack Publishing, Sheffield, 130-143.

Rotherham, I.D. (2010) 'Cultural Severance and the End of Tradition', *Landscape Archaeology and Ecology*, **8**, 178-199.

Rotherham, I.D. (2011a) *A Landscape History Approach to the Assessment of Ancient Woodlands.* In: Wallace, E.B. (ed.) *Woodlands: Ecology, Management and Conservation.* Nova Science Publishers Inc., USA, 161-184.

Rotherham, I.D. (2011b) *Animals, Man & Treescapes – perceptions of the past in the present.* In: Rotherham, I.D. & Handley, C. (eds.) (2011) *Animals, Man and Treescapes: The interactions between grazing animals, people and wooded landscapes,* Wildtrack Publishing, Sheffield, 1-32.

Rotherham, I.D. (ed.) (2012a) *Trees, Man, & Grazing Animals – A European perspective on trees and grazed treescapes.* EARTHSCAN, London (in press).

Rotherham, I.D. (2012b) *Re-interpreting wooded landscapes, shadow woods and the impacts of grazing.* In: Rotherham, I.D. (ed.) (2012a) *Trees, Man, & Grazing Animals – A European perspective on trees and grazed treescapes.* EARTHSCAN, London (in press).

Rotherham, I.D. & Ardron, P.A. (eds.) (2001) *Ecclesall Woods Millenium Archaeology Project.* Sheffield Hallam University, Sheffield.

Rotherham, I.D. & Ardron, P.A. (2006) The Archaeology of Woodland Landscapes: issues for managers based on the case-study of Sheffield, England and four thousand years of human impact. *Arboricultural Journal,* **29 (4)**, 229-243.

Rotherham, I.D. & Avison, C. (1997) *Owler Car Wood: a report on its historic landscape features and proposed management.* Sheffield Centre for Ecology and Environmental Management, Sheffield Hallam University, Sheffield.

Rotherham, I.D. & Avison, C. (1998) *Sustainable Woodlands for people and Nature? The relevance of landscape history to a vision of forest management.* In: *Woodland in the Landscape: Past and Future Perspectives.* Atherden, M.A. & Butlin, R.A. (eds.), The proceedings of the one-day conference at the University College of Ripon and York St John, PLACE, York, 194-199.

Rotherham, I.D. & Doram, G.P. (1992) A Preliminary Study of the Vegetation of Ecclesall Woods in Relation to Former Management. *Sorby Record,* **29**, 60-70.

Rotherham, I.D. & Egan, D. (2005) *The Economics of Fuel Wood, Charcoal and Coal: An Interpretation of Coppice Management of British Woodlands.* In: Agnoletti, M., Armiero, M., Barca, S. and Corona, G. (eds.), *History and Sustainability.* European Society for Environmental History, University of Florence, Florence, Italy, 100-104

Rotherham, I.D. & Handley, C. (eds.) (2011) *Animals, Man and Treescapes: The interactions between grazing animals, people and wooded landscapes.* Wildtrack Publishing, Sheffield.

Rotherham, I.D., Jones, M., Smith, L. & Handley, C. (eds.) (2008) *The Woodland Heritage Manual: A Guide to Investigating Wooded Landscapes.* Wildtrack Publishing, Sheffield.

Rotherham, I.D. & Jones, M. (2000a) Seeing the Woodman in the Trees – Some preliminary thoughts on Derbyshire's ancient coppice woods. *Peak District Journal of Natural History and Archaeology*, **2**, 7-18.

Rotherham, I.D. & Jones, M. (2000b) *The Impact of Economic, Social and Political Factors on the Ecology of Small English Woodlands: a Case Study of the Ancient Woods in South Yorkshire, England.* In: Agnoletti, M. and Anderson, S. (Eds.), *Forest History: International Studies in Socio-economic and Forest ecosystem change.* CAB International, Wallingford, Oxford, 397-410.

Rotherham, I.D. & Vickers, A.D. (1999) *Managing Urban Woodland - a study of the response of Bluebells to coppicing and seasonal differences between years.* Sheffield Hallam University and South Yorkshire Forest Partnership, Sheffield.

Skeggs, S. (1999) Various Botanical and Social Factors and Their Effects on an Urban Woodland inReading, Berkshire. *Arboricultural Journal*, **23 (3)**, 209-232.

Vera, F.H.W. (2000) *Grazing Ecology and Forest History.* CABI Publishing, Oxon.

Vickers, A.D. & Rotherham, I.D. (2000) The response of Bluebell (*Hyacinthoides non-scripta*) to seasonal differences between years and woodland management. *Aspects of Applied Biology*, **58**, 1-8.

Vickers, A.D., Rotherham, I.D. & Rose, J.C. (2000) Vegetation succession and colonisation rates at the forest edge under different environmental conditions. *Aspects of Applied Biology*, **58**, 351-356.

Working the woodlands.